THE BOOK OF
DARWIN

THE BOOK OF DARWIN

Edited with an introduction
and commentary by

GEORGE GAYLORD SIMPSON

WASHINGTON SQUARE PRESS
PUBLISHED BY POCKET BOOKS NEW YORK

A WASHINGTON SQUARE PRESS *Original* Publication

A Washington Square Press Publication of
POCKET BOOKS, a division of Simon & Schuster, Inc.
1230 Avenue of the Americas, New York, N.Y. 10020

ISBN: 0-671-43126-9

First Washington Square Press Printing December, 1983

10 9 8 7 6 5 4 3 2 1

WASHINGTON SQUARE PRESS, WSP and colophon are
registered trademarks of Simon & Schuster, Inc.

Printed in the U.S.A.

Dedicated in retrospect to Erasmus Darwin (grandfather of Charles Darwin), Thomas Huxley (grandfather of Thomas Henry Huxley), and Josiah Wedgwood (grandfather of Emma Darwin née Wedgwood). Down to this day their descendants singly and severally have added immeasurably to the knowledge, enjoyment, and beauty of human life.

Acknowledgments

Here I may give thanks to a few people who helped directly in the preparation of this book and to a necessarily very small selection of the large number of those whose studies of Darwin and of evolution have inspired my own and have thus indirectly contributed to my comments here.

In the first category are my wife, Dr. Anne Roe, who has gone over the manuscript with corrections and comments, as she has for almost everything I have written. Mrs. Lindy Flynn has typed the whole manuscript from my scribbles and has assisted well in other ways also. John Thornton, executive editor of the Washington Square Press, had the original idea for the book, has been forbearing when it lagged behind for a time, and has throughout been encouraging. Marnie Hagmann, associate editor, has been very helpful.

Among those many less directly involved I may name first Norah Barlow, who showed me the manuscript of Darwin's autobiography and who compiled and wrote important books about her grandfather. Gavin de Beer not only wrote an excellent biography of Darwin but also edited and published many of Darwin's notes. Julian Huxley was an innovative Neo-Darwinian naturalist and also wrote with H. B. D. Kettlewell, another innovative Neo-Darwinian, a richly illustrated biography of Darwin. Theodosius Dobzhansky introduced me to the genetical aspects of the synthetic theory (but did not himself use that name for it). Ernst Mayr has helped my investigation of the relationship between systematics (including classification) and evolution, primarily of animals. Ledyard Stebbins and Verne Grant have done much the same for plants. Teachers no longer living include Arthur Tieje, Carl Dunbar, and Richard Swann Lull, all of whom taught me paleontology which later served in connecting this more closely with evolutionary theory. David Hull is among those whose work has given me some insight into the bearing of evolution and of Darwin on the philosophy and logic of science.

Included in the many whom I have not known well or in some cases at all, but who have been the most instructive specifically about Darwin's work, its development and outcomes, Charles Darwin's son Francis should be named first for the *Life and Letters* and then *More Letters*. (With a bit of luck I might have known Francis Darwin, as he died only a year before I first worked at the British Museum.) There also rise to mind Morse Peckham for the variorum *Origin of Species,* R. C. Stouffer for the reconstruction of most of the "big book," and H. E. Gruber and P. H. Barrett for *Darwin on Man.* For historical and background notes the list would be too long to give here, but as excellent samples I just mention Edward Manier *(The Young Darwin and his Cultural Circle),* Michael Ruse *(The Darwinian Revolution),* and Peter Vorzimmer *(Charles Darwin: The Years of Controversy).*

The centenary in 1959 of the publication of *The Origin of Species* brought forth a flood of celebrations and also of publications from short comments to ponderous works in three volumes. Among the publications I will only cite one that is excellent but that is among the least known: The Darwin Anniversary Issue in September, 1959, of the journal "Victorian Studies," with articles by eight authors. The summing up in the last eleven pages, signed "P.A.," is by Philip Appleman, whose book *Darwin* (revised 1979) is also to be commended.

Tucson, Arizona
February, 1982

Contents

THE BOOK OF
DARWIN

1

A Prologue

Almost all humans meditate on the nature of the world in which they live, on their place in it and on their relationships to it. That may be the most distinct characteristic of *Homo sapiens* as compared with other species. It is true even of most of those who do not explicitly dwell on it, for it is basic to the myriad of religions, past and present, which are so extremely diverse and in respects other than this are for the most part mutually exclusive. Even atheism, usually considered a nonreligion, is fundamentally concerned with concepts of human existence and of the universe so it shares this concern, if little else, with all religions and with all systems of philosophy.

From time to time exceptional humans have considered the strictly objective world in its various aspects and have drawn new and revolutionary conclusions from their observations. Such objective study is the activity of science as distinct from but not necessarily averse to the nonscientific approaches of religions to consideration of our place in this vast and largely mysterious universe. This book is partly by and partly about Charles Darwin, one of those exceptional persons who have revolutionized both the scientific and the philosophical aspects of thought about those matters.

As a background to the Darwinian revolution, some comments on an earlier revolution of thought in a different field will assist understanding. Let us therefore briefly consider the much earlier Copernican revolution. The Pole Mikolaj Kopernik wrote in

13

Latin, as did almost all European savants of his day, and he Latinized his name as Nicolaus Copernicus. He was born in 1473 and died in 1543. He was educated in astronomy, canon law and medicine, but became more involved in astronomy, and sometime around 1507 he began especially to observe and to ponder about the solar system: the sun with its daily passage and the other celestial lights equally orderly but more complex in their wanderings, for which they were called planets. (*Planetae* meant "wanderers" in late, nonclassical Latin.) Copernicus reached a startling conclusion: perhaps the sun and the planets are not moving around the earth in their various ways but the earth, too, is a planet and all are moving in simple orbits around the central sun. About 1530 he wrote a manuscript to that effect with a Latin title translatable as "On the revolutions of the celestial orbs."

Copernicus was a churchman even more than a scientist. He became a canon of a cathedral, and when he finally wrote down his extraordinary concept of the solar system he dedicated it to Pope Paul III, but it was not put into print for some thirteen years. It was finally printed in 1543, and Copernicus was on his deathbed when he vaguely saw a printed copy. Without his knowledge a statement had been inserted saying that his description of the solar system was not meant to be taken literally. It was only a simplified artifice for calculation of the complex movements of the planets other than earth, which could continue to be taken as unmoving.

With Copernicus dead and his heresy explained away, his theory attracted little attention until Galileo Galilei (1564–1642), in a work about spots on the sun published in 1613, made clear that his extensive astronomical studies had convinced him that the Copernican view of the solar system was correct. As word got around, in 1616 Galileo was summoned to Rome and admonished by the Pope that this view was contrary to the holy faith. Nevertheless in 1632 he published another work, called (in Italian) "Dialogue on the two chief systems of the world." In this he again asserted that the Copernican system was correct. This time he was formally tried by the Inquisition, and to save himself he was forced to deny that the earth and [other] planets revolve around the sun. On his way to exile he was heard to say, in words that have become famous, *"E pur si muove"*—"And nevertheless it [the earth] does move!"

Centuries after Galileo it was at last generally accepted that he and Copernicus before him had been right. When I was a child (I was born in 1902), there were still some eccentrics who insisted that the earth is flat and does not revolve around the sun. Now if anyone denied that the earth is a globe, going around the sun, somewhat off center, in one of a vast number of galaxies, he would simply be laughed at as idiotic or insane. What was theological dogma in the centuries of Copernicus and of Galileo has been accordingly abandoned in church tenets as well as in science.

What does this have to do with Darwin? A great deal. Even more in detail than may appear at first sight. Copernicus was a trained theologian who became a scientist. So was Darwin. Copernicus started a major revolution in cosmography which was contrary to the theological dogma he had been taught. Darwin started a revolution in biology even more important for our concepts of our places and roles in the universe and even more in conflict with the almost universally accepted dogmas of the religion dominant in his time and society. Bothered by the conflict, Copernicus hesitated about fifteen years between fully verbalizing his revolution in thought and publishing it. Darwin hesitated almost exactly the same length of time. Both Copernican cosmography and Darwinian biology evoked antagonism bitter to the point of unreasoning attack. Copernicus was saved this by his timely death, but it fell with full force on his follower Galileo. Darwin lived through the first and much of the worst of it, partly by leading a somewhat reclusive but still highly productive life and partly by the aid of less reclusive and more outspoken defenders, notably Thomas Henry Huxley (1825–95). The attack on Copernican theory weakened and finally fell off in the course of some two and a half centuries or so. The attack on Darwinism has gone on so far for barely a century and a quarter. Things move faster in our days, and the attack has waxed and waned without being constant, yet just now we seem to be in a waxing stage again, with attacks on Darwinism almost back to the fluency, idiocy and popularity in some quarters last seen in the days of William Jennings Bryan, who was already widely repudiated when he died in 1925.

Some understanding of Darwin's character and of his life and work, not only as regards evolution but in other fields of science as well, will not wholly explain but will somewhat clarify the peculiar anomaly evident in the lag in full acceptance of the Copernican revolution first and then much later the Darwinian revolution. In both cases a major, perhaps the major, element of opposition is an underlying fear. People used to live on a stable earth, the unchanging center of a finite universe bounded by a great sphere sprinkled with stars and with the sun steadily circling the earth while, more slowly and eccentrically, the planets moved about the steadfast earth and the reliably circling sun. People knew where they stood: on solid ground right in the center of the universe. But it turned out that they do not. They live on an earth that is a mere spot rapidly moving in the awesome abyss of space. This struck terror in most of those who had been comfortably assured by generally held dogmas.

People got used to that particular correction of long-enduring prehistoric errors, but it took about ten generations before the terror was essentially ended. Still most people had the reassurance of the unchanging nature and superiority of their own kind. This, too, had been a human conviction in prehistoric times and became a dogma of various religions. In most of the dominant religions it was and by some still is held that the first humans were created, in exactly the form they have now, by a god, or a pantheon of gods, or some other supernatural entity. Even before Darwin there had been speculation that the creation of the human species might have been more gradual, even that it might have been by what we now call evolution. For example, Lamarck, who lived from 1744 to 1829 and whose science and philosophy were essentially those of the eighteenth century, wrote that living things continuously change through a circle from least perfect to most perfect organisms, with mankind the most perfect. For him, this evolution (he did not use that term) was itself the creation of God. No one paid a great deal of attention to that view, which was indeed merely a speculation not supported by objective evidence. Some others also speculated about evolution well into the nineteenth century, but it was Darwin who painstakingly gathered evidence which finally could not rationally be explained by anything but evolution (a term that Darwin did use, but not always). This, too, was contrary to dogma generally accepted in Darwin's own milieu and more widely. Like the Copernican revolution, this one made most people feel insecure and terrified some of them. The less they understood Darwin and the evolutionary scientists who followed him, the more they might cling to the safety blanket of creationism.

Most of the current minority but vociferous attackers of Darwinism and evolutionism—not identical things—display abysmal ignorance of what Darwin actually wrote, how he developed his views on evolution and life in general, what sort of background he had and what sort of man he was. It is a purpose of this book to supply at least a minimum of such knowledge through verbatim transcripts of Darwin's writings on a variety of topics, with commentaries placing them in their historical and contemporary contexts. Another purpose is to introduce readers to a fascinating man and something of his interesting life, both physical and intellectual.

It remains to be said here at the beginning of this book that it is not an attack on any religion. Darwin did cease to be a Christian, but he recorded, not intending it for publication, that when he wrote *The Origin of Species* he was a theist and that in some respects he later became not an atheist but an agnostic. As a scientist he sought always for more and more observable facts and then for the most probable, or most rational, explanation of them. Speaking now for myself I see no excuse for warfare between religion and science. Each has its own sphere, and friction arises only when either one is invaded by the other. Creationism, whether you believe in it or not, is strictly religious and it simply is not rational to speak of "scientific" creationism. Evolutionism, which is not confined to Darwinism, is a science, and it likewise is not rational to speak of "religious" evolutionism.

Surely the world we live in is full of mystery. We do not know how or by what it was created. Scientific study can neither deny nor affirm a concept of creation by a literally ineffable someone or something, nor can a scientist object to calling the creator "god," uncapitalized and undescribable. Once the universe and its laws of nature existed, it was a universe in at least one small part of which evolution occurred. Consideration of creation, unknown and unknowable in objective terms, is religion. Evolution, the incompletely known, the objectively knowable fact, is science.

So now let us turn to Darwin, the genius who, though fallible as all of us are, revolutionized scientific scrutiny and knowledge of our origins and of our physical relationships to nature and the universe.

2

A Bomb Is Dropped

On the evening of the first of July, 1858, the venerable and prestigious Linnean Society met to hear a paper read by George Bentham (1800–1884), a famous botanist of that time. Charles Lyell (1797–1875), the great man who was one of the founders of geology as a science, and Joseph D. Hooker (1817–1911), an eminent botanist, had arranged almost at the last moment to have two communications read to the Society before Bentham's paper. One was by their close friend Charles Darwin (1809–82), a member of the Society and already famous as a geologist, paleontologist and naturalist, and the other by Alfred Russel Wallace (1823–1913), a naturalist also known by them, especially for his book *A Narrative of Travels on the Amazon and Rio Negro* (still being read in 1982). Neither author was present at the meeting; Darwin remained at home because of illness and a death in the family, and Wallace was in the East Indies, or Malay Archipelago as it was then called. (Most of it is now Indonesia.) The communications were read by the secretary of the Society. Darwin's communication, reprinted in full on the following pages, was in two sections: the first was an extract from an unpublished manuscript written in 1844 and the second an abstract from a letter dated September 5, 1857, from Darwin to his American correspondent Asa Gray (1810–88), a professor at Harvard, which he made the center for botanical studies in the Western Hemisphere. Wallace's contribution was a long letter to Darwin sent from Ternate in the Malay Archipelago in February 1858.

ON THE VARIATION OF ORGANIC BEINGS IN A STATE OF NATURE

ON THE NATURAL MEANS OF SELECTION; ON THE COMPARISON OF DOMESTIC RACES AND TRUE SPECIES

By Charles Darwin

De Candolle, in an eloquent passage, has declared that all nature is at war, one organism with another, or with external nature. Seeing the contented face of nature, this may at first well be doubted: but reflection will inevitably prove it to be true. The war, however, is not constant, but recurrent in a slight degree at short periods, and more severely at occasional more distant periods; and hence its effects are easily overlooked. It is the doctrine of Malthus applied in most cases with tenfold force. As in every climate there are seasons, for each of its inhabitants, of greater and less abundance, so all annually breed; and the moral restraint which in some small degree checks the increase of mankind is entirely lost. Even slow-breeding mankind has doubled in twenty-five years; and if he could increase his food with greater ease, he would double in less time. But for animals without artificial means, the amount of food for each species must, *on an average,* be constant, whereas the increase of all organisms tends to be geometrical, and in a vast majority of cases at an enormous ratio. Suppose in a certain spot there are eight pairs of birds, and that *only* four pairs of them annually (including double hatches) rear only four young, and that these go on rearing their young at the same rate, then at the end of seven years (a short life, excluding violent deaths, for any bird) there will be 2048 birds, instead of the original sixteen. As this increase is quite impossible, we must conclude either that birds do not rear nearly half their young, or that the average life of a bird is, from accident, not nearly seven years. Both checks probably concur. The same kind of calculation applied to all plants and animals affords results more or less striking, but in very few instances more striking than in man.

Many practical illustrations of this rapid tendency to increase are on record, among which, during peculiar seasons, are the extraordinary numbers of certain animals; for instance, during the years 1826 to 1828, in La Plata, when from drought some millions of cattle perished, the whole country actually *swarmed* with mice. Now I think it cannot be doubted that during the breeding season all the mice (with the exception of a few males or females in excess) ordinarily pair, and therefore that this astounding increase during three years must be attributed to a greater number than usual surviving the first year, and then breeding, and so on till the third year, when their numbers were brought down to their usual limits on the return of wet weather. Where man has introduced plants and animals into a new and favourable country, there are many accounts in how surprisingly few years the whole country has become stocked with them. This increase would necessarily stop as soon as the country was fully stocked; and yet we have every reason to believe, from what is known of wild animals, that *all* would pair in the spring. In the majority of cases it is most difficult to imagine where the check falls—though generally, no doubt, on the seeds, eggs, and young; but when we remember how impossible, even in mankind (so much better known than any other animal), it is to infer from repeated casual observations what the average duration of life is, or to discover the different percentage of deaths to births in different countries, we ought to feel no surprise at our being unable to discover where the check falls in any animal or plant. It should always be remembered, that in most cases the checks are recurrent yearly in a small, regular degree, and in an extreme degree during unusually cold, hot, dry, or wet years, according to the constitution of the being in question. Lighten any check in the least degree, and the geometrical powers of increase in every organism will almost instantly increase the average number of the favoured species. Nature may be compared to a surface on which rest ten thousand sharp wedges touching each other and driven inwards by incessant blows. Fully to realize these views much reflection is requisite. Malthus on man should be studied; and all such cases as those of the mice in La Plata, of the cattle and horses when first turned out in South America, of the birds by our calculation, etc., should be well considered. Reflect on the enormous multiplying power *inherent and annually in action* in all animals; reflect on the countless seeds scattered by a hundred ingenious contrivances, year after year, over the whole face of the land; and yet we have every reason to suppose that the average percentage of each of the inhabitants of a country usually remains constant. Finally, let it be borne in mind that this average number of individuals (the external conditions remaining the same) in each country is kept up by recurrent struggles against other species or against external nature (as on the borders of the arctic regions, where the cold checks life), and that ordinarily each individual of every species holds its place, either by its own struggle and capacity of acquiring nourishment in some period of its life, from the egg upwards; or by the struggle of its parents (in short-lived organisms, when the main check occurs at longer intervals) with other individuals of the *same* or *different* species.

But let the external conditions of a country alter. If in a small degree, the relative proportions of the inhabitants will in most cases simply be slightly changed; but let the number of inhabitants be small, as on an island, and free access to it from other countries be circumscribed, and let the change of conditions continue progressing (forming new stations), in such a case the original inhabitants must cease to be as perfectly adapted to the changed conditions as they were originally. It has been shown in a former part of this work, that such changes of external conditions would, from their acting on the reproductive system, probably cause the organization of those beings which were most affected to become, as under domestication, plastic. Now, can it be doubted, from the struggle each individual has to obtain subsistence, that any minute variation in structure, habits, or instincts, adapting that individual better to the new conditions, would tell upon its vigour and health? In the struggle it would have a better *chance* of surviving; and those of its offspring which inherited the variation, be it ever so slight, would also have a better *chance*. Yearly more are bred than can survive; the smallest grain in the balance, in the long run, must tell on which death shall fall, and which shall survive. Let this work of selection on the one hand, and death on the other, go on for a thousand generations, who will pretend to affirm that it would produce no effect, when we remember what, in a few years, Bakewell effected in cattle, and Western in sheep, by this identical principle of selection?

To give an imaginary example from changes in progress on an island: let the organization of a canine animal which preyed chiefly on rabbits, but sometimes on hares, become slightly plastic; let these same changes cause the number of rabbits very slowly to decrease, and the number of hares to increase; the effect of this would be that the fox or dog would be driven to try to catch more hares: his organization, however, being slightly plastic, those individuals with the lightest forms, longest limbs, and best eyesight, let the difference be ever so small, would be slightly favoured, and would tend to live longer, and to survive during that time of the year when food was scarcest; they would also rear more young, which would tend to inherit these slight peculiarities. The less fleet ones would be rigidly destroyed. I can see no more reason to doubt that these causes in a thousand generations would produce a marked effect, and adapt the form of the fox or dog to the catching of hares instead of rabbits, than that greyhounds can be improved by selection and careful breeding. So would it be with plants under similar circumstances. If the number of individuals of a species with plumed seeds could be increased by greater powers of dissemination within its own area (that is, if the check to increase fell chiefly on the seeds), those seeds which were provided with ever so little more down, would in the long run be most disseminated; hence a greater number of seeds thus formed would germinate, and would tend to produce plants inheriting the slightly better-adapted down.

Besides this natural means of selection, by which those individuals are preserved, whether in their egg, or larval, or mature state, which are best adapted to the place they fill in nature, there is a second agency at work in most unisexual animals, tending to produce the same effect, namely the struggle of the males for the females. These struggles are generally decided by the law of battle, but in the case of birds, apparently, by the charms of their song, by their beauty or their power of courtship, as in the dancing rock-thrush of Guiana. The most vigorous and healthy males, implying perfect adaptation, must generally gain the victory in their contests. This kind of selection, however, is less rigorous than the other; it does not require the death of the less successful, but gives to them fewer descendants. The struggle falls, moreover, at a time of year when food is generally abundant, and perhaps the effect chiefly produced would be the modification of the secondary sexual characters, which are not related to the power of obtaining food, or to defence from enemies, but to fighting with or rivalling other males. The result of this struggle amongst the males may be compared in some respects to that produced by those agriculturists, who pay less attention to the careful selection of all their young animals, and more to the occasional use of a choice male.

ABSTRACT OF A LETTER FROM CHARLES DARWIN
TO PROFESSOR ASA GRAY

OF BOSTON, U.S.A., DATED DOWN,
5 SEPTEMBER 1857

It is wonderful what the principle of selection by man, that is the picking out of individuals with any desired quality, and breeding from them, and again picking out, can do. Even breeders have been astounded at their own results. They can act on differences inappreciable to an uneducated eye. Selection has been *methodically* followed in *Europe* for only the last half century; but it was occasionally, and even in some degree methodically, followed in the most ancient times. There must have been also a kind of unconscious selection from a remote period, namely in the preservation of the individual animals (without any thought of their offspring) most useful to each race of man in his particular circumstances. The 'roguing', as nurserymen call the destroying of varieties which depart from their type, is a kind of selection. I am convinced that intentional and occasional selection has been the main agent in the production of our domestic races; but however this may be, its great power of modification has been indisputably shown in later times. Selection acts only by the accumulation of slight or greater variations, caused by external conditions, or by the mere fact that in generation the child is not absolutely similar to its parent. Man, by this power of accumulating variations, adapts living beings to his wants—may be said to make the wool of one sheep good for carpets, of another for cloth, etc.

Now suppose there were a being who did not judge by mere external appearances, but who could study the whole internal organization, who was never capricious, and should go on selecting for one object during millions of generations; who will say what he might not effect? In nature we have some *slight* variation occasionally in all parts; and I think it can be shown that changed conditions of existence is the main cause of the child not exactly resembling its parents; and in nature geology shows us what changes have taken place, and are taking place. We have almost unlimited time; no one but a practical geologist can fully appreciate this. Think of the Glacial period, during the whole of which the same species at least of shells have existed; there must have been during this period millions on millions of generations.

I think it can be shown that there is such an unerring power at work in *Natural Selection* (the title of my book), which selects exclusively for the good of each organic being. The elder de Candolle, W. Herbert, and Lyell have written excellently on the struggle for life; but even they have not written strongly enough. Reflect that every being (even the elephant) breeds at such a rate, that in a few years, or at most a few centuries, the surface of the earth would not hold the progeny of one pair. I have found it hard constantly to bear in mind that the increase of every single species is checked during some part of its life, or during some shortly recurrent generation. Only a few of those annually born can live to propagate their kind. What a trifling difference must often determine which shall survive, and which perish!

Now take the case of a country undergoing some change. This will tend to cause some of its inhabitants to vary slightly—not but that I believe most beings vary at all times enough for selection to act on them. Some of its inhabitants will be exterminated; and the remainder will be exposed to the mutual action of a different set of inhabitants, which I believe to be far more important to the life of each being than mere climate. Considering the infinitely various methods which living beings follow to obtain food by struggling with other organisms, to escape danger at various times of life, to have their eggs or seeds disseminated, etc., I cannot doubt that during millions of generations individuals of a species will be occasionally born with some slight variation, profitable to some part of their economy. Such individuals will have a better chance of surviving, and of propagating their new and slightly different structure; and the modification may be slowly increased by the accumulative action of natural selection to any profitable extent. The variety thus formed will either coexist with, or, more commonly, will exterminate its parent form. An organic being like the woodpecker or mistletoe, may thus come to be adapted to a score of contingencies—natural selection accumulating those slight variations in all parts of its structure, which are in any way useful to it during any part of its life.

Multiform difficulties will occur to every one, with respect to this theory. Many can, I think, be satisfactorily answered. *Natura non facit saltum* answers some of the most obvious. The slowness of the change, and only a very few individuals undergoing change at any one time, answers others. The extreme imperfection of our geological records answers others.

Another principle, which may be called the principle of divergence, plays, I believe, an important part in the origin of species. The same spot will support more life if occupied by very diverse forms. We see this in the many generic forms in a square yard of turf, and in the plants or insects on any little uniform islet, belonging almost invariably to as many genera and families as species. We can understand the meaning of this fact amongst the higher animals, whose habits we understand. We know that it has been experimentally shown that a plot of land will yield a greater weight if sown with several species and genera of grasses, than if sown with only two or three species. Now, every organic being, by propagating so rapidly, may be said to be striving its utmost to increase in numbers. So it will be with the offspring of any species after it has become diversified into varieties, or subspecies, or true species. And it follows, I think, from the foregoing facts, that the varying offspring of each species will try (only few will succeed) to seize on as many and as diverse places in the economy of nature as possible. Each new variety or species, when formed, will generally take the place of, and thus exterminate its less well-fitted parent. This I believe to be the origin of the classification and affinities of organic beings at all times; for organic beings always *seem* to branch and sub-branch like the limbs of a tree from a common trunk, the flourishing and diverging twigs destroying the less vigorous—the dead and lost branches rudely representing extinct genera and families.

This sketch is *most* imperfect; but in so short a space I cannot make it better. Your imagination must fill up very wide blanks.[1]

This novel communication, which was a forerunner of the work that would bring about a revolution in science, might be expected to have put the group of listening naturalists in a frenzy. It did not. Presented unexpectedly and briefly, it was evidently too much for the staid audience to absorb. There was no real discussion. As Hooker later wrote, the statement was "too novel and too ominous for the old School to enter the lists before armouring." In other words they had need but not yet time to think it over. The president of the Society, Thomas Bell, although an old friend of Darwin's, remained silent at the meeting and later opposed Darwin's views. Bentham, whose paper the members had come to hear, was and remained a firm antievolutionist. He withdrew his Linnean Society paper.

The bomb had been dropped, but those present did not yet know what had hit them.

The incidents that led up to this meeting and hence, as will later appear, to publication of *The Origin of Species* in the following year have been recounted and discussed many times. They must be more briefly outlined here. The background goes back to 1837, the year after Darwin's return from his voyage around the world in the *Beagle*. He was heavily involved with the narrative of that

voyage, with extensive publications on his geological observations and on the animals, living and fossil, collected on the
voyage, as well as with his personal life, which was leading to a
long, happy and fruitful marriage to his cousin Emma Wedgwood.
Yet in 1837 he started his first notebook on the origin of species,
and although much else also absorbed him, this subject never left
his mind for all the rest of his life.

In 1842 Darwin wrote a rather brief and rough outline of his
views on evolution and on the main Darwinian concept, natural
selection. In poor health, he had almost an obsession about the
possibility of his dying without passing on his great theory, and in
1844 he wrote a more complete version of it and of the rapidly
accumulating evidence for it. This was not intended for publication unless he did die without finishing what he called the "big
book." Until the meeting in 1858 only a few of Darwin's closest
friends and correspondents knew that he had become a thorough-
going evolutionist and hoped to write a book on the subject when
he was confident that an enormous accumulation of evidence
would warrant positive conclusions. On October 3, 1856, he
wrote to his second cousin, W. D. Fox, with whom he was on
close terms:

> . . . I remember you protested against Lyell's advice of
> writing a *sketch* of my species doctrines. Well, when I began I
> found it such unsatisfactory work that I have desisted, and am
> now drawing up my work as perfect as my materials of
> nineteen years' collecting suffice, but do not intend to stop to
> perfect any line of investigation beyond current work. Thus far
> and no farther I shall follow Lyell's urgent advice . . . I find to
> my sorrow it will run to quite a big book.[2]

On February 8, 1858, Darwin wrote to Fox:

> . . . I am working very hard at my book, perhaps too hard.
> It will be very big . . . I am like Croesus overwhelmed with my
> riches in facts, and I mean to make my book as perfect as ever
> I can. I shall not go to press at soonest for a couple of years.[3]

In fact the "big book" was destined never to go to press as
such, although most of the material in the thirteen chapters
written in draft was incorporated in *The Origin of Species* and
later books. Continuation of work on the "big book" was
abruptly stopped on June 18, 1858, when Darwin received a letter
and manuscript from Wallace.

Wallace was a brilliant naturalist and in other ways, some of them quite eccentric, an interesting man. He deserves to have books written about him, and several have been. In this book about Darwin and Darwinism he enters only at this point. Wallace was supporting his travels and field observations in the East Indies by collecting specimens, especially insects and birds, for sale to collectors and museums. He was also thinking deeply about biogeography and is one of the founders of that subject as a science. His occupation further made him ponder on the origin of the species observed and collected. Without any knowledge of Darwin's work on the same subject, he reached an almost identical theory of evolution involving natural selection. The manuscript was sent to Darwin for comment. It took Darwin aback. He had worked on this subject for twenty-one years and was far along in preparing it for publication, and here was a short manuscript that independently expressed the most essential points of his own progressing "big book." Darwin sent Wallace's manuscript on for Lyell to read, and in his accompanying letter he wrote:

"I never saw a more striking coincidence; if Wallace had my MS. sketch written out in 1842, he could not have made a better short abstract! Even his terms now stand as heads of my chapters."

Although humanly crushed at the thought of a forestalling of the results of his long antecedent work, Darwin felt obliged "in honour" to arrange the publication of Wallace's paper before his own book, despite the long priority of his work. This had been started twenty-one years before, when Wallace was only fourteen years old. When Darwin's first sketch of his theory was written in 1842, Wallace was nineteen and had not yet started his career as a naturalist. There is thus no possible question about Darwin's priority on the theory of natural selection. (A paper published by Wallace in 1855 is sometimes brought into this discussion, but it was devoted to biogeography, only hinted at evolution and said nothing about natural selection.) After much heart-wringing Darwin asked for the advice of his "two best and kindest friends," Lyell and Hooker. They strongly advised that Wallace's paper and an abstract of Darwin's theory should be read at the same meeting of the Linnean Society and published simultaneously.

It is pleasant to record that Wallace always recognized Darwin's priority as regards natural selection and did not consider himself a coauthor of the theory they reached independently but Wallace years after Darwin. Wallace, fourteen years younger than Darwin, outlived him by thirty-one years and always revered the elder evolutionist. On the basic issues they differed only in that Wallace did not accept that mankind evolved in the same way as other species of animals.

After the Linnean meeting Darwin wisely decided not to wait the years it would take him to finish the "big book" in full and to prepare an abstract of it for prompt publication. That was *The Origin of Species,* an "abstract" 490 pages long! It was published on November 26, 1859. To it we will return in later chapters. First we must go back to what may be called the preparatory years that changed a somewhat indeterminate and at times even a frivolous youth into—well, into not *a* but *the* Darwin.

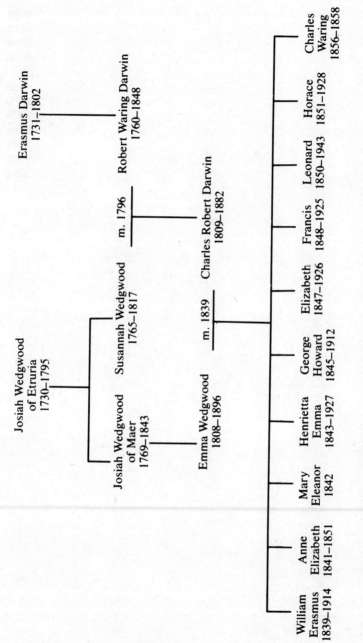

A PARTIAL GENEALOGY OF CHARLES DARWIN AND HIS FAMILY

Erasmus Darwin
1731–1802

Robert Waring Darwin
1760–1848

m. 1796

Josiah Wedgwood
of Etruria
1730–1795

Susannah Wedgwood
1765–1817

Josiah Wedgwood
of Maer
1769–1843

Emma Wedgwood
1808–1896

Charles Robert Darwin
1809–1882

m. 1839

William
Erasmus
1839–1914

Anne
Elizabeth
1841–1851

Mary
Eleanor
1842

Henrietta
Emma
1843–1927

George
Howard
1845–1912

Elizabeth
1847–1926

Francis
1848–1925

Leonard
1850–1943

Horace
1851–1928

Charles
Waring
1856–1858

3

Search for a Profession

Charles Darwin was born on February 12, 1809, the same day and year as Abraham Lincoln. It is impressive, but obviously is only a coincidence, that two of the great men of the nineteenth century, who were to lead such different lives but to reach equal renown, were born at the same time at such wide distance and in such different circumstances.

Charles Darwin was born into an affluent upper-class family, his father, Robert Darwin, a highly successful physician, son of Erasmus Darwin, also a physician and a poet who wrote at length, touching on ideas of evolution then circulating on pre-Darwinian and, as it turned out, non-Darwinian grounds. The infant was christened Charles Robert, but the "Robert," after his father, was almost never used by Charles. His mother, who married his father in 1796, was Susannah Wedgwood, daughter of Josiah Wedgwood of Etruria who had carried the old Wedgwood ceramics to the height of beauty and popularity that has persisted to this day. Josiah Wedgwood's son, also named Josiah, was distinguished as the Josiah Wedgwood of Maer, his adult home. Emma Wedgwood, whom Charles Darwin married, was the daughter of Josiah of Maer, and hence first cousin to Charles. Marrying cousins was not looked askance at in the family: the Josiah Wedgwood of Etruria had married an only slightly more distant Wedgwood relative. Thus Charles and Emma both descended from at least two branches of Wedgwoods. This is some evidence that consanguineous marriages can produce superior and not inferior offspring.

As shown here in the partial family tree on page 29, the marriage of Charles and Emma was fruitful. They produced ten children. Three of them died young, a proportion not unusual then even in physicians' grandchildren, but the others had extended lives, Leonard reaching the prodigious age of ninety-three. Six of the children married, and descendants of Charles and Emma are still living now.

The story of Charles Darwin's youth and the wavering course up to his embarking on the *Beagle* is best documented in his autobiography and is here given by extracts from the earlier parts of that document. It was written mainly in 1876, when he was sixty-seven years old, but some additions or changes were made up until the year of his death at age seventy-three in 1882. The autobiography was not intended for publication but, as he prefaced it, was written because he "thought the attempt would amuse me, and might possibly interest my children or their children." He added that, "I have attempted to write the following account of myself as if I were a dead man in another world looking back at my own life . . . I have taken no pains about my style of writing." Shortly after Darwin's death his seventh child and third son, Francis, undertook to compile and edit a two-volume work on "The Life and Letters of Charles Darwin." He decided to include the autobiography as Chapter II of that work, but there arose much disagreement among the family members: the wife and mother, Emma, and the then surviving seven sons and daughters. Usually on the best of terms, they did not agree as to what of the autobiography meant for them could or should be made public. Francis did publish most of the autobiography but with the prefatory note that, "in a narrative of a personal and intimate kind written for his wife and children, passages should occur which must here be omitted."

The original manuscript survived, and long after Emma and all of the first generation children who had objected to publication of parts or all of it were dead, the whole, unexpurgated autobiography was transcribed and edited by one of Charles Darwin's granddaughters, Norah Barlow, and published in 1958. (By courtesy of Lady Barlow, the present commentator was able to consult Darwin's original handscript before its publication; Darwin's writing was almost as illegible as my own.) While approving this edition and recommending it for researchers, I have nevertheless taken the excerpts for the present book from the first publication of the autobiography in the version approved by Darwin's wife and all his then surviving children. Careful comparison of the expurgated and unexpurgated editions shows that little new and relevant to the life and character of Darwin himself is involved in the earlier suppressed passages. Practically all of them fall into three categories:

1. Some are personal, not derogatory and sometimes especially loving remarks about the family itself. That it was a loved and loving family is clear enough from other sources, and these corroborations were probably excised from a Victorian sense of modesty or privacy.

2. Some are ill-tempered or merely personal remarks about certain of Darwin's colleagues and contemporaries. For example, it was no secret that after earlier friendship, Richard Owen (1804–92) had become Darwin's bitter enemy, and it is obvious without Darwin's autobiographical remark that Owen's change toward him was motivated by jealousy at Darwin's success. It was also obvious that Darwin disliked Spencer and some others. On the other hand it is hard to see why his expressions of great good will and appreciation of Hooker and Huxley were considered to call for deletion. This, too, was widely known before the autobiography was written.

3. Almost everything that Darwin said about religion was expurgated from the autobiography, clearly by wish of Emma, who remained a devoted Christian while Charles moved from Christianity to theism to agnosticism, as he had made plain in publication outside of the autobiography. He was a little more explicit or emphatic in the autobiography; for example, saying that if Christianity were true, it would condemn his father, brother and almost all his best friends to everlasting punishment "and this is a damnable doctrine." Emma asked to have this deleted, with a note that (in her opinion) very few would now call that Christianity. Despite their divergence in religion, Emma and Charles had always remained happy and congenial together.

Now let us set the scene for excerpts from the autobiography that will take Darwin up to 1831, then in the following chapter to the next, in many ways to the most important, phase of his life, his voyage on the *Beagle*.

Darwin was born in Mount House, a roomy, three-story, rather plain edifice in Shrewsbury. It has been lately made over for offices of the government and bears no special notice of the Darwins, but the room where Charles was born and the one that he and his brother converted into a childish laboratory were identified for me when I visited the house some years ago. Charles had three older sisters and one older brother. Later another sister was born. His earliest schooling was by his sister Caroline, nine years older than he. She was not impressed by him as a scholar. His mother died in 1817, when he was eight, and shortly thereafter he spent a year in a day school run by a Reverend G. Case, minister of a Unitarian chapel.

The autobiography may be taken up from here:

In the summer of 1818 I went to Dr. Butler's great school in Shrewsbury, and remained there for seven years till Midsummer 1825, when I was sixteen years old. I boarded at this school, so that I had the great advantage of living the life of a true schoolboy; but as the distance was hardly more than a mile to my home, I very often ran there in the longer intervals between the callings over and before locking up at night. This, I think, was in many ways advantageous to me by keeping up home affections and interests. I remember in the early part of my school life that I often had to run very quickly to be in time, and from being a fleet runner was generally successful; but when in doubt I prayed earnestly to God to help me, and I well remember that I attributed my success to the prayers and not to my quick running, and marvelled how generally I was aided.

I have heard my father and elder sister say that I had, as a very young boy, a strong taste for long solitary walks; but what I thought about I know not. I often became quite absorbed, and once, whilst returning to school on the summit of the old fortifications round Shrewsbury, which had been converted into a public foot-path with no parapet on one side, I walked off and fell to the ground, but the height was only seven or eight feet. Nevertheless the number of thoughts which passed through my mind during this very short, but sudden and wholly unexpected fall, was astonishing, and seem hardly compatible with what physiologists have, I believe, proved about each thought requiring quite an appreciable amount of time.

Nothing could have been worse for the development of my mind than Dr. Butler's school, as it was strictly classical, nothing else being taught, except a little ancient geography and history. The school as a means of education to me was simply a blank. During my whole life I have been singularly incapable of mastering any language. Especial attention was paid to verse-making, and this I could never do well. I had many friends, and got together a good collection of old verses, which by patching together, sometimes aided by other boys, I could work into any subject. Much attention was paid to learning by heart the lessons of the previous day; this I could effect with great facility, learning forty or fifty lines of Virgil or Homer, whilst I was in morning chapel; but this exercise was utterly useless, for every verse was forgotten in forty-eight hours. I was not idle, and with the exception of versification, generally worked conscientiously at my classics, not using cribs. The sole pleasure I ever received from such studies, was from some of the odes of Horace, which I admired greatly.

When I left the school I was for my age neither high nor low in it; and I believe that I was considered by all my masters and by my father as a very ordinary boy, rather below the common standard in intellect. To my deep mortification my father once said to me, "You care for nothing but shooting, dogs, and rat-catching, and you will be a disgrace to yourself and all your family." But my father, who was the kindest man I ever knew and whose memory I love with all my heart, must have been angry and somewhat unjust when he used such words.

Looking back as well as I can at my character during my school life, the only qualities which at this period promised well for the future, were, that I had strong and diversified tastes, much zeal for whatever interested me, and a keen pleasure in understanding any complex subject or thing. I was taught Euclid by a private tutor, and I distinctly remember the intense satisfaction which the clear geometrical proofs gave me. I remember, with equal distinctness, the delight which my uncle gave me (the father of Francis Galton) by explaining the principle of the vernier of a barometer. With respect to diversified tastes, independently of science, I was fond of reading various books, and I used to sit for hours reading the historical plays of Shakespeare, generally in an old window in the thick walls of the school. I read also other poetry, such as Thomson's 'Seasons,' and the recently published poems of Byron and Scott. I mention this because later in life I wholly lost, to my great regret, all pleasure from poetry of any kind, including Shakespeare. In connection with pleasure from poetry, I may add that in 1822 a vivid delight in scenery was first awakened in my mind, during a riding tour on the borders of Wales, and this has lasted longer than any other aesthetic pleasure.

Early in my school days a boy had a copy of the 'Wonders of the World,' which I often read, and disputed with other boys about the veracity of some of the statements; and I believe that this book first gave me a wish to travel in remote countries, which was ultimately fulfilled by the voyage of the *Beagle*. In the latter part of my school life I became passionately fond of shooting; I do not believe that any one could have shown more zeal for the most holy cause than I did for shooting birds. How well I remember killing my first snipe, and my excitement was so great that I had much difficulty in reloading my gun from the trembling of my hands. This taste long continued, and I became a very good shot. When at Cambridge I used to practice throwing up my gun to my shoulder before a looking-glass to see that I threw it up straight. Another and better plan was to get a friend to wave about a lighted candle, and then to fire at it with a cap on the nipple, and if the aim was accurate the little puff of air would blow out the candle. The explosion of the cap caused a sharp crack, and I was told that the tutor of the college remarked, "What an extraordinary thing it is, Mr. Darwin seems to spend hours in cracking a horse-whip in his room, for I often hear the crack when I pass under his windows."

I had many friends amongst the schoolboys, whom I loved dearly, and I think that my disposition was then very affectionate.

With respect to science, I continued collecting minerals with much zeal, but quite unscientifically—all that I cared about was a new-*named* mineral, and I hardly attempted to classify them. I must have observed insects with some little care, for when ten years old (1819) I went for three weeks to Plas Edwards on the sea-coast in Wales, I was very much interested and surprised at seeing a large black and scarlet Hemipterous insect, many moths (Zygaena), and a Cicindela which are not found in Shropshire. I almost made up my mind to begin collecting all the insects which I could find dead, for on consulting my sister I concluded that it was not right to kill insects for the sake of making a collection. From reading White's 'Selborne,' I took much pleasure in watching the habits of birds, and even made notes on the subject. In my simplicity I remember wondering why every gentleman did not become an ornithologist.

Towards the close of my school life, my brother worked hard at chemistry, and made a fair laboratory with proper apparatus in the tool-house in the garden, and I was allowed to aid him as a servant in most of his experiments. He made all the gases and many compounds, and I read with great care several books on chemistry, such as Henry and Parkes' 'Chemical Catechism.' The subject interested me greatly, and we often used to go on working till rather late at night. This was the best part of my education at school, for it showed me practically the meaning of experimental science. The fact that we worked at chemistry somehow got known at school, and as it was an unprecedented fact, I was nicknamed "Gas." I was also once publicly rebuked by the head-master, Dr. Butler, for thus wasting my time on such useless subjects; and he called me very unjustly a "poco curante," and as I did not understand what he meant, it seemed to me a fearful reproach.

As I was doing no good at school, my father wisely took me away at a rather earlier age than usual, and sent me (Oct. 1825) to Edinburgh University with my brother, where I stayed for two years or sessions. My brother was completing his medical studies, though I do not believe he ever really intended to practise, and I was sent there to commence them. But soon after this period I became convinced from various small circumstances that my father would leave me property enough to subsist on with some comfort, though I never imagined that I should be so rich a man as I am; but my belief was sufficient to check any strenuous efforts to learn medicine.

The instruction at Edinburgh was altogether by lectures, and these were intolerably dull, with the exception of those on chemistry by Hope; but to my mind there are no advantages and many disadvantages in lectures compared with reading. Dr. Duncan's lectures on Materia

Medica at 8 o'clock on a winter's morning are something fearful to remember. Dr. —— made his lectures on human anatomy as dull as he was himself, and the subject disgusted me. It has proved one of the greatest evils in my life that I was not urged to practise dissection, for I should soon have got over my disgust; and the practise would have been invaluable for all my future work. This has been an irremediable evil, as well as my incapacity to draw. I also attended regularly the clinical wards in the hospital. Some of the cases distressed me a good deal, and I still have vivid pictures before me of some of them; but I was not so foolish as to allow this to lessen my attendance. I cannot understand why this part of my medical course did not interest me in a greater degree; for during the summer before coming to Edinburgh I began attending some of the poor people, chiefly children and women in Shrewsbury: I wrote down as full an account as I could of the case with all the symptoms, and read them aloud to my father, who suggested further inquiries and advised me what medicines to give, which I made up myself. At one time I had at least a dozen patients, and I felt a keen interest in the work. My father, who was by far the best judge of character whom I ever knew, declared that I should make a successful physician,—meaning by this one who would get many patients. He maintained that the chief element of success was exciting confidence; but what he saw in me which convinced him that I should create confidence I know not. I also attended on two occasions the operating theatre in the hospital at Edinburgh, and saw two very bad operations, one on a child, but I rushed away before they were completed. Nor did I ever attend again, for hardly any inducement would have been strong enough to make me do so; this being long before the blessed days of chloroform. The two cases fairly haunted me for many a long year.

My brother stayed only one year at the University, so that during the second year I was left to my own resources; and this was an advantage, for I became well acquainted with several young men fond of natural science. One of these was Ainsworth, who afterwards published his travels in Assyria; he was a Wernerian geologist, and knew a little about many subjects. Dr. Coldstream was a very different young man, prim, formal, highly religious, and most kind-hearted; he afterwards published some good zoological articles. A third young man was Hardie, who would, I think, have made a good botanist, but died early in India. Lastly, Dr. Grant, my senior by several years, but how I became acquainted with him I cannot remember; he published some first-rate zoological papers, but after coming to London as Professor in University College, he did nothing more in science, a fact which has always been inexplicable to me. I knew him well; he was dry and formal in manner, with much enthusiasm beneath this outer crust. He one day, when we were walking together, burst forth in high admiration of Lamarck and his views on evolution. I listened in silent astonishment, and as far as I can judge without any effect on my mind. I had previously read the 'Zoono-mia' of my grandfather, in which similar views are maintained, but without producing any effect on me. Nevertheless it is probable that the hearing rather early in life such views maintained and praised may have favoured my upholding them under a different form in my 'Origin of Species.' At this time I admired greatly the 'Zoonomia'; but on reading it a second time after an interval of ten or fifteen years, I was much disappointed; the proportion of speculation being so large to the facts given.

Drs. Grant and Coldstream attended much to marine Zoology, and I often accompanied the former to collect animals in the tidal pools, which I dissected as well as I could. I also became friends with some of the Newhaven fishermen, and sometimes accompanied them when they trawled for oysters, and thus got many specimens. But from not having had any regular practise in dissection, and from possessing only a wretched microscope, my attempts were very poor. Nevertheless I made one interesting little discovery, and read, about the beginning of the year 1826, a short paper on the subject before the Plinian Society. This was that the so-called ova of Flustra had the power of independent movement by means of cilia, and were in fact larvae. In another short paper I showed that the little globular bodies which had been supposed to be the young state of *Fucus loreus* were the egg-cases of the wormlike *Pontobdella muricata*.

The Plinian Society was encouraged and, I believe, founded by Professor Jameson: it consisted of students and met in an underground room in the University for the sake of reading papers on natural science and discussing them. I used regularly to attend, and the meetings had a good effect on me in stimulating my zeal and giving me new congenial acquaintances. One evening a poor young man got up, and after stammering for a prodigious length of time, blushing crimson, he at last slowly got out the words, "Mr. President, I have forgotten what I was going to say." The poor fellow looked quite overwhelmed, and all the members were so surprised that no one could think of a word to say to cover his confusion. The papers which were read to our little society were not printed, so that I had not the satisfaction of seeing my paper in print; but I believe Dr. Grant noticed my small discovery in his excellent memoir on Flustra.

I was also a member of the Royal Medical Society, and attended pretty regularly; but as the subjects were exclusively medical, I did not much care about them. Much rubbish was talked there, but there were some good speakers, of whom the best was the present Sir J. Kay-Shuttleworth. Dr. Grant took me occasionally to the meetings of the Wernerian Society, where various papers on natural history were read, discussed, and afterwards published in the 'Transactions.' I heard Audubon deliver there some interesting discourses on the habits of N. American birds, sneering somewhat unjustly at Waterton. By the way, a negro lived in Edinburgh, who had travelled with Waterton, and gained his livelihood by stuffing birds, which he did excellently: he gave me lessons for payment, and I used often to sit with him, for he was a very pleasant and intelligent man.

Mr. Leonard Horner also took me once to a meeting of the Royal Society of Edinburgh, where I saw Sir Walter Scott in the chair as President, and he apologised to the meeting as not feeling fitted for such a position. I looked at him and on the whole scene with some awe and reverence, and I think it was owing to this visit during my youth, and to my having attended the Royal Medical Society, that I felt the honour of being elected a few years ago an honorary member of both these Societies, more than any other similar honour. If I had been told at that time that I should one day have been thus honoured, I declare that I should have thought it as ridiculous and improbable, as if I had been told that I should be elected King of England.

During my second year at Edinburgh I attended ——'s lectures on Geology and Zoology, but they were incredibly dull. The sole effect they produced on me was the determination never as long as I lived to read a book on Geology, or in any way to study the science. Yet I feel sure that I was prepared for a philosophical treatment of the subject; for an old Mr. Cotton in Shropshire, who knew a good deal about rocks, had pointed out to me two or three years previously a well-known large erratic boulder in the town of Shrewsbury, called the "bell-stone"; he told me that there was no rock of the same kind nearer than Cumberland or Scotland, and he solemnly assured me that the world would come to an end before any one would be able to explain how this stone came where it now lay. This produced a deep impression on me, and I meditated over this wonderful stone. So that I felt the keenest delight when I first read of the action of icebergs in transporting boulders, and I gloried in the progress of Geology. Equally striking is the fact that I, though now only sixty-seven years old, heard the Professor, in a field lecture at Salisbury Craigs, discoursing on a trap-dyke, with amygdaloidal margins and the strata indurated on each side, with volcanic rocks all around us, say that it was a fissure filled with sediment from above, adding with a sneer that there were men who maintained that it had been injected from beneath in a molten condition. When I think of this lecture, I do not wonder that I determined never to attend to Geology.

From attending ——'s lectures, I became acquainted with the curator of the museum, Mr. Macgillivray, who afterwards published a large and excellent book on the birds of Scotland. I had much interesting natural history talk with him, and he was very kind to me. He gave me some rare shells, for I at that time collected marine mollusca, but with no great zeal.

My summer vacations during these two years were wholly given up to amusements, though I always had some book in hand, which I read with interest. During the summer of 1826 I took a long walking tour with two friends with knapsacks on our backs through North Wales. We walked thirty miles most days, including one day the ascent of Snowdon. I also went with my sister a riding tour in North Wales, a servant with saddle-bags carrying our clothes. The autumns were devoted to shooting chiefly at Mr. Owen's, at Woodhouse, and at my Uncle Jos's, at Maer. My zeal was so great that I used to place my shooting-boots open by my bed-side when I went to bed, so as not to lose half a minute in putting them on in the morning; and on one occasion I reached a distant part of the Maer estate, on the 20th of August for black-game shooting, before I could see: I then toiled on with the game-keeper the whole day through thick heath and young Scotch firs.

I kept an exact record of every bird which I shot throughout the whole season. One day when shooting at Woodhouse with Captain Owen, the eldest son, and Major Hill, his cousin, afterwards Lord Berwick, both of whom I liked very much, I thought myself shamefully used, for every time after I had fired and thought that I had killed a bird, one of the two acted as if loading his gun, and cried out, "You must not count that bird, for I fired at the same time," and the game-keeper, perceiving the joke, backed them up. After some hours they told me the joke, but it was no joke to me, for I had shot a large number of birds, but did not know how many, and could not add them to my list, which I used to do by making a knot in a piece of string tied to a button-hole. This my wicked friends had perceived.

How I did enjoy shooting! but I think that I must have been half-consciously ashamed of my zeal, for I tried to persuade myself that shooting was almost an intellectual employment; it required so much skill to judge where to find most game and to hunt the dogs well.

One of my autumnal visits to Maer in 1827 was memorable from meeting there Sir J. Mackintosh, who was the best converser I ever listened to. I heard afterwards with a glow of pride that he had said, "There is something in that young man that interests me." This must have been chiefly due to his perceiving that I listened with much interest to everything which he said, for I was as ignorant as a pig about his subjects of history, politics, and moral philosophy. To hear of praise from an eminent person, though no doubt apt or certain to excite vanity, is, I think, good for a young man, as it helps to keep him in the right course.

My visits to Maer during these two or three succeeding years were quite delightful, independently of the autumnal shooting. Life there was perfectly free; the country was very pleasant for walking or riding; and in the evening there was much very agreeable conversation, not so personal as it generally is in large family parties, together with music. In the summer the whole family used often to sit on the steps of the old portico, with the flower-garden in front, and with the steep wooded bank opposite the house reflected in the lake, with here and there a fish rising or a water-bird paddling about. Nothing has left a more vivid picture on my mind than these evenings at Maer. I was also attached to and greatly revered my Uncle Jos; he was silent and reserved, so as to be a rather awful man; but he sometimes talked openly with me. He was the very type of an upright man, with the clearest judgment. I do not believe that any power on earth could have made him swerve an inch from what he considered the right course. I used to apply to him in my mind the well-known ode of Horace, now forgotten by me, in which the words "nec vultus tyranni, &c.," come in.

Cambridge 1828–1831.—After having spent two sessions in Edinburgh, my father perceived, or he heard from my sisters, that I did not like the thought of being a physician, so he proposed that I should become a clergyman. He was very properly vehement against my turning into an idle sporting man, which then seemed my probable destination. I asked for some time to consider, as from what little I had heard or thought on the subject I had scruples about declaring my belief in all the dogmas of the Church of England; though otherwise I liked the thought of being a country clergyman. Accordingly I read with care 'Pearson on the Creed,' and a few other books on divinity; and as I did not then in the least doubt the strict and literal truth of every word in the Bible, I soon persuaded myself that our Creed must be fully accepted.

Considering how fiercely I have been attacked by the orthodox, it seems ludicrous that I once intended to be a clergyman. Nor was this intention and my father's wish ever formally given up, but died a natural death when, on leaving Cambridge, I joined the *Beagle* as naturalist. . . .

As it was decided that I should be a clergyman, it was necessary that I should go to one of the English universities and take a degree; but as I had never opened a classical book since leaving school, I found to my dismay, that in the two intervening years I had actually forgotten, incredible as it may appear, almost everything which I had learnt, even to some few of the Greek letters. I did not therefore proceed to Cambridge at the usual time in October, but worked with a private tutor in Shrewsbury, and went to Cambridge after the Christmas vacation, early in 1828. I soon recovered my school standard of knowledge, and could translate easy Greek books, such as Homer and the Greek Testament, with moderate facility.

During the three years which I spent at Cambridge my time was wasted, as far as the academical studies were concerned, as completely as at Edinburgh and at school. I attempted mathematics, and even went during the summer of 1828 with a private tutor (a very dull man) to Barmouth, but I got on very slowly. The work was repugnant to me, chiefly from my not being able to see any meaning in the early steps in algebra. This impatience was very foolish, and in after years I have deeply regretted that I did not proceed far enough at least to understand something of the great leading principles of mathematics, for men thus endowed seem to have an extra sense. But I do not believe that I should ever have succeeded beyond a very low grade. With respect to Classics I did nothing except attend a few compulsory college lectures, and the attendance was almost nominal. In my second year I had to work for a month or two to pass the Little-Go, which I did easily. Again, in my last year I worked with some earnestness for my final degree of B.A., and brushed up on my Classics, together with a little Algebra and Euclid, which latter gave me much pleasure, as it did at school. In order to pass the B.A. examination, it was also necessary to get up Paley's 'Evidences of Christianity,' and his 'Moral Philosophy.' This was done in a thorough manner, and I am convinced that I could have written out the whole of the 'Evidences' with perfect correctness, but not of course in the clear language of Paley. The logic of this book and, as I may add, of his 'Natural Theology,' gave me as much delight as did Euclid. The careful study of these works, without attempting to learn any part by rote, was the only part of the academical course which, as I then felt and as I still believe, was of the least use to me in the education of my mind. I did not at that time trouble myself about Paley's premises; and taking these on trust, I was charmed and convinced by the long line of argumentation. By answering well the examination questions in Paley, by doing Euclid well, and by not failing miserably in Classics, I gained a good place among the οἱ πολλοὶ or crowd of men who do not go in for honours. Oddly enough, I cannot remember how high I stood, and my memory fluctuates between the fifth, tenth, or twelfth, name on the list.

Public lectures on several branches were given in the University, attendance being quite voluntary; but I was so sickened with lectures at Edinburgh that I did not even attend Sedgwick's eloquent and interesting lectures. Had I done so I should probably have become a geologist earlier than I did. I attended, however, Henslow's lectures on Botany, and liked them much for their extreme clearness, and the admirable illustrations; but I did not study botany. Henslow used to take his pupils, including several of the older members of the University, field excursions, on foot or in coaches, to distant places, or in a barge down the river, and lectured on the rarer plants and animals which were observed. These excursions were delightful.

Although, as we shall presently see, there were some redeeming features in my life at Cambridge, my time was sadly wasted there, and worse than wasted. From my passion for shooting and for hunting, and, when this failed, for riding across country, I got into a sporting set, including some dissipated low-minded young men. We used often to dine together in the evening, though these dinners often included men of a higher stamp, and we sometimes drank too much, with jolly singing and playing at cards afterwards. I know that I ought to feel ashamed of days and evenings thus spent, but as some of my friends were very pleasant, and we were all in the highest spirits, I cannot help looking back to these times with much pleasure.

But I am glad to think that I had many other friends of a widely different nature. I was very intimate with Whitley, who was afterwards Senior Wrangler, and we used continually to take long walks together. He inoculated me with a taste for pictures and good engravings, of which I bought some. I frequently went to the Fitzwilliam Gallery, and my taste must have been fairly good, for I certainly admired the best pictures, which I discussed with the old curator. I read also with much interest Sir Joshua Reynolds' book. This taste, though not natural to me, lasted for several years, and many of the pictures in the National Gallery in London gave me much pleasure; that of Sebastian del Piombo exciting in me a sense of sublimity.

I also got into a musical set, I believe by means of my warm-hearted friend, Herbert, who took a high wrangler's degree. From associating with these men, and hearing them play, I acquired a strong taste for music, and used very often to time my walks so as to hear on week days the anthem in King's College Chapel. This gave me intense pleasure, so that my backbone would sometimes shiver. I am sure that there was no affectation or mere imitation in this taste, for I used generally to go by myself to King's College, and I sometimes hired the chorister boys to sing in my rooms. Nevertheless I am so utterly destitute of an ear, that I cannot perceive a discord, or keep time and hum a tune correctly; and it is a mystery how I could possibly have derived pleasure from music.

My musical friends soon perceived my state, and sometimes amused themselves by making me pass an examination, which consisted in ascertaining how many tunes I could recognise when they were played rather more quickly or slowly than usual. 'God save the King,' when thus played, was a sore puzzle. There was another man with almost as bad an ear as I had, and strange to say he played a little on the flute. Once I had the triumph of beating him in one of our musical examinations.

But no pursuit at Cambridge was followed with nearly so much eagerness or gave me so much pleasure as collecting beetles. It was the mere passion for collecting, for I did not dissect them, and rarely compared their external characters with published descriptions, but got them named anyhow. I will give a proof of my zeal: one day, on tearing off some old bark, I saw two rare beetles, and seized one in each hand; then I saw a third and new kind, which I could not bear to lose, so I popped the one which I held in my right hand into my mouth. Alas! It ejected some intensely acrid fluid, which burnt my tongue so that I was forced to spit the beetle out, which was lost, as was the third one.

I was very successful in collecting, and invented two new methods; I employed a labourer to scrape during the winter, moss off old trees and place it in a large bag, and likewise to collect the rubbish at the bottom of the barges in which reeds are brought from the fens, and thus I got some very rare species. No poet ever felt more delighted at seeing his first poem published than I did at seeing, in Stephens' 'Illustrations of British Insects,' the magic words, "captured by C. Darwin, Esq." I was introduced to entomology by my second cousin, W. Darwin Fox, a clever and most pleasant man, who was then at Christ's College, and with whom I became extremely intimate. Afterwards I became well acquainted, and went out collecting, with Albert Way of Trinity, who in after years became a well-known archæologist; also with H. Thompson of the same College, afterwards a leading agriculturist, chairman of a great railway, and Member of Parliament. It seems therefore that a taste for collecting beetles is some indication of future success in life! . . .

I have not as yet mentioned a circumstance which influenced my whole career more than any other. This was my friendship with Professor Henslow. Before coming up to Cambridge, I had heard of him from my brother as a man who knew every branch of science, and I was accordingly prepared to reverence him. He kept open house once every week when all undergraduates, and some older members of the University, who were attached to science, used to meet in the evening. I soon got, through Fox, an invitation, and went there regularly. Before long I became well acquainted with Henslow, and during the latter half of my time at Cambridge took long walks with him on most days; so that I was called by some of the dons "the man who walks with Henslow"; and in the evening I was very often asked to join his family dinner. His knowledge was great in botany, entomology, chemistry, mineralogy, and geology. His strongest taste was to draw conclusions from long-continued minute observations. His judgment was excellent, and his whole mind well balanced; but I do not suppose that any one would say that he possessed much original genius. He was deeply religious, and so orthodox that he told me one day he should be grieved if a single word of the Thirty-nine Articles were altered. His moral qualities were in every way admirable. He was free from every tinge of vanity or other petty feeling; and I never saw a man who thought so little about himself or his own concerns. His temper was imperturbably good, with the most winning and courteous manners; yet, as I have seen, he could be roused by any bad action to the warmest indignation and prompt action. . . .

Henslow's benevolence was unbounded, as he proved by his many excellent schemes for his poor parishioners, when in after years he held the living of Hitcham. My intimacy with such a man ought to have been, and I hope was, an inestimable benefit. I cannot resist mentioning a trifling incident, which showed his kind consideration. Whilst examining some pollen-grains on a damp surface, I saw the tubes exserted, and instantly rushed off to communicate my surprising discovery to him. Now I do not suppose any other professor of botany could have helped laughing at my coming in such a hurry to make such a communication. But he agreed how interesting the phenomenon was, and explained its meaning, but made me clearly understand how well it was known; so I left him not in the least mortified, but well pleased at having discovered for myself so remarkable a fact, but determined not to be in such a hurry again to communicate my discoveries.

Dr. Whewell was one of the older and distinguished men who sometimes visited Henslow, and on several occasions I walked home with him at night. Next to Sir J. Mackintosh he was the best converser on grave subjects to whom I ever listened. Leonard Jenyns, who afterwards published some good essays in Natural History, often stayed with Henslow, who was his brother-in-law. I visited him at his parsonage on the borders of the Fens [Swaffham Bulbeck], and had many a good walk and talk with him about Natural History . . . These men and others of the same standing, together with Henslow, used sometimes to take distant excursions into the country, which I was allowed to join, and they were most agreeable.

Looking back, I infer that there must have been something in me a little superior to the common run of youths, otherwise the above-mentioned men, so much older than me and higher in academical position, would never have allowed me to associate with them. Certainly I was not aware of any such superiority, and I remember one of my sporting friends, Turner, who saw me at work with my beetles, saying that I should some day be a Fellow of the Royal Society, and the notion seemed to me preposterous.

During my last year at Cambridge, I read with care and profound interest Humboldt's 'Personal Narrative.' This work, and Sir J. Herschel's 'Introduction to the Study of Natural Philosophy,' stirred up in me a burning zeal to add even the most humble contribution to the noble structure of Natural Science. No one or a dozen other books influenced me nearly so much as these two. I copied out from Humboldt long passages about Teneriffe, and read them aloud on one of the above-mentioned excursions, to (I think) Henslow, Ramsay, and Dawes, for on a previous occasion I had talked about the glories of Teneriffe, and some of the party declared they would endeavour to go there; but I think that they were only half in earnest. I was, however, quite in earnest, and got an introduction to a merchant in London to enquire about ships; but the scheme was, of course, knocked on the head by the voyage of the *Beagle*.

My summer vacations were given up to collecting beetles, to some reading, and short tours. In the autumn my whole time was devoted to shooting, chiefly at Woodhouse and Maer, and sometimes with young Eyton of Eyton. Upon the whole the three years which I spent at Cambridge were the most joyful in my happy life; for I was then in excellent health, and almost always in high spirits.

As I had at first come up to Cambridge at Christmas, I was forced to keep two terms after passing my final examination, at the commencement of 1831; and Henslow then persuaded me to begin the study of geology. Therefore on my return to Shropshire I examined sections, and coloured a map of parts round Shrewsbury. Professor Sedgwick intended to visit North Wales in the beginning of August to pursue his famous geological investigations amongst the older rocks, and Henslow asked him to allow me to accompany him. Accordingly he came and slept at my father's house.

A short conversation with him during this evening produced a strong impression on my mind. Whilst examining an old gravel-pit near Shrewsbury, a labourer told me that he had found in it a large worn tropical Volute shell, such as may be seen on the chimney-pieces of cottages; and as he would not sell the shell, I was convinced that he had really found it in the pit. I told Sedgwick of the fact, and he at once said (no doubt truly) that it must have been thrown away by some one into the pit; but then added, if really embedded there it would be the greatest misfortune to geology, as it would overthrow all that we know about the superficial deposits of the Midland Counties. These gravel-beds belong in fact to the glacial period, and in after years I found in them broken arctic shells. But I was then utterly astonished at Sedgwick not being delighted at so wonderful a fact as a tropical shell being found near the surface in the middle of England. Nothing before had ever made me thoroughly realise, though I had read various scientific books, that science consists in grouping facts so that general laws or conclusions may be drawn from them.

Next morning we started for Llangollen, Conway, Bangor, and Capel Curig. This tour was of decided use in teaching me a little how to make out the geology of a country. Sedgwick often sent me on a line parallel to his, telling me to bring back specimens of the rocks and to mark the stratification on a map. I have little doubt that he did this for my good, as I was too ignorant to have aided him. On this tour I had a striking instance of how easy it is to overlook phenomena, however conspicuous, before they have been observed by any one. We spent many hours in Cwm Idwal, examining all the rocks with extreme care, as Sedgwick was anxious to find fossils in them; but neither of us saw a trace of the wonderful glacial phenomena all around us; we did not notice the plainly scored rocks, the perched boulders, the lateral and terminal moraines. Yet these phenomena are so conspicuous that, as I declared in a paper published many years afterwards in the 'Philosophical Magazine,' a house burnt down by fire did not tell its story more plainly than did this valley. If it had still been filled by a glacier, the phenomena would have been less distinct than they are now.

At Capel Curig I left Sedgwick and went in a straight line by compass and map across the mountains to Barmouth, never following any track unless it coincided with my course. I thus came on some strange wild places, and enjoyed much this manner of travelling. I visited Barmouth to see some Cambridge friends who were reading there, and thence returned to Shrewsbury and to Maer for shooting; for at that time I should have thought myself mad to give up the first days of partridge-shooting for geology or any other science.[1]

Although many persons and some more or less technical matters are mentioned in the foregoing pages from Darwin's autobiography, it does not seem necessary to identify or define them all in notes. The general feeling of an energetic young man with as yet no clear course before him is well conveyed in these pages. I may, however, clarify or add interest if I comment briefly on a few points.

"Poco curante," the epithet applied to young Darwin by Dr. Butler at the Shrewsbury School (a "public school" in the British

sense) and understood by Darwin only as some sort of put down, is an Italian expression meaning simply "not very attentive." If a keen young student was not attentive, this would seem to reflect discredit more on the teacher than on the student.

"White's 'Selborne' " mentioned here on page 36 is Gilbert White's *Natural History and Antiquities of Selborne,* published in 1789, a charming book still read today in later editions.

The Werner mentioned was the German Abraham Gottlob Werner (1750–1817), a very famous geologist in his day. He was the leader of "neptunian" geology, which maintained that all the rocks of the earth's crust were sedimentary. That view was already becoming obsolete when Darwin was at Edinburgh, and this accounts for Darwin's disgust with the Wernerian geology taught there and with the professor's failure to see that a dike ("dyke" in Darwin's spelling) was obviously igneous. As will appear later, Lyellian geology replaced Wernerian (and others) from 1830 on. It made Darwin an enthusiastic and able geologist, and Lyell became a close friend of Darwin's for the rest of his life.

Zoonomia, here mentioned as having been read first with admiration and later with disappointment, was a poem by Charles Darwin's grandfather Erasmus. This was not mentioned in the first edition of *The Origin of Species,* but Darwin later wrote "An Historical Sketch" as an introduction to *The Origin,* then in a footnote noted that his grandfather had "anticipated the views and erroneous grounds of opinion of Lamarck." *Zoonomia* was published in 1794, Lamarck's *Philosophie Zoologique* in 1809.

Maer, mentioned several times and specifically as visited in 1827, was the home of Charles Darwin's uncle Josiah Wedgwood and thus also of Josiah's daughter and Charles's cousin Emma Wedgwood, about nineteen years of age at the time of that one of many visits. Emma is not mentioned in the autobiography just here, but twelve years later, in 1839, she became Darwin's wife.

At Cambridge Darwin was in Christ's College. It is one of the ironic twists of history that William Paley (1743–1805) also attended Cambridge in Christ's College and later wrote homilies, notably one on "Natural Theology," which delighted Darwin when he was at Cambridge, but which it was Darwin's fate to put wholly in the wrong when he wrote *The Origin of Species.*

When Darwin wrote his autobiography he could not recall whether he was fifth, tenth or twelfth in his class at Cambridge. He was tenth.

Darwin's meeting Henslow and Sedgwick at Cambridge gave a new turn to his life and had much to do with his becoming a great scientist rather than a sporting rector. John Stevens Henslow (1796–1861) started his academic career as a geologist but became the Professor of Botany at Cambridge in 1827 and held that position until his death. He retained an interest in geology, indeed in all natural sciences, encouraged this bent in Darwin, was instrumental in getting Darwin a post on the *Beagle,* saw to the receipt and care of the many specimens that Darwin sent back from ports touched on by that ship, and maintained a warm friendship with the whole Darwin family all the rest of his life. Adam Sedgwick (1785–1873) along with Lyell and almost contemporary with him, was one of the great pioneers of geology in Britain. As noted in the last passage of the autobiography quoted in this chapter, it was Sedgwick who gave Darwin his first experience with fully professional field geology. Unlike Henslow, however, Sedgwick did not remain particularly friendly with Darwin and in fact later attacked him for writing *The Origin of Species*.

The autobiography goes on to the preliminaries of the voyage of the *Beagle* and then to the voyage itself, and the present chapter closes at this crucial point. I now add only that to keep things in bounds I have omitted some short parts of the autobiography as they did not seem to be particularly useful for the purpose here, that of showing Darwin's interests and development as a boy and young man. The sign . . . indicates that some following matter is omitted.

4

The Voyage

His voyage on the *Beagle* was by far the most important physical adventure of Darwin's life. It was important to him as an adventure and is enthusiastically so seen in the journal and in the many letters he wrote during the voyage. However as he also made clear it was even more important, in fact crucial, in turning him to science as a life work: first to geology, then to systematic biology, and for years almost clandestinely to evolutionary biology. The latter interest, for which he is most remembered, was brought into the open by the Linnean meeting in 1858, here recounted in Chapter 2, and then fully in *The Origin of Species* in 1859, here to be considered especially in Chapter 7.

The circumstances of Darwin's going on the *Beagle* are adequately but briefly noted in the excerpt from the autobiography given below. The ship was a ten-gun brig, a vessel of the Royal Navy, dispatched by the Admiralty not with bellicose intent but to chart the coast and islands of southern South America and then to return to England by way of the Pacific, Indian Ocean and Atlantic. The survey had been begun by the same ship in 1826–30. After its return to England Captain Robert Fitz-Roy (1805–65) was placed in command. After some delays the *Beagle* sailed from Devonport on December 27, 1831, and it finally returned to England at Falmouth on October 2, 1836. Among other places visited in sequence were Madeira, the Canary Islands, Cape Verde, Bahia, Rio de Janeiro, Montevideo, Buenos Aires, the Falkland Islands, many places in Patagonia and on and around

Tierra del Fuego and along the west coast of South America, including Valdivia, Valparaiso and Lima, then (most importantly for Darwin, as it turned out) the Galápagos Islands, onward to the Society Islands in mid-Pacific, New Zealand, Sydney, Tasmania and King George's Sound in Australia, Keeling Island and Mauritius in the Indian Ocean, the Cape Colony in Africa, St. Helena and Ascension Islands in the South Atlantic, and so back to England via Brazil again and the Azores.

Later in this chapter extracts will be given from Darwin's journal and some other sources especially illustrative of Darwin's character and his personal development, and leading to his most important later work. First we must get him onto the *Beagle*, together with some comments on its importance to him and on his relationship with Fitz-Roy.

On returning home from my short geological tour in North Wales, I found a letter from Henslow, informing me that Captain Fitz-Roy was willing to give up part of his own cabin to any young man who would volunteer to go with him without pay as naturalist to the Voyage of the *Beagle*. I have given, as I believe, in my MS. Journal an account of all the circumstances which then occurred; I will here only say that I was instantly eager to accept the offer, but my father strongly objected, adding the words, fortunate for me, "If you can find any man of common sense who advises you to go I will give my consent." So I wrote that evening and refused the offer. On the next morning I went to Maer to be ready for September 1st, and, whilst out shooting, my uncle sent for me, offering to drive me over to Shrewsbury and talk with my father, as my uncle thought it would be wise in me to accept the offer. My father always maintained that he was one of the most sensible men in the world, and he at once consented in the kindest manner. I had been rather extravagant at Cambridge, and to console my father said, "that I should be deuced clever to spend more than my allowance whilst on board the *Beagle;*" but he answered with a smile, "But they tell me you are very clever."

Next day I started for Cambridge to see Henslow, and thence to London to see Fitz-Roy, and all was soon arranged. Afterwards, on becoming very intimate with Fitz-Roy, I heard that I had run a very narrow risk of being rejected, on account of the shape of my nose! He was an ardent disciple of Lavater, and was convinced that he could judge of a man's character by the outline of his features; and he doubted whether any one with my nose could possess sufficient energy and determination for the voyage. But I think he was afterwards well satisfied that my nose had spoken falsely.

Fitz-Roy's character was a singular one, with very many noble features: he was devoted to his duty, generous to a fault, bold, determined, and indomitably energetic, and an ardent friend to all under his sway. He would undertake any sort of trouble to assist those whom he thought deserved assistance. He was a handsome man, strikingly like a gentleman, with highly courteous manners, which resembled those of his maternal uncle, the famous Lord Castlereagh, as I was told by the Minister at Rio. Nevertheless he must have inherited much in his appearance from Charles II., for Dr. Wallich gave me a collection of photographs which he had made, and I was struck with the resemblance of one to Fitz-Roy; and on looking at the name, I found it Ch. E. Sobieski Stuart, Count d'Albanie, a descendant of the same monarch.

Fitz-Roy's temper was a most unfortunate one. It was usually worst in the early morning, and with his eagle eye he could generally detect something amiss about the ship, and was then unsparing in his blame. He was very kind to me, but was a man very difficult to live with on the intimate terms which necessarily followed from our messing by ourselves in the same cabin. We had several quarrels; for instance, early in the voyage at Bahia, in Brazil, he defended and praised slavery, which I abominated, and told me that he had just visited a great slave-owner, who had called up many of his slaves and asked them whether they were happy, and whether they wished to be free, and all answered "No." I then asked him, perhaps with a sneer, whether he thought that the answer of slaves in the presence of their master was worth anything? This made him excessively angry, and he said that as I doubted his word we could not live any longer together. I thought that I should have been compelled to leave the ship; but as soon as the news spread, which it did quickly, as the captain sent for the first lieutenant to assuage his anger by abusing me, I was deeply gratified by receiving an invitation from all the gun-room officers to mess with them. But after a few hours Fitz-Roy showed his usual magnanimity by sending an officer to me with an apology and a request that I would continue to live with him.

His character was in several respects one of the most noble which I have ever known.

The voyage of the *Beagle* has been by far the most important event in my life, and has determined my whole career; yet it depended on so small a circumstance as my uncle offering to drive me thirty miles to Shrewsbury, which few uncles would have done, and on such a trifle as the shape of my nose. I have always felt that I owe to the voyage the first real training or education of my mind; I was led to attend closely to several branches of natural history, and thus my powers of observation were improved, though they were always fairly developed.

The investigation of the geology of all the places visited was far more important, as reasoning here comes into play. On first examining a new district nothing can appear more hopeless than the chaos of rocks; but by recording the stratification and nature of the rocks and fossils at many points, always reasoning and predicting what will be found elsewhere, light soon begins to dawn on the district, and the structure of the whole becomes more or less intelligible. I had brought with me the first volume of Lyell's 'Principles of Geology,' which I studied attentively; and the book was of the highest service to me in many ways. The very first place which I examined, namely St. Jago in the Cape de Verde islands, showed me clearly the wonderful superiority of Lyell's manner of treating geology, compared with that of any other author, whose works I had with me or ever afterwards read.

Another of my occupations was collecting animals of all classes, briefly describing and roughly dissecting many of the marine ones; but from not being able to draw, and from not having sufficient anatomical knowledge, a great pile of MS. which I made during the voyage has proved almost useless. I thus lost much time, with the exception of that spent in acquiring some knowledge of the Crustaceans, as this was of service when in after years I undertook a monograph of the Cirripedia.

During some part of the day I wrote my Journal, and took much pains in describing carefully and vividly all that I had seen; and this was good practice. My Journal served also, in part, as letters to my home, and portions were sent to England whenever there was an opportunity.

The above various special studies were, however, of no importance compared with the habit of energetic industry and of concentrated attention to whatever I was engaged in, which I then acquired. Everything about which I thought or read was made to bear directly on what I had seen or was likely to see; and this habit of mind was continued during the five years of the voyage. I feel sure that it was this training which has enabled me to do whatever I have done in science.

Looking backwards, I can now perceive how my love for science gradually preponderated over every other taste. During the first two years my old passion for shooting survived in nearly full force, and I shot myself all the birds and animals for my collection; but gradually I gave up my gun more and more, and finally altogether, to my servant, as shooting interfered with my work, more especially with making out the geological structure of a country. I discovered, though unconsciously and insensibly, that the pleasure of observing and reasoning was a much higher one than that of skill and sport. That my mind became developed through my pursuits during the voyage is rendered probable by a remark made by my father, who was the most acute observer whom I ever saw, of a sceptical disposition, and far from being a believer in phrenology; for on first seeing me after the voyage, he turned round to my sisters, and exclaimed, "Why, the shape of his head is quite altered."

To return to the voyage. On September 11th (1831), I paid a flying visit with Fitz-Roy to the *Beagle* at Plymouth. Thence to Shrewsbury to wish my father and sisters a long farewell. On October 24th I took up my residence at Plymouth, and remained there until December 27th, when the *Beagle* finally left the shores of England for her circumnavigation of the world.[1]

As noted in Chapter 3, it was Henslow who proposed Darwin to Fitz-Roy as a suitable person to accompany him on the *Beagle*.

Although Fitz-Roy's primary duty was charting and navigating, his orders also included obtaining geological and other information about the places visited. As no official provision was made for personnel or funds for these activities, Fitz-Roy arranged for them on his own, although also providing no pay. When Darwin's father finally agreed to the arrangement, he continued Charles's allowance. His father's doubts about Charles's frugality were justified. Many of Charles's letters home, generally to his sisters Catherine and Caroline, asked that his father transfer more money to his account.

Fitz-Roy's judgment of a man's character by his physiognomy was a fad of the times, and Johann Lavater (1741–1801) was a then still famous quack, poet, mystic, theologist and physiognomist. Profile pictures do show that Darwin had a short, almost a buttonlike nose, while Fitz-Roy had a tremendous, jutting beak. (Perhaps this embarrassed him and made him touchy about noses?) Phrenology, mentioned elsewhere in the autobiography, was a similar quack fad of the times, involving "reading" the bumps on people's heads, an idea due to F. J. Gall (1758–1828). While studying for the ministry Darwin had been told that the bumps on his head were particularly suited for that profession, and this explains his father's chaffing remark that after the voyage the shape of Charles's head had been "quite altered."

As Darwin chose at this point in his autobiography to discuss Fitz-Roy's character as "singular," quarrelsome and yet noble, a few words here may summarize his life after the voyage of the *Beagle*. Born in 1805, he was only 23 when he was made Captain of the *Beagle*. After a few other posts, he was made governor of New Zealand in 1843, but his temper and temperament brought about his recall two years later. He retired from the navy in 1850. He developed England's first meteorological service and also a system of gale warnings for shipping. He is now highly honored as a pioneer of meteorology. However at the time he was often criticized for failure of predictions, as meteorologists still are, and perhaps as much in a fit of temper as of despondency, he committed suicide in 1865.

So ended a life sad on the whole, but one not wasted and worthy of honoring. We are likely now to remember and honor Fitz-Roy most for his part in introducing Darwin to the breadth and depth of the world and its phenomena, geological, botanical and zoological. Darwin himself continued to express gratitude to him to the day of Fitz-Roy's death, which considerably preceded Darwin's. This was in spite of their quite different temperaments and, as developed almost immediately after their voyage together, their diametrically opposite reactions to the sights and experiences they had shared. Both started the voyage as not particularly thoughtful but also not doubtful of the Semitic creation stories then—as in some cases now—orthodox for various Christian sects as well. Hardly had they returned to England when Fitz-Roy wrote at great length and most earnestly adjuring all, and especially the young, to accept those stories as the Truth of God for their souls' sakes. Darwin returned from the voyage with some doubts and within a year began to record facts and judgments that finally proved beyond intelligent doubt that the stories in the Book of Genesis may be beautiful parables but that all of nature proclaims that the factual interpretation is quite otherwise.

In spite of its sad end Fitz-Roy's work produced charts of previously unmapped lands so accurate that they continued to be the best available for a century or more, and he later made basic contributions to steam navigation, to weather observation and to other useful arts and sciences.

So let us turn back to Darwin, and first to the effect on this young Englishman of emotions and beauties far from his native soil. Although he had been interested enough and busy enough with marine life and land geology on earlier stops, it was in Bahia, or San Salvador, that he first encountered tropical scenery and foliage. (Bahia is a state in northern Brazil; San Salvador or Salvador, its capital, is often also called by the name of the state.) The impression made on the budding naturalist follows in his own words:

BAHIA, OR SAN SALVADOR. BRAZIL, FEB. 29TH.— The day has past delightfully. Delight itself, however, is a weak term to express the feelings of a naturalist who, for the first time, has been wandering by himself in a Brazilian forest. Among the multitude of striking objects, the general luxuriance of the vegetation bears away the victory. The elegance of the grasses, the novelty of the parasitical plants, the beauty of the flowers, the glossy green of the foliage, all tend to this end. A most paradoxical mixture of sound and silence pervades the shady parts of the wood. The noise from the insects is so loud, that it may be heard even in a vessel anchored several hundred yards from the shore; yet within the recesses of the forest a universal silence appears to reign. To a person fond of natural history, such a day as this, brings with it a deeper pleasure than he ever can hope again to experience. After wandering about for some hours, I returned to the landing-place; but, before reaching it, I was overtaken by a tropical storm. I tried to find shelter under a tree which was so thick, that it would never have been penetrated by common English rain; but here, in a couple of minutes, a little torrent flowed down the trunk. It is to this violence of the rain we must attribute the verdure at the bottom of the thickest woods: if the showers were like those of a colder clime, the greater part would be absorbed or evaporated before it reached the ground. I will not at present attempt to describe the gaudy scenery of this noble bay, because, in our homeward voyage, we called here a second time, and I shall then have occasion to remark on it.

The geology of the surrounding country possesses little interest. Throughout the coast of Brazil, and certainly for a considerable space inland, from the Rio Plata to Cape St. Roque, lat. 5° S., a distance of more than 2000 geographical miles, wherever solid rock occurs, it belongs to a granitic formation. The circumstance of this enormous area being thus constituted of materials, which almost every geologist believes to have been crystallized by the action of heat under pressure, gives rise to many curious reflections. Was this effect produced beneath the depths of a profound ocean? or did a covering of strata formerly extend over it, which has since been removed? Can we believe that any power, acting for a time short of infinity, could have denuded the granite over so many thousand square leagues?[2]

The first visit to Bahia was on the last day of February, 1832 (a leap year). Darwin did return there four years later, early in August 1836, and then did "have occasion to remark on it" as follows:

Upon leaving Ascension the ship's head was directed towards the coast of South America, and on August 1st, we anchored at Bahia or San Salvador. We staid here four days, in which time I took several long walks. I was glad to find my enjoyment of tropical scenery had not decreased even in the slightest degree, from the want of novelty. The elements of the scenery are so simple, that they are worth mentioning, as a proof on what trifling circumstances exquisite natural beauty depends.

The country may be described as a level plain of about three hundred feet in elevation, which in every part has been worn into flat-bottomed valleys. This structure is remarkable in a granitic land, but is nearly universal in all those softer formations, of which plains usually are composed. The whole surface is covered by various kinds of stately trees, interspersed with patches of cultivated ground, out of which houses, convents, and chapels arise. It must be remembered that within the tropics, the wild luxuriance of nature is not lost even in the vicinity of large cities; for the natural vegetation of the hedges and hill-sides, overpowers in picturesque effect the artificial labour of man. Hence, there are only a few spots where the bright red soil affords a strong contrast with the universal clothing of green. From the edges of the plain there are distant glimpses either of the ocean, or of the great bay bordered by low wooded shores, and on the surface of which numerous boats and canoes show their white sails. Excepting from these points, the range of vision is very limited: following the level pathways, on each hand alternate peeps into the wooded valleys below can alone be obtained. Finally, I may add that the houses, and especially the sacred edifices, are built in a peculiar and rather fantastic style of architecture. They are all whitewashed; so that when illuminated by the brilliant sun of midday, and as seen against the pale blue sky of the horizon, they stand out more like shadows than substantial buildings.

Such are the elements of the scenery, but to paint the effect is a hopeless endeavour. Learned naturalists describe these scenes of the tropics by naming a multitude of objects, and mentioning some characteristic feature of each. To a learned traveller, this possibly may communicate some definite ideas: but who else from seeing a plant in an herbarium can imagine its appearance when growing in its native soil? Who from seeing choice plants in a hothouse can magnify some into the dimensions of forest trees, and crowd others into an entangled jungle? Who when examining in the cabinet of the entomologist the gay exotic butterflies, and singular cicadas, will associate with these objects, the ceaseless harsh music of the latter, and the lazy flight of the former,—the sure accompaniments of the still, glowing, noonday of the tropics. It is, when the sun has attained its greatest height, that such views should be beheld: then the dense splendid foliage of the mango hides the ground with its darkest shade, whilst the upper branches are rendered from the profusion of light of the most brilliant green. In the temperate zones, as it appears to me, the case is different, the vegetation there is not so dark or so rich, and hence the rays of the declining sun, tinged of a red, purple, or yellow colour, add most to the beauties of the scenery of those climes.

When quietly walking along the shady pathways, and admiring each successive view, one wishes to find language to express one's ideas. Epithet after epithet is found too weak to convey to those, who have not visited the intertropical regions, the sensation of delight which the mind experiences. I have said the plants in a hothouse fail to communicate a just idea of the vegetation, yet I must recur to it. The land is one great wild, untidy, luxuriant hothouse, which nature made for her managerie, but man has taken possession of it, and has studded it with gay houses and formal gardens. How great would be the desire in every admirer of nature to behold, if such were possible, another planet; yet to every one in Europe, it may be truly said, that at the distance of a few degrees from his native soil, the glories of another world are open to him. In my last walk, I stopped again and again to gaze on these beauties, and endeavoured to fix for ever in my mind an impression, which at the time I knew, sooner or later must fail. The form of the orange-tree, the cocoa-nut, the palm, the mango, the tree-fern, the banana, will remain clear and separate; but the thousand beauties which unite these into one perfect scene must fade away; yet they will leave, like a tale heard in childhood, a picture full of indistinct, but most beautiful figures.[3]

The *Beagle* reached Rio on April 4, 1832, and Darwin stayed ashore until July 5. The early part of that long stay was largely spent traveling with an English owner of an estate more than a hundred miles from Rio. Much of the time he found the local people surly and inhospitable, but he also stayed at two large *fazendas* (the Portuguese equivalent of Spanish *haciendas*). Here the hospitality was almost overwhelming. At that time such establishments depended entirely on black slave labor. It is surprising to find Darwin saying of the first of these hospitable *fazendas* that, "On such fazendas as these, I have no doubt the slaves pass happy and contented lives." It was just such a remark by Fitz-Roy that had caused Darwin to quarrel with him and to be banished briefly from the Captain's cabin on the *Beagle*. At the other *fazenda* where Darwin spent some time he came to see slavery in a very different light, and he commented on its "inhumanity" and "degradation" and spoke of his own "disgust" and "shame" and of the lack of any such feelings by the *fazendeiro*.

Back in Rio, he lived in a cottage on Botofogo Bay. He was understandably enthusiastic about the local scenery and took many walks and excursions devoted especially to observation of the flora and fauna.

The *Beagle* left Rio on July 5, 1832, and anchored at Monte Video (written as two words by Darwin) just three weeks later. In Uruguay Darwin spent ten weeks in and about Maldonado, a province directly east of Montevideo terminating at Punta del Este, a name now more widely known than Maldonado. In this region he made "a nearly perfect collection of the animals, birds, and reptiles."

On July 24, 1833, the *Beagle* sailed from Maldonado and on August 3 she arrived off the mouth of the Rio Negro, the river considered to divide central from southern Argentina, the latter still referred to as Patagonia, an old term for a region no longer officially so called but divided into several provinces. Darwin went a few miles up the river to a town "indifferently called El Carmen or Patagones." It is now called Carmen de Patagones and is on the left (north) bank of the river, hence in what is now the extreme south of the Province of Buenos Aires, while Viedma, a larger town facing it on the other bank, is at the northern edge of Patagonia in the Province of Rio Negro. Darwin decided to leave the *Beagle* temporarily and to go overland from here to Buenos Ayres, as he spelled the name of that city. This was one of several overland treks that Darwin took; most important among them was one later taken across the Andes from Chile to Argentina and back, as will be noted later.

The pampas to be crossed were still swarming with Indians. Darwin visited an encampment of cavalry under General Rosas, engaged in deliberately killing off as many Indians as possible. This was so successful that soon no tribal Indians remained in that vast region. Without further contact with what was referred to as a war but was in plain fact a massacre, Darwin went on to Bahía Blanca, then the only settlement between the Rio Negro and Buenos Aires. In this region Darwin made further geological observations and also found and collected bones of prehistoric and for the most part extinct mammals. Darwin later noted that it was mainly the knowledge of such fossils, their relationships with earlier and later animals in the same region, and observations of the fauna of the Galápagos Islands that most inspired him to make the further studies that led to *The Origin of Species*. His account of the region of Bahía Blanca thus is of great historical interest for Darwinists and evolutionists.

The Beagle arrived on the 24th of August, and a week afterwards sailed for the Plata. With Captain Fitzroy's consent I was left behind, to travel by land to Buenos Ayres. I will here add some observations, which were made during this visit, and on a previous occasion, when the Beagle was employed in surveying the harbour [at Bahía Blanca]. Not much can be made out respecting the geology. At the distance of some miles inland, an escarpment of a great argillaceo-calcareous formation of rock extends. The space near the coast consists of plains of hardened mud, and broad bands of sand-dunes, which present appearances, that can easily be accounted for by a rise of the land; and of this phenomenon, although to a trifling amount, we have other proofs.

At Punta Alta, a low cliff, about twenty feet high, exposes a mass of partly consolidated shingle, irregularly interstratified with a reddish muddy clay, and containing numerous recent shells. We may believe a similar accumulation would now take place, on any point, where tides and waves were opposed. In the gravel a considerable number of bones were embedded. Mr. Owen, who has undertaken the description of these remains, has not yet examined them with care; but the following list may give some idea of their nature: 1st, a tolerably perfect head of a megatherium, and a fragment and teeth of two others; 2d, an animal of the order Edentata, as large as a pony, and with great scratching claws; 3d and 4th, two great Edentata related to the megatherium, and both fully as large as an ox or horse; 5th, another equally large animal, closely allied or perhaps identical with the Toxodon (hereafter to be described), which had very flat grinding teeth, somewhat resembling those of a rodent; 6th, a large piece of the tesselated covering like that of the armadillo, but of gigantic size; 7th, a tusk which in its prismatic form, and in the disposition of the enamel, closely resembles that of the African boar; it is probable that it belonged to the same animal with the singular flat grinders. Lastly, a tooth in the same state of decay with the others: its broken condition does not allow Mr. Owen, without further comparison, to come to any definite conclusion; but the part that is perfect, resembles in every respect the tooth of the common horse. All these remains were found embedded in a beach which is covered at spring tides; and the space in which they were collected could not have exceeded one hundred and fifty yards square. It is a remarkable circumstance that so many different species should be found together; and it proves how numerous in kind the ancient inhabitants of this country must have been.

At the distance of about thirty miles, in another cliff of red earth, I found several fragments of bones. Among them were the teeth of a rodent, much narrower, but even larger than those of the *Hydrochoerus capybara;* the animal which has been mentioned as exceeding in dimensions every existing member of its order [rodentia]. There was also part of the head of a Ctenomys; the species being different from the Tucutuco, but with a close general resemblance [small rodents].

The remains at Punta Alta were associated, as before remarked, with shells of existing species. These have not as yet been examined with scrupulous care, but it may be safely asserted, that they are most closely similar to the species now living in the same bay: it is also very remarkable, that not only the species, but the proportional numbers of each kind, are nearly the same with those now cast up on the pebble beaches. There are eleven marine species (some in an imperfect state), and one terrestrial. If I had not collected living specimens from the same bay, some of the fossils would have been thought extinct; for Mr. Sowerby, who was kind enough to look at my collection, had not previously seen them. We may feel certain that the bones have not been washed out of an older formation, and embedded in a more recent one, because the remains of one of the Edentata were lying in their proper relative position (and partly so in a second case); which could not have happened, without the carcass had been washed to the spot where the skeleton is now entombed.

We here have a strong confirmation of the remarkable law so often insisted on by Mr. Lyell, namely, that the "longevity of the species in the mammalia, is upon the whole inferior to that of the testacea." When we proceed to the southern part of Patagonia, I shall have occasion to describe the case of an extinct camel, from which the same result may be deduced.

From the shells being littoral species (including one terrestrial), and from the character of the deposit, we may feel absolutely certain that the remains were embedded in a shallow sea, not far from the coast. From the position of the skeleton being undisturbed, and likewise from the fact that full-grown serpulae were attached to some of the bones, we know that the mass could not have been accumulated on the beach itself. At the present time, part of the bed is daily washed by the tide, while another part has been raised a few feet above the level of the sea. Hence we may infer, that the elevation has here been trifling, since the period when the mammalia, now extinct, were living. This conclusion is in harmony with several other considerations (such as the recent character of the beds underlying the Pampas deposit), but which I have not space in this work to enter on.

From the general structure of the coast of this part of South America, we are compelled to believe, that the changes of level have all (at least of late) been in one direction, and that they have been very gradual. If, then, we look back to the period when these quadrupeds lived, the land probably stood at a level, less elevated only by a few fathoms than at present. Therefore, its general configuration since that epoch cannot have been greatly modified; a conclusion which certainly would be drawn from the close similarity in every respect, between the shells now living in the bay (as well as in the case of the one terrestrial species) with those which formerly lived there.

The surrounding country, as may have been gathered from this journal, is of a very desert character. Trees nowhere occur, and only a few bushes, which are chiefly confined to depressions among the sand-hillocks, or to the borders of the saline marshes. Here, then, is an apparent difficulty: we have the strongest evidence that there has occurred no great physical change to modify the features of the country, yet in former days, numerous large animals were supported on the plains now covered by a thin and scanty vegetation.

That large animals require a luxuriant vegetation, has been a general assumption, which has passed from one work to another. I do not hesitate, however, to say that it is completely false; and that it has vitiated the reasoning of geologists, on some points of great interest in the ancient history of the world. The prejudice has probably been derived from India, and the Indian islands, where troops of elephants, noble forests, and impenetrable jungles, are associated together in every account. If, on the other hand, we refer to any work of travels through the southern parts of Africa, we shall find allusions in almost every page either to the desert character of the country, or to the numbers of large animals inhabiting it. The same thing is rendered evident by the many sketches which have been published of various parts of the interior. When the Beagle was at Cape Town, I rode a few leagues into the country, which at least was sufficient to render that which I had read more fully intelligible.[4]

Important as they were for him and still are for us, Darwin's discoveries of fossil mammals were far from being the first made in South America or in the Argentinian pampas that he was traversing. The first such discovery on record was a nearly complete skeleton of a giant ground sloth sent in 1789 to Madrid, where it is still on display. Drawings of it were sent to Cuvier in Paris where in 1812 he described and figured the animal and named it *Megatherium,* "big beast." Despite the enormous difference in size and some other characters, Cuvier classified this correctly as an edentate related to the living tree sloths of South America. Darwin thus had a basis for recognizing one of his finds as a "head of a megatherium." He also recognized several specimens as being other sorts of giant Edentata, and some of these were named by Richard Owen in *The Zoology of the Voyage of H.M.S. Beagle.* Owen also supported Darwin's identification of a horse tooth and that it belonged with the old, largely extinct fauna. Owen wrote of this, "This evidence of the former existence of a genus *[Equus],* which, as regards South America, had become extinct, and has a second time been introduced into that Continent [i.e., by the Spaniards as domesticated animals], is not one of the least interesting of Mr. Darwin's palaeontological discoveries." In his oblique way of expression, Owen was indicating that it *was* one of the *most* interesting discoveries.

The Zoology of the Voyage had not yet been published when Darwin wrote the first published edition of his Journal, but Darwin could here use the name *Toxodon* because Owen had given this name and a somewhat confusing discussion of Darwin's specimen of this genus in the proceedings of the Geological Society of London in 1837.

Although there are somewhat older fossils at Monte Hermosa, not far from Bahía Blanca, Darwin's judgment was correct that those from Bahía Blanca, or Punta Alta near that settlement, are comparatively young as fossils go. They were all Pleistocene, and probably rather late Pleistocene, hence only tens of thousands rather than millions of years old.

Darwin arrived in Buenos Aires on September 20 and then on September 27 set out by land northwestward for Santa Fé, some 200 miles distant on the banks of the Rio Paraná, one of the two main tributaries of the Río de la Plata, which is not strictly a river in the usual sense but rather an estuary into which the Paraná, the Uruguay and several smaller streams empty. Along the way to Santa Fé, or St. Fé as he wrote it, Darwin crossed the Río Tercero, a small tributary of the Paraná from the west, where some previous explorers had recorded the occurrence of fossils. Darwin's prize was an upper molar of *Toxodon* demonstrating its peculiar bowed form to which it owes the name Owen later gave it (from Greek *toxon,* "bow" and Greek *odon,* "tooth"). Darwin there also found scraps of teeth that he recognized as being from some species of mastodons. The local men told him that immense bones of such animals were found weathering out from deep in the ground. They concluded that these were remains of burrowing animals. Santa Fé is on the right bank of the Rio Paraná, and on the other bank is the town St. Fé Bajada, then with a population of some 6000, a large number for that time and region. There Darwin found many more fossils, including "a large piece, nearly four feet across, of the giant armadillo-like case." That was certainly a glyptodont, which Darwin cannot have had means to collect, but in his travels in Argentina he did pick up scraps of the bony armor of those tanklike animals, which Owen recognized as being like *Glyptodon,* an extinct edentate.

After that upcountry jaunt Darwin made a second and last visit to Uruguay. On an excursion into the country there—the Banda Oriental as it was then known—he made a fascinating acquisition at an expense which was not excessive for the son of a wealthy father:

NOVEMBER 26TH.—I set out on my return in a direct line for Monte Video. Having heard of some giant's bones at a neighbouring farm-house on the Sarandis, a small stream entering the Rio Negro, I rode there accompanied by my host, and purchased for the value of eighteen pence, the head of an animal equalling in size that of the hippopotamus. Mr. Owen in a paper read before the Geological Society, has called this very extraordinary animal, Toxodon, from the curvature of its teeth. The following notice is taken from the proceedings of that society: Mr. Owen says, judging from the portion of the skeleton preserved, the Toxodon, as far as dental characters have weight, must be referred to the rodent order. But from that order it deviates in the relative position of its supernumerary incisors, in the number and direction of the curvature of its molars, and in some other respects. It again deviates, in several parts of its structure which Mr. Owen enumerated, both from the *Rodentia,* and the existing *Pachydermata,* and it manifests an affinity to the *Dinotherium* and the *Cetaceous* order. Mr. Owen, however, observed, that "the development of the nasal cavity and the presence of frontal sinuses, renders it extremely improbable that the habits of the *Toxodon* were so exclusively aquatic as would result from the total absence of hinder extremities; and concludes, therefore, that it was a quadruped, and not a Cetacean; and that it manifested an additional step in the gradation of mammiferous forms leading from the *Rodentia,* through the *Pachydermata* to the *Cetacea;* a gradation of which the water-hog of

South America (*Hydrochaerus capybara*) already indicates the commencement amongst existing *Rodentia*, of which order it is interesting to observe this species is the largest, while at the same time it is peculiar to the continent in which the remains of the gigantic *Toxodon* were discovered."

The people at the farm-house told me that the remains were exposed, by a flood having washed down part of a bank of earth. When found, the head was quite perfect; but the boys knocked the teeth out with stones, and then set up the head as a mark to throw at. By a most fortunate chance, I found a perfect tooth, which exactly fits one of the sockets in this skull, embedded by itself on the banks of the Rio Tercero, at the distance of about 180 miles from this place. Near the Toxodon I found the fragments of the head of an animal, rather larger than the horse, which has some points of resemblance with the Toxodon, and others perhaps with the Edentata. The head of this animal, as well as that of the Toxodon, and especially the former, appear so fresh, that it is difficult to believe they have lain buried for ages under ground. The bone contains so much animal matter, that when heated in the flame of a spirit-lamp, it not only exhales a very strong animal odour, but likewise burns with a slight flame.[5]

Owen was the greatest comparative anatomist and vertebrate paleontologist of the mid-nineteenth century, and it would hardly be fair to consider his account of the affinities of *Toxodon* as nonsense, but it certainly seems so in retrospect. By "affinity" he did not mean a relationship implying ancestry in common, and his placing of *Toxodon* as a step in gradation from the Rodentia through the Pachydermata (a term now long abandoned that included most of the larger hoofed mammals) to the Cetacea did not imply that such a gradation had some natural origin or significance. *Toxodon* belongs to an extinct group of hoofed mammals, the Notoungulata ("southern ungulates"), almost confined to South America, of which Owen and other paleontologists then had no clear notion. Owen outlived Darwin by ten years and *The Origin of Species* by thirty-three years, but he never accepted Darwinian evolution and only hinted darkly that he had a better idea, which, however, he never shared with the world.

Darwin returned to Buenos Aires and on December 6, 1833, the *Beagle* left the Río de la Plata never to return and sailed southward along the coast of Patagonia, with various stops, Fitz-Roy mapping and Darwin geologizing. At Port St. Julian (Puerto San Julián) Darwin again found and collected Pleistocene mammals and brooded over their significance, as related in the following passage from his published journal:

On the south side of the harbour, a cliff of about ninety feet in height intersects a plain constituted of the formations above described; and its surface is strewed over with recent marine shells. The gravel, however, differently from that in every other locality, is covered by a very irregular and thin bed of a reddish loam, containing a few small calcareous concretions. The matter somewhat resembles that of the Pampas, and probably owes its origin either to a small stream having formerly entered the sea at that spot, or to a mud-bank similar to those now existing at the head of the harbour. In one spot this earthy matter filled up a hollow, or gully, worn quite through the gravel, and in this mass a group of large bones was embedded. The animal to which they belonged, must have lived, as in the case at Bahia Blanca, at a period long subsequent to the existence of the shells now inhabiting the coast. We may feel sure of this, because the formation of the lower terrace or plain, must necessarily have been posterior to those above it, and on the surface of the two higher ones, sea-shells of recent species are scattered. From the small physical change, which the last one hundred feet elevation of the continent could have produced, the climate, as well as the general condition of Patagonia, probably was nearly the same, at the time when the animal was embedded, as it now is. This conclusion is moreover supported by the identity of the shells belonging to the two ages. Then immediately occurred the difficulty, how could any large quadruped have subsisted on these wretched deserts in lat. 49° 15′? I had no idea at the time, to what kind of animal these remains belonged. The puzzle, however, was soon solved when Mr. Owen examined them; for he considers that they formed part of an animal allied to the guanaco or llama, but fully as large as the true camel. As all the existing members of the family of Camelidae are inhabitants of the most sterile countries, so may we suppose was this extinct kind. The structure of the cervical vertebrae, the transverse processes not being perforated for the vertebral artery, indicates its affinity: some other parts, however, of its structure, probably are anomalous.

The most important result of this discovery, is the confirmation of the law that existing animals have a close relation in form with extinct species. As the guanaco is the characteristic quadruped of Patagonia, and the vicuna of the snow-clad summits of the Cordillera, so in bygone days, this gigantic species of the same family must have been conspicuous on the southern plains. We see this same relation of type between the existing and fossil Ctenomys, between the capybara (but less plainly, as shown by Mr. Owen) and the gigantic Toxodon; and lastly, between the living and extinct Edentata. At the present day, in South America, there exist probably nineteen species of this order, distributed into several genera; while throughout the rest of the world there are but five. If, then, there is a relation between the living and the dead, we should expect that the Edentata would be numerous in the fossil state. I need only reply by enumerating the megatherium, and the three or four other great species, discovered at Bahia Blanca; the remains of some of which are also abundant over the whole immense territory of La Plata. I have already pointed out the singular relation between the armadilloes and their great prototypes, even in a point apparently of so little importance as their external covering.

The order of rodents at the present day, is most conspicuous in South America, on account of the vast number and size of the species, and the multitude of individuals: according to the same law, we should expect to find their representatives in a fossil state. Mr. Owen has shown how far the Toxodon is thus related; and it is moreover not improbable that another large animal has likewise a similar affinity.

The teeth of the rodent nearly equalling in size those of the Capybara, which were discovered near Bahia Blanca, must also be remembered.

The law of the succession of types, although subject to some remarkable exceptions, must possess the highest interest to every philosophical naturalist, and was first clearly observed in regard to Australia, where fossil remains of a large and extinct species of Kangaroo and other marsupial animals were discovered buried in a cave. In America the most marked change among the mammalia has been the loss of several species of Mastodon, of an elephant, and of the horse. These Pachydermata appear formerly to have had a range over the world, like that which deer and antelopes now hold. If Buffon had known of these gigantic armadilloes, llamas, great rodents, and lost pachydermata, he would have said with a greater semblance of truth, that the creative force in America had lost its vigour, rather than that it had never possessed such powers.

It is impossible to reflect without the deepest astonishment, on the changed state of this continent. Formerly it must have swarmed with great monsters, like the southern parts of Africa, but now we find only the tapir, guanaco, armadillo, and capybara; mere pigmies compared to the antecedent races. The greater number, if not all, of these extinct quadrupeds lived at a very recent period; and many of them were contemporaries of the existing molluscs. Since their loss, no very great physical changes can have taken place in the nature of the country. What then has exterminated so many living creatures? In the Pampas, the great sepulchre of such remains, there are no signs of violence, but on the contrary, of the most quiet and scarcely sensible changes. At Bahia Blanca I endeavoured to show the probability that the ancient Edentata, like the present species, lived in a dry and sterile country, such as now is found in that neighbourhood. With respect to the camel-like llama of Patagonia, the same grounds which, before knowing more than the size of the remains, perplexed me, by not allowing any great change of climate, now that we can guess the habits of the animal, are strangely confirmed. What shall we say of the death of the fossil horse? Did those plains fail in pasture, which afterwards were overrun by thousands and tens of thousands of the successors of the fresh stock introduced with the Spanish colonist? In some countries, we may believe, that a number of species subsequently introduced, by consuming the food of the antecedent races, may have caused their extermination; but we can scarcely credit that the armadillo has devoured the food of the immense Megatherium, the capybara of the Toxodon, or the guanaco of the camel-like kind. But granting that all such changes have been small, yet we are so profoundly ignorant concerning the physiological relations, on which the life, and even health (as shown by epidemics) of any existing species depends, that we argue with still less safety about either the life or death of any extinct kind.[6]

Here again Owen and Darwin, accepting Owen's views on affinities, went astray because it would not yet be evident that the fossils in South America included not only many ancestral or closely related to those still living on that continent but also others of bizarre evolutionary sidelines that became extinct along with all their really close relatives. The large fossil mammal found there and named *Macrauchenia* by Owen in *The Zoology of the Voyage of H.M.S. Beagle* was believed to have affinity with the llamas and their kin, South American camels, and hence with the family Camelidae. In fact although it did have a deceptively somewhat camel-like build, it was radically different in detail. It belonged to a completely distinct order, the Litopterna, that evolved in South America long before the llamas and other camelids invaded from North America. Thus this particular clue to evolution, on the basis of extinct species having living relatives in the same regions, went astray. At this point it might be considered just a hunch. Nevertheless it was one that eventually helped to lead Darwin into Darwinism. The principle is generally correct. In most cases living mammals do have ancestors or other close relatives among species found as fossils in the same region.

To sum up the general subject of the collection of fossil mammals by Darwin, the following paragraph by Darwin at the end of Owen's report on the fossil mammals in the first volume of *The Zoology of the Voyage of H.M.S. Beagle* is here given.

FOSSIL MAMMALIA.

With respect to the geological contemporaneity of the fossils collected by him, Mr. Darwin subjoins the following observations:—

"The remains of the following animals were embedded together at Punta Alta in Bahia Blanca:—The *Megatherium Cuvierii, Megalonyx Jeffersonii, Mylodon Darwinii, Scelidotherium leptocephalum, Toxodon*

Platensis (?) a Horse and a small Dasypodoid quadruped, mentioned p. 107; at St. Fé in Entre Rios, a Horse, a Mastodon, Toxodon Platensis, and some large animal with a tesselated osseous dermal covering; on the banks of the Tercero the Mastodon, Toxodon, and, according to the Jesuit Falkner, some animal with the same kind of covering; near the Rio Negro in Banda Oriental, the Toxodon Platensis, Glossotherium, and some animal with the same kind of covering. To these two latter animals the Glyptodon clavipes, described by Mr. Owen in the Geological Transactions, may, from the locality where it was discovered, and from the similarity of the deposit which covers the greater part of Banda Oriental, almost certainly be added, as having been contemporaneous. From nearly the same reasons, it is probable that the Rodents found at Monte Hermoso in Bahia Blanca, co-existed with the several gigantic mammifers from Punta Alta. I have, also, shown in the Introduction, that the Macrauchenia Patachonica, must have been coeval, or nearly so, with the last mentioned animals. Although we have no evidence of the geological age of the deposits in some of the localities just specified, yet from the presence of the same fossil mammifers in others, of the age of which we have fair means of judging, (in relation to the usual standard of comparison, of the amount of change in the specific forms of the invertebrate inhabitants of the sea,) we may safely infer that most of the animals described in this volume, and likewise the Glyptodon, were strictly contemporaneous, and that all lived at about the same very recent period in the earth's history. Moreover, as some of the fossil animals, discovered in such extraordinary numbers by M. Lund in the caves of Brazil, are identical or closely related with some of those, which lately lived together in La Plata and Patagonia, a certain degree of light is thus thrown on the antiquity of the ancient Fauna of Brazil, which otherwise would have been left involved in complete darkness."

Here it becomes necessary to omit much that is of great human as well as historical and scientific interest. The original edition of Darwin's Journal of Researches, which has become known as The Voyage of the Beagle, ran to 629 pages. The part that must now be skipped in order to keep the present book within its different size and purpose is full not only of fascinating natural history but also of adventures with Indians, earthquakes, and other incidents in one of the most interesting parts of the world at a most interesting period in its history. I therefore skip all but one point between Darwin's departure from San Julián until his passage of the cordillera of the Andes about a year later. The reader is strongly urged for his or her own pleasure to read Darwin's own account in full, one of the most fascinating books of travel and adventure ever written. The one small item I do not entirely omit in this year in 1834–35 is a remark in connection with Darwin's visit to the Falkland Islands in March 1834:

The only quadruped native to the island, is a large wolf-like fox, which is common to both East and West Falkland. I have no doubt it is a peculiar species, and confined to this archipelago; because many sealers, Gauchos, and Indians, who have visited these islands, all maintain that no such animal is found in any part of South America. Molina, from a similarity of habits, thought this was the same with his "culpeu;" but I have seen both and they are quite distinct . . . As far as I am aware, there is no other instance in any part of the world, of so small a mass of broken land, distant from a continent possessing so large a quadruped peculiar to itself.[7]

In the part devoted to recent mammals in *The Zoology of the Voyage of H.M.S. Beagle,* there is a color plate of one of these large foxes (based on a specimen collected by Fitz-Roy) and a description in Latin and English by George R. Waterhouse. A following note by Darwin ends with the statement that ". . . it cannot, I think, be doubted, that as these islands are now becoming colonized, before the paper is decayed on which this animal has been figured, it will be ranked amongst those species which have vanished from the face of the earth." The paper of that volume has not yet decayed, and indeed the Falkland fox has been extinct since about 1876.

In *The Origin of Species* (p. 393 of the first edition), Darwin makes a point that oceanic islands generally lack amphibians and he adds, "why, on the theory of creation, they should not have been created there, it would be difficult to explain." He then goes on to say that he had never found a clear instance of a native terrestrial mammal inhabiting an island situated more than 300 miles from a continent or large continental island. The "wolf-like fox" of the Falklands is noted as "nearest to an exception" but he argues that these islands cannot be considered as (truly) oceanic. That among mammals only bats, which can fly, commonly occur on oceanic islands is both an important aspect of biogeography and a strong argument against creationism. It is rather curious that Darwin did not remark in *The Origin of Species* on the fact that these foxes, being isolated on the Falklands, had become specifically distinct from South American continental foxes evidently with the same ancestry. This is an excellent example of one of the ways in which speciation has occurred as a factor in evolution.

For the whole of 1834 and approximately the first half of 1835, the *Beagle* continued with the charting of the southern end of South America, including the coast of Argentina from the Río de la Plata to Cape Horn and the coast of Chile, which is a maze of islands and inlets in its southern part. Darwin was on the ship during much of this time, but as his own interests were more ashore he took many short excursions on land and a few long ones. Several of his longer land travels have already been mentioned, especially in connection with his searches for fossil mammals. At this point there are special reasons for reference to his trek from Santiago, Chile, over the Andes to Mendoza, Argentina, and return.

Darwin left Santiago on March 18, 1835, and returned on April 10th. He was struck, as every traveler is, by the immensity and grandeur of the Andes and, as every geologist is, by the complication of their rocky structure. Darwin was by now more than an amateur in geology. He had brought from England the first volume of Charles Lyell's epoch-making work *Principles of Geology,* published in 1830, and a copy of the second volume, published in 1832, reached him in Montevideo. Darwin studied these assiduously on the voyage, and Lyellian geology quite blotted out the disgust with geology that he had acquired from his earlier Wernerian professor. As a sample of Darwin's now (for its time) sophisticated geologizing, here is a short extract from the account of his climbing up to the Portillo pass, the more southern and more difficult of the two reachable from Santiago.

MARCH 21ST.—We set out early in the morning, and continued to follow the course of the river, which by this time had become small, till we arrived at the foot of the ridge that separates the waters flowing into the Pacific and Atlantic oceans. The road, which as yet had been good, with a steady but very gradual ascent, now changed into a steep zigzag track. The Cordillera in this part consists of two principal ranges; the passes across which attain respectively an elevation of 13,210 and 14,365 feet. The first great line (consisting of course of many subordinate ones) is called Peuquenes. It divides the waters, and therefore likewise the republics of Chile and Mendoza. To the eastward, a mountainous and elevated region separates it from the second range (called the Portillo) overlooking the Pampas. The streams from the intermediate tract find a passage a little way to the southward through this second line.

I will here give a very brief sketch of the geological structure of these mountains: first, of the Peuquenes, or western line; for the constitution of the two ranges is totally different. The lowest stratified rock is a dull red or purple claystone porphyry, of many varieties, alternating with conglomerates, and breccia composed of a similar substance: this formation attains a thickness of more than a mile. Above it there is a grand mass of gypsum, which alternates, passes into, and is replaced by, red sandstone, conglomerates, and black calcareous clay-slate. I hardly dare venture to guess the thickness of this second division; but I have already said some of the beds of gypsum alone attain a thickness of at least two thousand feet. Even at the very crest of the Peuquenes, at the height of 13,210 feet, and above it, the black clay-slate contained numerous marine remains, amongst which a gryphaea is the most abundant, likewise shells, resembling turritellae, terebratulae, and an ammonite. It is an old story, but not the less wonderful, to hear of shells, which formerly were crawling about at the bottom of the sea, being now elevated nearly fourteen thousand feet above its level. The formation probably is of the age of the central parts of the secondary series of Europe.

These great piles of strata have been penetrated, upheaved, and overturned, in the most extraordinary manner, by masses of injected rock, equalling mountains in size. On the bare sides of the hills, complicated dikes, and wedges of variously-coloured porphyries and other stones, are seen traversing the strata in every possible form and direction; proving also by their intersections, successive periods of violence. The rock which composes the axis of these great lines of dislocation, at a distance very closely resembles granite, but on examination, it is found rarely to contain any quartz; and instead of ordinary felspar, albite.

The metamorphic action has been very great, as might have been expected from the close proximity of such grand masses of rock, which were injected when in a liquefied state from heat. When it is known, first, that the stratified porphyries have flowed as streams of submarine lava under an enormous pressure, and that the mechanical beds separating them owe their origin to explosions from the same submarine craters; secondly, that the whole mass in the lower part has generally been so completely fused into one solid rock by metamorphic action, that the lines of division can only be traced with much difficulty; and thirdly, that masses of porphyry, undistinguishable by their mineralogical characters from the two first kinds, have been subsequently injected;—the extreme complication of the whole will readily be believed.[8]

From the fossils mentioned the "black clay-slate" (evidently a dark shale) was Cretaceous in age, which is close enough to Darwin's estimate of the age as being that of the central parts of the secondary series, which was the term then used for the Mesozoic. Darwin's petrology, necessarily that of his time and used as in Lyell, was correct in rejecting the designation of a rock as granite because it rarely contained quartz, which by definition is always a constituent of granite. However, granite does often contain the "felspar" (usually spelled "feldspar") albite. Darwin's "ordinary felspar" would be orthoclase, which is usual in granite and is often pink.

After crossing the main range, the Portillo, the descent to the plains was rapid, and after spending a night in a small village Darwin went on to Mendoza, still the metropolis of this region, as related as follows in the *Journal of Researches:*

We crossed the Luxan, which is a river of considerable size, though its course towards the sea-coast is very imperfectly known. It is even doubtful whether, in passing over the plains, it is evaporated, or whether it forms a tributary of the Sauce or Colorado. We slept in the village, which is a small place surrounded by gardens, and forms the most southern part, that is cultivated, of the province of Mendoza; it is five leagues south of the capital. At night I experienced an attack (for it deserves no less a name) of the *Benchuca* (a species of Reduvius) the great black bug of the Pampas. It is most disgusting to feel soft wingless insects, about an inch long, crawling over one's body. Before sucking they are quite thin, but afterwards become round and bloated with blood, and in this state they are easily crushed. They are also found in the northern parts of Chile and in Peru. One which I caught at Iquique was very empty. When placed on the table, and though surrounded by people, if a finger was presented, the bold insect would immediately draw its sucker, make a charge, and if allowed, draw blood. No pain was caused by the wound. It was curious to watch its body during the act of sucking, as it changed in less than ten minutes, from being as flat as a wafer to a globular form. This one feast, for which the benchuca was indebted to one of the officers, kept it fat during four whole months; but, after the first fortnight, the insect was quite ready to have another suck.

MARCH 27TH.—We rode on to Mendoza. The country was beautifully cultivated, and resembled Chile. This neighbourhood is celebrated for its fruit; and certainly nothing could appear more flourishing than the vineyards and the orchards of figs, peaches, and olives. We bought watermelons nearly twice as large as a man's head, most deliciously cool and well-flavoured, for a halfpenny apiece; and for the value of threepence, half a wheelbarrowful of peaches. The cultivated and enclosed part of this province is very small; there is little more than that which we passed through between Luxan and the capital. The land, as in Chile, entirely owes its fertility to artificial irrigation; and it is really wonderful to observe how abundantly productive a barren traversia is rendered by this simple process.[9]

In spite of his admiration of the fruits, Darwin found that the city of Mendoza had "a stupid forlorn aspect." Most modern visitors find it charming, and most of the abundant, good Argentinian wine comes from that area.

Darwin moved on almost immediately and returned to Santiago by the more northern pass, Uspallata, which has become the main route of surface travel between Chile and Argentina. On

April 10, 1835, Darwin was back in Santiago, and after another excursion along and near the coast southward from Santiago, he went off on the *Beagle* for a time in Peru and then to the Galápagos, of which more later.

The trip to Mendoza has been given brief but special notice here for two reasons: first, to provide a glimpse of Darwin as an accomplished and enthusiastic geologist, and second, to discuss the perennial subject of Darwin's chronic illness. As to the first, it can be supplemented interestingly by an extract from a letter Darwin wrote in Lima to his cousin W. D. Fox:

> I am glad to hear you have some thoughts of beginning geology. I hope you will; there is so much larger a field for thought than in the other branches of Natural History. I am become a zealous disciple of Mr. Lyell's views, as known in his admirable book. . . . Geology is a capital science to begin, as it requires nothing but a little reading, thinking, and hammering.

There will be more about geology, as this was the field in which Darwin first became an established scientist, but here some remarks on his health are introduced because his years of chronic illness have sometimes been considered as having a relationship to his voyage and specifically to his visits to Peru and western Argentina. Darwin was seasick most of the time while he was at sea, as his correspondence and journal make highly evident. He spent as much time ashore as he possibly could, weeks and even months on end during the "voyage," and there seems to have had no more health problems than most world travelers. It is possible that his seasickness had a bearing on the fact that after the voyage on the *Beagle* Darwin never again left Great Britain, which before air travel could only be done in a boat or ship.

Shortly after his return to England, in 1837 at the latest, Darwin was afflicted with illness, which came and went to some extent but which kept him a semi-invalid for the rest of his life. As the most constant symptom was sickness in the usual English sense of that word, that is, nausea and vomiting, the prior long seasickness makes it impossible to be sure when in fact his chronic illness began. Everyone who has written much about Darwin has mentioned that illness and has usually expressed an opinion about its origin. (The most detailed account is *To Be an Invalid* by Ralph Colp, Jr., University of Chicago Press, 1977.) There are many chronic illnesses with similar symptoms that were never recognized, or diagnosed, let alone cured during Darwin's lifetime. Two among them could have been contracted during the visit to Peru and western Argentina. The *"benchuca"* by which he was bitten near Mendoza was a reduviid or conenose bug, probably *Triatoma*. It is now known to be a common vector that frequently transmits trypanosomiasis from mammalian hosts, such as rodents or armadillos, to humans. This is related to African sleeping sickness, but in South America it causes Chagas' disease (pronounced shah'-gahs, named for a Brazilian doctor), which has chronic symptoms quite like Darwin's. Also particularly rife in the area traversed by Darwin on that trip was brucellosis, a bacterial disease then common in domesticated and some wild animals, often transmitted to humans, and likewise with a chronic form quite similar to Darwin's illness. Pain often accompanied Darwin's attacks, and from time to time he also had skin rashes and heart palpitations, which were probably passing allergies or other problems not necessarily related to his chronic disabilities. The doctors he consulted, including his father, never reached a firm diagnosis, and medication or hydropathy—a fad at the time—seemed to have no effect. There is really no clear basis for any diagnosis made during his lifetime or for any of the multiple guesses made without direct evidence by later writers: "suppressed gout" (whatever that may be), addiction to snuff, "refractive anomaly of the eyes," hypoglycemia, porphyria, arsenic poisoning (some of the many medicines given him contained arsenic), epilepsy (Darwin said he had "fits," but evidently he meant only stomach attacks), allergy to pigeons and various others, a few possible but many ridiculous.

A frequently mentioned idea is that Darwin's illness was not physical but purely neurotic or psychosomatic. That was and is the way out for a doctor who cannot really diagnose his patient's disease, and of course it is the bread and butter for psychoanalysts. Anyone with a greatly extended chronic physical disease is likely to become somewhat neurotic and occasionally depressed, but those are results, not causes of physical illness. The tests now known to be appropriate for a host of physical diseases, such as trypanosomiasis or brucellosis, were mostly unknown and in any case not applied and recorded while Darwin was alive. Thus there really is no way to identify his chronic ailment and we will never know with certainty what it was. (Every writer on Darwin has a guess, which does no harm if frankly guesswork; my guess is that he had chronic brucellosis.)

In spite of that disability Darwin lived to the age of seventy-three, even now not considered a particularly early death. During that life he accomplished far more than has almost anyone else regardless of length of life. Toward the end of his autobiography, which was written about six years before his death, Darwin explained in a simple way and with his usual excessive modesty how he could do so much in spite of physical adversity:

"My habits are methodical, and this has been of not a little use for my particular line of work. Lastly, I have had ample leisure from not having to earn my own bread. Even ill-health, though it has annihilated several years of my life, has saved me from the distractions of society and amusement.")

And now back to the *Beagle* and on to the Galápagos Islands, which provided the third set of observations that, as Darwin later remarked, caused him to be "haunted" by the origin of species. (The first was the presence of fossil mammals in South America, as discussed earlier in this chapter, and the second the observation that in South America "closely allied animals replace one another in proceeding southwards over the Continent." Quoted from the "Autobiography.")

On September 15, 1835, the *Beagle* arrived at the Galápagos Islands, possessions of Ecuador and some five to six hundred miles out in the Pacific west of the South American mainland. On September 17 Darwin landed on Chatham Island, easternmost of the Galápagos, and the *Beagle* spent some time sailing around it. Darwin spent one night on shore, where he found the lava fields, parched surface and weedy vegetation unattractive, although he learned at once that "the greater number of its inhabitants, both vegetable and animal, [are] found nowhere else."[10] As the Galápagos are now much studied and visited, especially by those interested in natural history and in Darwin's connection with these islands, it will be helpful here to list them and to point out that each island has two names, one English and one Spanish:

ENGLISH NAME	SPANISH NAME	COMMENT
Chatham	San Cristobal	Easternmost island.
Hood	Española	Small island, south of Chatham.
Charles	Floreana	Somewhat larger, west of Hood.
Indefatigable	Santa Cruz	Large, near the center of the group.
Seymour	Baltra	Small, just off the north coast of Indefatigable.
Barrington	Santa Fé	Small, southwest of Indefatigable.
Duncan	Pinzón	Small, west of Indefatigable, between it and Albemarle.

ENGLISH NAME	SPANISH NAME	COMMENT
James	Santiago	Large, northwest of Indefatigable.
Albemarle	Isabel	Much the largest island, with a long, crooked line of high volcanic peaks.
Narborough	Fernandina	Large, just west of Albemarle and almost surrounded by the latter on three sides.

Abingdon (Pinta), Bindloe (Marchenal) and Tower (Genovesa) are small or moderate-sized islands north of the main group. A bay on Tower Island is named after Darwin. So far to the northwest as hardly to seem part of the archipelago are two quite small islands, Wenman, also called Wolf, and Culpepper, also called Darwin. Within the archipelago itself there are also several very small islands or mere rocks and some reefs. An active research station is now maintained by the Charles Darwin Foundation at Academy Bay on Indefatigable Island.

Darwin's general summary of the flora and fauna is given as follows in the *Journal of Researches*.

I will now offer a few general observations on the natural history of these islands. I endeavoured to make as nearly a perfect collection in every branch as time permitted. The plants have not yet been examined, but Professor Henslow, who has kindly undertaken the description of them, informs me that there are probably many new species, and perhaps even some new genera. They all have an extremely weedy character, and it would scarcely have been supposed, that they had grown at an inconsiderable elevation directly under the equator. In the lower and sterile parts, the bush, which from its minute brown leaves chiefly gives the leafless appearance to the brushwood, is one of the Euphorbiaceæ. In the same region an acacia and a cactus *(Opuntia Galapageia)*, with large oval compressed articulations, springing from a cylindrical stem, are in some parts common. These are the only trees which in that part afford any shade. Near the summits of the different islands, the vegetation has a very different character; ferns and coarse grasses are abundant; and the commonest tree is one of the Compositæ. Tree-ferns are not present. One of the most singular characters of the Flora, considering the position of this archipelago, is the absence of every member of the palm family. Cocos Island, on the other hand, which is the nearest point of land, takes its name from the great number of cocoa-nut trees on it. From the presence of the Opuntias and some other plants, the vegetation partakes more of the character of that of America than of any other country.

Of mammalia a large kind of mouse forms a well-marked species.

From its large thin ears, and other characters, it approaches in form a section of the genus, which is confined to the sterile regions of South America. There is also a rat, which Mr. Waterhouse believes is probably distinct from the English kind; but I cannot help suspecting that it is only the same altered by the peculiar conditions of its new country.

In my collections from these islands, Mr. Gould considers that there are twenty-six different species of land birds. With the exception of one, all probably are undescribed kinds, which inhabit this archipelago, and no other part of the world. Among the waders and waterfowl it is more difficult, without detailed comparison, to say what are new. But a water-sail which lives near the summits of the mountains, is undescribed, as perhaps is a Totanus and a heron. The only kind of gull which is found among these islands, is also new; when the wandering habits of this genus are considered, this is a very remarkable circumstance. The species most closely allied to it, comes from the Strait of Magellan. Of the other aquatic birds, the species appear the same with well-known American birds.

The general character of the plumage of these birds is extremely plain, and like the Flora possesses little beauty. Although the species are thus peculiar to the archipelago, yet nearly all in their general structure, habits, colour of feathers, and even tone of voice, are strictly American. The following brief list will give an idea of their kinds. 1st. A buzzard, having many of the characters of Polyborus or Caracara; and in its habits not to be distinguished from that peculiar South American genus; 2d. Two owls; 3d. Three species of tyrant-flycatchers—a form strictly American. One of these appears identical with a common kind (*Muscicapa coronata?* Lath.), which has a very wide range, from La Plata throughout Brazil to Mexico; 4th. A sylvicola, an American form, and especially common in the northern division of the continent; 5th. Three species of mocking-birds, a genus common to both Americas; 6th. A finch, with a stiff tail and a long claw to its hinder toe, closely allied to a North American genus; 7th. A swallow belonging to the American division of that genus; 8th. A dove, like, but distinct from, the Chilian species; 9th. A group of finches, of which Mr. Gould considers there are thirteen species; and these he has distributed into four new sub-genera. These birds are the most singular of any in the archipelago. They all agree in many points; namely, in a peculiar structure of their bill, short tails, general form, and in their plumage. The females are gray or brown, but the old cocks jet-black. All the species, excepting two, feed in flocks on the ground, and have very similar habits. It is very remarkable that a nearly perfect gradation of structure in this one group can be traced in the form of the beak, from one exceeding in dimensions that of the largest gros-beak, to another differing but little from that of a warbler. Of the aquatic birds I have already remarked that some are peculiar to these islands, and some common to North and South America.

We will now turn to the order of reptiles, which forms, perhaps, the most striking feature in the zoology of these islands. The species are not numerous, but the number of individuals of each kind, is extraordinarily great. There is one kind both of the turtle and tortoise; of lizards four; and of snakes about the same number.

I will first describe the habits of the tortoise *(Testudo Indicus)* which has been so frequently alluded to. These animals are found, I believe, in all the islands of the Archipelago; certainly in the greater number. They frequent in preference the high damp parts, but likewise inhabit the lower and arid districts. I have already mentioned proofs, from the numbers which have been taken in a single day, how very numerous they must be. Some individuals grow to an immense size: Mr. Lawson, an Englishman, who had at the time of our visit charge of the colony, told us that he had seen several so large, that it required six or eight men to lift them from the ground; and that some had afforded as much as two hundred pounds of meat. The old males are the largest, the females rarely growing to so great a size. The male can readily be distinguished from the female by the greater length of its tail. The tortoises which live on those islands where there is no water, or in the lower and arid parts of the others, chiefly feed on the succulent cactus. Those which frequent the higher and damp regions, eat the leaves of various trees, a kind of berry (called guayavita) which is acid and austere, and likewise a pale green filamentous lichen, that hangs in tresses from the boughs of the trees.

The tortoise is very fond of water, drinking large quantities, and wallowing in the mud. The larger islands alone possess springs, and these are always situated towards the central parts, and at a considerable elevation. The tortoises, therefore, which frequent the lower districts, when thirsty, are obliged to travel from a long distance. Hence broad and well-beaten paths radiate off in every direction from the wells even down to the sea-coast; and the Spaniards by following them up, first discovered the watering-places. When I landed at Chatham Island, I could not imagine what animal travelled so methodically along the well-chosen tracks. Near the springs it was a curious spectacle to behold many of these great monsters; one set eagerly travelling onwards with out-stretched necks, and another set returning, after having drunk their fill. When the tortoise arrives at the spring, quite regardless of any spectator, it buries its head in the water above its eyes, and greedily swallows great mouthfuls, at the rate of about ten in a minute. The inhabitants say each animal stays three or four days in the neighbourhood of the water, and then returns to the lower country; but they differed in their accounts respecting the frequency of these visits. The animal probably regulates them according to the nature of the food which it has consumed. It is, however, certain, that tortoises can subsist even on those islands where there is no other water, than what falls during a few rainy days in the year.[11]

The "large kind of mouse" mentioned by Darwin is a rice rat of the genus now called *Oryzomys*. Several species are now known from the Galápagos. *Oryzomys* is extremely abundant in southern North America and all over South America. It is readily rafted out to sea and so it must have been to the Galápagos long enough ago to have evolved into new species there. The rat that Darwin thought might have been a modified English rat may have been another *Oryzomys* or, most likely, it was a true *Rattus* that went ashore from one of the many ships that for years had stopped there to water and to take tortoises for food. The finches assigned by John Gould to thirteen species are those now famous as Darwin's finches, now mentioned or figured in almost all books on evolutionary biology. A later remark on these is made in the next extract from Darwin's account. The tortoises mentioned by Darwin as of a single species are now called *Geochelone elephantopus* and are supposed to have evolved in isolation on various islands into fifteen subspecies, ten each on a single island and five on the major peaks of the largest and most complex island, Albemarle. Some of the subspecies have been completely killed off by humans, and others are in danger.

Some pages later Darwin summed up certain aspects of the fauna in a way especially significant in view of his later thoughts on evolution.

I will not here attempt to come to any definite conclusions, as the species have not been accurately examined; but we may infer, that, with the exception of a few wanderers, the organic beings found on this archipelago are peculiar to it; and yet that their general form strongly partakes of an American character. It would be impossible for any one accustomed to the birds of Chile and La Plata to be placed on these islands, and not to feel convinced that he was, as far as the organic world was concerned, on American ground. This similarity in type, between distant islands and continents, while the species are distinct, has scarcely been sufficiently noticed. The circumstance would be explained, according to the views of some authors, by saying that the creative power had acted according to the same law over a wide area.

It has been mentioned, that the inhabitants can distinguish the tortoises, according to the islands whence they are brought. I was also informed that many of the islands possess trees and plants which do not occur on the others. For instance the berry-bearing tree, called Guyavita, which is common on James Island, certainly is not found on Charles Island, though appearing equally well fitted for it. Unfortunately, I was not aware of these facts till my collection was nearly completed: it never occurred to me, that the productions of islands only a few miles apart, and placed under the same physical conditions, would be dissimilar. I therefore did not attempt to make a series of specimens from the separate islands. It is the fate of every voyager, when he has just discovered what object in any place is more particularly worthy of his attention, to be hurried from it. In the case of the mocking-bird, I ascertained (and have brought home the specimens) that one species (*Orpheus trifasciatus,* Gould) is exclusively found in Charles Island; a second *(O. parvulus)* on Albemarle Island; and a third *(O. melanotus)* common to James and Chatham Islands. The two last species are closely allied, but the first would be considered by every naturalist as quite distinct. I examined many specimens in the different islands, and in each the respective kind was *alone* present. These birds agree in general plumage, structure, and habits; so that the different species replace each other in the economy of the different islands. These species are not characterized by the markings on the plumage alone, but likewise by the size and form of the bill, and other differences. I have stated, that in the thirteen species of ground-finches, a nearly perfect gradation may be traced, from a beak extraordinarily thick, to one so fine, that it may be compared to that of a warbler. I very much suspect, that certain members of the series are confined to different islands; therefore, if the collection had been made on any *one* island, it would not have presented so perfect a gradation. It is clear, that if several islands have each their peculiar species of the same genera, when these are placed together, they will have a wide range of character. But there is not space in this work, to enter on this curious subject.[12]

In *The Zoology of the Voyage of H.M.S. Beagle,* John Gould made the identifications and diagnoses of new genera and species of finches and also drew beautiful plates of eight of the thirteen species, which were then lithographed by Mrs. Gould. However as Gould left for Australia before finishing the text, this was almost all written by Darwin himself. The following significant comment is by Darwin:

This singular genus appears to be confined to the islands of the Galapagos Archipelago. It is very numerous, both in individuals and in species, so that it forms the most striking feature in their ornithology. The characters of the species of Geospiza, as well as of the following allied subgenera, run closely into each other in a most remarkable manner.

In my Journal of Researches, p. 475, I have given my reasons for believing that in some cases the separate islands possess their own representatives of the different species, and this almost necessarily would cause a fine gradation in their characters. Unfortunately I did not suspect this fact until it was too late to distinguish the specimens from the different islands of the group; but from the collection made for Captain FitzRoy, I have been able in some small measure to rectify this omission.

In each species of these genera a perfect gradation in colouring might,

I think, be formed from one jet black to another pale brown. My observations showed that the former were invariably the males; but Mr. Bynoe, the surgeon of the Beagle, who opened many specimens, assured me that he found two quite black specimens of one of the smaller species of Geospiza, which certainly were females: this, however, undoubtedly is an exception to the general fact; and is analogous to those cases, which Mr. Blyth has recorded of female linnets and some other birds, in a state of high constitutional vigour, assuming the brighter plumage of the male. The jet black birds, in cases where there could be no doubt in regard to the species, were in singularly few proportional numbers to the brown ones: I can only account for this by the supposition that the intense black colour is attained only by three-year-old birds. I may here mention, that the time of year (beginning of October) in which my collection was made, probably corresponds, as far as the purposes of incubation are concerned, with our autumn. The several species of Geospiza are undistinguishable from each other in habits; they often form, together with the species of the following subgenera, and likewise with doves, large irregular flocks. They frequent the rocky and extremely arid parts of the land sparingly covered with almost naked bushes, near the coasts; for here they find, by scratching in the cindery soil with their powerful beaks and claws, the seeds of grasses and other plants, which rapidly spring up during the short rainy season, and as rapidly disappear. They often eat small portions of the succulent leaves of the *Opuntia Galapageia,* probably for the sake of the moisture contained in them: in this dry climate the birds suffer much from the want of water, and these finches, as well as others, daily crowd round the small and scanty wells, which are found on some of the islands. I seldom, however, saw these birds in the upper and damp region, which supports a thriving vegetation; excepting on the cleared and cultivated fields near the houses in Charles Island, where, as I was informed by the colonists, they do much injury by digging up roots and seeds from a depth of even six inches.[13]

For each species of "Darwin's finches," Darwin gave what information he had as to its place of occurrence, thanks mainly to Fitz-Roy, as the preceding passage indicates. The data given are as follows:

SPECIES	KNOWN DISTRIBUTION
Geospiza magnirostris	Charles and Chatham Islands. (Darwin added: "I have strong reasons for believing this species is not found in James's Island.")
Geospiza strenua	James and Chatham Islands
Geospiza fortis	Charles and Chatham Islands
Geospiza nebulosa	Charles Island
Geospiza fuliginosa	Chatham and James' Island

SPECIES	KNOWN DISTRIBUTION
Geospiza dentirostris	Galápagos Archipelago
Geospiza parvala	James' Island
Geospiza dubia	Chatham Island
Camarhynchus psittaculus	James' Island
Camarhynchus crassirostris	Charles Island? (Darwin added: "I am nearly certain this species is not found in James Island. I believe it came from Charles Island, and probably there replaces the *C. psittaculus* of James Island.")
Cactornis scandens	James' Island
Cacturnis assimilis	Galápagos Archipelago
Certhidea olivacea	Chatham and James Island. (Darwin added that he thought his specimens came from both islands but was only sure of James Island.)

(Comment: the varied use of "James's," "James' " and "James" follows that in the publication.)

Darwin was always avid for facts, and even at this early stage in his career he was a close and careful observer and recorder of anything that would eventually bear on the "mystery of mysteries—the first appearance of new beings on earth." He still spoke and wrote of creation, but it is evident that he was beginning to have doubts. It is thus curious that on the Galápagos he made no record of where a particular specimen of birds, or particularly of the finches now called "Darwin's," was collected. It is perhaps even more curious that Fitz-Roy, who tended to be critical of Darwin's painstaking collections, did make some such records, even though these were not complete and in some cases not surely accurate.

. The distribution and characteristics of these finches have become a crowning example of, and a clinching argument for, evolution. Since Darwin they have been studied in great and precise detail, notably in David Lack's book *Darwin's Finches* (1947). As the preceding extract from the *Journal of Researches* shows, Darwin himself did not go beyond noting the gradation of variation in the finches' bills and a mere suspicion "that certain members of the series are confined to different islands." In *The Origin of Species* Darwin did not specify the finches in particular but referred to the Galápagos fauna as an example of the inhabitants of an archipelago, though specifically distinct, being closely allied to those of the nearest continent. In the first edition of *The Origin of Species* he wrote further that ". . . the several islands of the Galápagos Archipelago are tenanted . . . by very closely related species; so that the inhabitants of each separate island, though mostly distinct, are related in an incomparably closer degree to each other than to the inhabitants of any other part of the world." In the fifth (and sixth, last) edition he made this statement more positive: "Thus each separate island of the Galápagos Archipelago is tenanted, and the fact is a marvelous one, by distinct species." He did not make this statement explicitly about the finches, but he certainly had them in mind. After publication of *The Origin of Species* Darwin argued at some length with his friend Lyell, who was at first skeptical about evolution but was later convinced, and the Galápagos fauna entered into this.

That Darwin was already at least halfway to becoming an evolutionist is evident in a remark in one of his notebooks published by Lady Barlow (one of his granddaughters) in 1963. After some notes on the birds and tortoises of the Galápagos, he wrote, "If there is the slightest foundation for these remarks the zoology of Archipelagoes—will be well worth examining; for such facts would undermine the stability of species." What was evidently already in Darwin's mind here was that the presence of some closely similar and yet distinct kinds of birds and tortoises on the various islands could perhaps be explained by their divergence as different species from a single ancestral species. That would indeed undermine the belief that species do not evolve— the conclusion here only glimpsed but later established by Darwin.

The *Beagle* sailed from the Galápagos on October 20, 1835. This virtually ended the parts of the voyage which, in retrospect, Darwin considered those that set him on the way to evolution as fact and as a process for which explanatory theories and principles must be considered. He had also added to his knowledge and zest for other natural sciences, up to this point about evenly divided between zoology and geology, with quite a bit of botany thrown in. In the long voyages to Tahiti, New Zealand and Australia across the Pacific and then to the Cocos, or Keeling, Islands and Mauritius across the Indian Ocean, his observations and thoughts turned more to atolls, or lagoon islands, barrier reefs and fringing reefs. Although these abound in zoological phenomena, as everyone knows, Darwin's consideration of them as we shall see was more from a geological point of view.

5

The Maturing Scientist

When Darwin finally reached England on October 2, 1836, he cleared his paraphernalia and last collections from the *Beagle* and then hastened to reunite with his family at Shrewsbury and visit with his childhood friends and close relatives at Maer. Apart from these personal matters, his first concern was to see what could be made of his collections and observations. For that he turned to Henslow in Cambridge. During the voyage, whenever possible, Darwin had sent boxes of specimens, mineral, plant and animal, to Henslow for care until his return. They had corresponded whenever possible on so long and interrupted a journey, and Henslow had sent Darwin books and news. Now Darwin visited Cambridge and with Henslow undertook the onerous task of sorting out the collections. A major problem was to arrange to have the specimens identified and described, especially as concerned the vertebrate animals.

Darwin also had to report on his activities during the cruise. It was Fitz-Roy's intention to have this combined with his report, but Darwin balked. His edited journal was first published in 1839, as Volume III of the narrative reports, under the title of *Journal of Researches into the Geology and Natural History of the Various Countries Visited by H.M.S. Beagle.* Most of the excerpts here given in Chapters 2 to 4 are taken from that edition, its title condensed to *Journal of Researches.* This was later somewhat expanded and emended and published in 1845 as an independent volume. It is this edition, sometimes with minor further changes, that has been most often reprinted and is generally available today, sometimes simply titled as *The Voyage of the Beagle*.

Darwin further took upon himself the editorship of publications on the vertebrate animals collected during the voyages and of getting sometimes reluctant specialists in the various groups to work on these. They were published in five parts, collected in three sumptuous volumes. Part I (1840) on fossil mammals was by Richard Owen, then Professor of Anatomy and Physiology in the Royal College of Surgeons and on good terms with Darwin although he later became bitterly opposed to Darwin, as has been mentioned. Part II (1839) on (recent) Mammalia was by George Waterhouse, then Curator of the Zoological Society of London. Part III (1841) was devoted to the birds, and as noted in Chapter 4 of this book the new names and Latin diagnoses were by John Gould, described only as a Fellow of the Linnean Society, but the accompanying text was by Darwin himself. There is also an appendix by T. C. Eyton, another Fellow of the Linnean Society, with anatomical descriptions of twelve species, specimens of which were evidently brought back whole, probably in alcohol. Part IV (1842) is by the Reverend Leonard Jenyns, likewise a Fellow of the Linnean Society. Localities were provided by Darwin and so were relatively brief notes on the colors of some of the fishes when alive. Part V (1843), the last part, is labeled "Reptiles," but using the broad sense of herpetology as a specialty it also includes amphibians, all of which in Darwin's collections were anurans, frogs and toads. The localities were of course provided by Darwin, but here he added less by way of comment than in the other parts of *The Zoology of the Voyage*. The author was Thomas Bell, Professor of Zoology in King's College and a Fellow of both the Royal Society and the Linnean Society. (The early recognition of Darwin's abilities and accomplishments is shown by the fact that when this large work was published under his editorship he was already a Fellow of the Royal Society, the most prestigious British scientific society.) Each part of this luxurious work contains many large illustrations, lithographed or engraved, and those of the mammals and birds were colored by hand. Copies of the original edition, never reprinted as such, were few and now fetch fabulous prices when available at all. An excellent facsimile was issued in 1980, but again in a small edition (750 copies with no reprints) and also expensive.

A discrepancy between *The Journal of Researches* and *The Zoology of the Voyage* may be mentioned. In the former Darwin wrote at length about the tortoises that gave the islands their Spanish name, but they are not mentioned among the reptiles in the latter work. The explanation is doubtless that Darwin did not include a specimen of these huge animals among those sent back to England for study.

When the zoology was well under way, Darwin undertook to write on the geology of the voyage. This was originally done in three separate books published by Smith, Elder in London. In 1842 there was issued *The Structure and Distribution of Coral Reefs Being the First Part of the Geology of the Voyage of the Beagle*. The second part, 1844, was *Geological Observations on the Volcanic Islands, Visited during the Voyage of H.M.S. Beagle*, and the third, 1846, was *Geological Observations on South America*. The second and third parts were later published in a single volume, without revision. The parts of this work are largely in a sequence reversed from that of the voyage itself. The first part on reefs and atolls embodies observations made in the latter part of the voyage, in the Pacific and Indian oceans, after the *Beagle* had left South America. The third part is also mainly devoted to islands in the Pacific and Indian oceans, but its first chapter is on the Cape Verde Islands (Darwin's "Cape de Verde Archipelago"), well out in the Atlantic, and the second chapter starts with Fernando Noronha, also in the Atlantic but not far off the Brazilian coast. Cape Verde and Fernando Noronha were both visited before the *Beagle* reached South America, but another Atlantic island, Terceira, discussed in Chapter II is in the Azores and was not visited until the *Beagle* was approaching England on its way home.

The first of these three geological books is the most interesting in several ways. It describes places and scenery, with reefs that are attractive to anyone who visits them in travels through the more tropical parts of the oceans and seas. Darwin formulated a theory of how fringing reefs, barrier reefs and atolls are formed and how they have succeeded each other in time. He made a meticulous collection of observed facts, examined then-current hypotheses as to their origins and relations, found evidence that contradicted those hypotheses, formed a new hypothesis, sought out anything that would falsify his hypothesis and found no such falsification, and thus arrived at an important, tenable theory. This is a model, a sort of paradigm, of truly scientific method. It shows how Darwin's mind was working as regards scientific problems, a method and an ability that would later result in the Darwinian theory of evolution. The work on reefs and atolls was all the more remarkable because it was done in a period when Darwin's health was even more troublesome than usual. In 1841 he remarked that he was recommencing on this study "after more than thirteen months interval," and it had been interrupted at least twice before that.

As background here, it is important that Lyell, whom Darwin always recognized as his mentor in geology, had devoted almost the whole of Chapter XVIII, "volume the second" of his *Principles of Geology* to reefs and atolls. This was published in 1832, after the *Beagle* had left England, but Darwin received a copy before he had visited a "coral" reef. "Coral" is given quotation marks because a "coral" reef embodies much more than "coral" strictly speaking. One may be sure that he studied this chapter of Lyell's most attentively while making his own observations of the "coral" islands and drawing deductions from them. It was and is generally known that "coral" reefs occur in three situations, as already mentioned above in passing. Fringing reefs occur attached to shores around islands, often of considerable height, composed of other materials and rocks. Barrier reefs occur at some distance from a shore, either low or high, with a channel or long lagoon of some depth between reef and shore. Atolls are low islands, much of them at or even a little below sea level, composed entirely of reef materials and their weathering products. These atoll reefs may be quite irregular in shape, but their determining feature is that they nearly or quite surround a usually rather shallow lagoon. They were known to the earliest navigators of the tropical Indian and Pacific oceans and their origin was a puzzle to early geologists.

Reduced to the simplest terms, Lyell's view was that the atoll lagoons occupied the craters of extinct volcanoes, generally with a partial filling of reeflike rock, and that the surrounding reefs themselves had grown up from the eroded rims of the ancient craters. Darwin certainly started with some bias toward that theory, or more precisely that hypothesis, but he soon encountered objections to it. In his book *The Structure and Distribution of Coral Reefs* he first described atolls in general and some in particular, notably Keeling Atoll and the numerous atolls of the Maldive Islands (Darwin called them the "Maldiva Archipelago"). Here followed chapters on barrier reefs and fringing, or shore, reefs, then one on distribution and growth of reefs, one on a theory of their formation (its essence given in Darwin's words below), and finally a chapter connecting theory and geographic distribution. Plates include maps of characteristic reefs and a large map of the tropics from the east coast of Africa to the west coast of South America and the West Indies, with the three main types of reefs and also the locations of active volcanoes overlaid in color.

Here follow the essentials of Darwin's new theory in his own words:

The facts stand thus; —there are many large tracts of ocean, without any high land, interspersed with reefs and islets, formed by the growth of those kinds of corals, which cannot live at great depths; and the existence of these reefs and low islets, in such numbers and at such distant points, is quite inexplicable, excepting on the theory, that the bases on which the reefs first became attached, slowly and successively sank beneath the level of the sea, whilst the corals continued to grow upwards. No positive facts are opposed to this view, and some general considerations render it probable. There is evidence of change in form, whether or not from subsidence, on some of these coral-islands; and there is evidence of subterranean disturbances beneath them. Will then the theory, to which we have thus been led, solve the curious problem, —what has given to each class of reef its peculiar form?

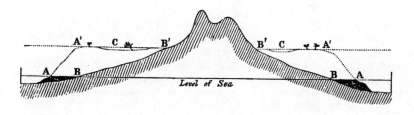

AA—Outer edge of the reef at the level of the sea.

BB—Shores of the island.

A'A'—Outer edge of the reef, after its upward growth during a period of subsidence.

CC—The lagoon-channel between the reef and the shores of the now encircled land.

B'B'—The shores of the now encircled island.

N.B. In this, and the following wood-cut, the subsidence of the land could only be represented by an apparent rise in the level of the sea.

Let us in imagination place within one of the subsiding areas, an island surrounded by a "fringing reef," —that kind, which alone offers no difficulty in the explanation of its origin. Let the unbroken lines and the oblique shading in the woodcut (No. 1) represent a vertical section through such an island; and the horizontal shading will represent the section of the reef. Now, as the island sinks down, either a few feet at a time or quite insensibly, we may safely infer from what we know of the conditions favourable to the growth of coral, that the living masses bathed by the surf on the margin of the reef, will soon regain the surface. The water, however, will encroach, little by little, on the shore, the island becoming lower and smaller, and the space between the edge of the reef and the beach proportionally broader. A section of the reef and island in this state, after a subsidence of several hundred feet, is given by the dotted lines: coral-islets are supposed to have been formed on the new reef, and a ship is anchored in the lagoon-channel. This section is in every respect that of an encircling barrier-reef; it is, in fact, a section taken E. and W. through the highest point of the encircled island of Bolabola. The same section is more clearly shown in the following woodcut (No. 2) by the unbroken lines. The width of the reef, and its slope both on the outer and inner side, will have been determined by the growing powers of the coral, under the conditions, (for instance the force of the breakers and of the currents) to which it has been exposed; and the lagoon-channel will be deeper or shallower, in proportion to the growth of the delicately branched corals within the reef, and to the accumulation of sediment, relatively, also, to the rate of subsidence and the length of the intervening stationary periods.

It is evident in this section, that a line drawn perpendicularly down from the outer edge of the new reef to the foundation of solid rock, exceeds by as many feet as there have been feet of subsidence, that small limit of depth at which the effective polypifers can live,—the corals having grown up, as the whole sank down, from a basis formed of other corals and their consolidated fragments. Thus the difficulty on this head, which before seemed so great, disappears.

As the space between the reef and the subsiding shore continued to increase in breadth and depth, and as the injurious effects of the sediment and fresh water borne down from the land were consequently lessened, the greater number of the channels, with which the reef in its fringing state must have been breached, especially those which fronted the smaller streams, will have become choked up by the growth of coral: on the windward side of the reef, where the coral grows most vigorously, the breaches will probably have first been closed. In barrier-reefs, therefore, the breaches kept open by draining the tidal waters of the lagoon-channel, will generally be placed on the leeward side, and they will still face the mouths of the larger streams, although removed beyond the influence of their sediment and fresh-water; —and this, it has been shown, is commonly the case.

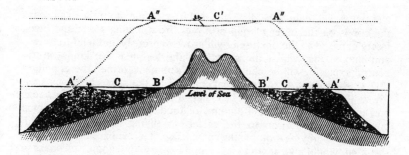

A'A'—Outer edges of the barrier-reef at the level of the sea. The cocoa-nut trees represent coral-islets formed on the reef.

CC—The lagoon-channel.

B'B'—The shores of the island, generally formed of low alluvial land and of coral detritus from the lagoon-channel.

A"A"—The outer edges of the reef now forming an atoll.

C'—The lagoon of the newly-formed atoll. According to the scale, the depth of the lagoon and of the lagoon-channel is exaggerated.

Referring to the above diagram, in which the newly-formed barrier-reef is represented by unbroken lines, instead of by dots as in the former woodcut, let the work of subsidence go on, and the doubly-pointed hill will form two small islands (or more, according to the number of the hills) included within one annular reef. Let the island continue subsiding, and the coral-reef will continue growing up on its own foundation, whilst the water gains inch by inch on the land, until the last and highest pinnacle is covered, and there remains a perfect atoll. A vertical section of this atoll is shown in the woodcut by the dotted lines; —a ship is anchored in its lagoon, but islets are not supposed yet to have been formed on the reef. The depth of the lagoon and the width and slope of the reef, will depend on the circumstances just referred to under barrier-reefs. Any further subsidence will produce no change in the atoll, except perhaps a diminution in its size, from the reef not growing vertically upwards; but should the currents of the sea act violently on it, and should the corals perish on part or on the whole of its margin, changes would result during subsidence which will be presently noticed. I may here observe, that a bank either of rock or of hardened sediment, level with the surface of the sea, and fringed with living coral, would (if not so small as to allow the central space to be quickly filled up with detritus) by subsidence be converted immediately into an atoll, without passing, as in the case of a reef fringing the shore of an island, through the intermediate form of a barrier-reef. If such a bank lay a few fathoms submerged, the simple growth of the coral without the aid of subsidence, would produce a structure scarcely to be distinguished from a true atoll; for in all cases the corals on the outer margin of a reef, from having space and being freely exposed to the open sea, will grow vigorously and tend to form a continuous ring, whilst the growth of the less massive kinds on the central expanse, will be checked by the sediment formed there, and by that washed inwards by the breakers; and as the space becomes shallower, their growth will, also, be checked by the impurities of the water, and probably by the small amount of food brought by the enfeebled currents, in proportion to the surface of living reefs studded with innumerable craving mouths: the subsidence of a reef based on a bank of this kind, would give depth to its central expanse or lagoon, steepness to its flanks, and through the free growth of the coral, symmetry to its outline: —I may here repeat that the larger groups of atolls in the Pacific and Indian oceans cannot be supposed to be founded on banks of this nature.

If, instead of the island in the diagram, the shore of a continent fringed by a reef had subsided, a great barrier-reef, like that on the N.E. coast of Australia, would have necessarily resulted; and it would have been separated from the main land by a deep-water channel, broad in proportion to the amount of subsidence, and to the less or greater inclination of the neighbouring coast-land. The effect of the continued subsidence of a great barrier-reef of this kind, and its probable conversion into a chain of separate atolls, will be noticed, when we discuss the apparent progressive disseverment of the larger Maldiva atolls.

We now are able to perceive that the close similarity in form, dimensions, structure, and relative position (which latter point will hereafter be more fully noticed) between fringing and encircling barrier-reefs, and between these latter and atolls, is the necessary result of the transformation, during subsidence, of the one class into the other. On this view, the three classes of reefs ought to graduate into each other. Reefs having an intermediate character between those of the fringing and barrier classes do exist; for instance, on the S.W. coast of Madagascar, a reef extends for several miles, within which there is a broad channel from seven to eight fathoms deep, but the sea does not deepen abruptly outside the reef. Such cases, however, are open to some doubts, for an old fringing reef, which had extended itself a little on a basis of its own formation, would hardly be distinguishable from a barrier-reef, produced by a small amount of subsidence, and with its lagoon-channel nearly filled up with sediment during a long stationary period. Between barrier-reefs, encircling either one lofty island or several small low ones, and atolls including a mere expanse of water, a striking series can be shown: in proof of this, I need only refer to the first plate at the end of this volume, which speaks more plainly to the eye, than any description could to the ear. The authorities from which the charts have been engraved, together with some remarks on them, are given on a separate page descriptive of the plates. At New Caledonia the barrier-reefs extend for 150 miles on each side of the submarine prolongation of the island; and at their northern extremity they appear broken up and converted into a vast atoll-formed reef, supporting a few low coral-islets: we may imagine that we here see the effects of subsidence actually in progress,—the water always encroaching on the northern end of the island, towards which the mountains slope down, and the reefs steadily building up their massive fabrics in the lines of their ancient growth.[1]

The island called Bolabola by Darwin is now usually called Bora Bora. It is a small high island with a barrier reef almost completely encircling it. It is in the Society Islands, or Tahiti Archipelago, some distance northwest of Tahiti itself. Darwin spent some days on Tahiti, which he admired, and without stopping at Bora Bora went from there to New Zealand, which on the whole he disliked. Darwin's plates in this book include fifteen charts of atolls and islands with fringing or barrier reefs.

Lyell's reaction to this contradiction of his own theory of atolls speaks well for his perspicacity and open mind. About this he wrote on May 24, 1837, to Sir John Herschel (1792–1871; an astronomer, son of the more famous astronomer Sir William Herschel) in part as follows:

> I am very full of Darwin's new theory of Coral Islands . . . I must give up my volcanic crater theory for ever, though it cost me a pang at first . . . [My] whole theory is knocked on the head, and the annular shape and central lagoon have nothing to do with volcanoes, nor even with a crateriform bottom.

Other geologists were not so open-minded. Some still clung to Lyell's theory although Lyell himself had abandoned it. Debate and disagreement on this subject went on throughout the rest of Darwin's life and for some years thereafter. In 1880 John (later Sir John) Murray (1841–1914), a leading oceanographer, rejected Darwin's view and substituted one of his own, which was still being mentioned, at least, well into the twentieth century. This dissent led Darwin to write on May 5, 1881, to Alexander Agassiz (1835–1910), also an oceanographer and son of the equally famous naturalist Louis Agassiz (1807–73):

> . . . You will have seen Mr. Murray's views on the forma-
> tion of atolls and barrier reefs. Before publishing my book I
> thought long over the same view . . . If I am wrong, the sooner
> I am knocked on the head and annihilated so much the better .
> . . I wish that some doubly rich millionaire would take it into
> his head to have borings made in some of the Pacific and

Indian atolls, and bring home cores for slicing from a depth of
500 or 600 feet . . .

It is ironic that Darwin died less than a year after writing that he
should be knocked on the head if he were wrong. It is still more
ironic that borings and soundings relevant to this subject were
indeed made long after his death not by "some doubly rich
millionaire" but, for the most part, by a doubly rich government.
These have fully corroborated Darwin's views so that the essentials of his theory are not now seriously doubted by any oceanographer or geologist. Intensive studies of ocean floors have also
gone farther than Darwin, but along the same lines, by discovery
that in the areas where atolls abound there are also sea mounts
that once reached above sea level but unlike those that formed
atolls are now hidden from sight in the depths of the sea. They are
called guyots (pronounced ghee-ohs) after Arnold Henry Guyot
(1807–84), a Swiss geologist who became a professor of geology
at Princeton University, where the geology building is also named
after him.

The other two geological volumes, on volcanic islands and on
the geology of (southern) South America were well received,
although Darwin complained to Lyell that *Geological Observations on the Volcanic Islands,* which cost him twelve months to
write, was not widely read. In fact neither this nor the South
American volume contains much that is strikingly new or contro-
versial, which probably contributed to their being well received
but little read. They were valued at the time as descriptive of
geological aspects of regions poorly known or unknown to previous geologists. They were also taken as largely substantiating
Lyell's views as applied to regions which had been unknown to
Lyell himself. Darwin was especially impressed by evidence of
changes of sea level relative to land (or land level relative to the
sea). In regional and volcanic geology Darwin was an observant
pioneer, but as he essentially abandoned geology, strictly speaking, in later years, more sophisticated interpretations were made
even in his lifetime, and have greatly changed since then.

Some of the geological phenomena that particularly intrigued
Darwin continue to do so for geologists to this day. An example is
the *rodados patagónicas* (Patagonian pebbles), the rounded
stones strewn widely over the nearly flat uplifted *mesetas* of
Patagonia east of the Andes. Darwin's hypothesis was that they
were of marine origin and indicated a rise of the sea to this level
which later was itself elevated well above the present sea level.

Later geologists have generally considered that the *rodados* originated from the eastern flank of the Andes and were spread by flooding waters over the *mesetas* at approximately their present level. There are nevertheless still doubts and disagreements as to the details of such a process.

As the geological-paleontological excerpts in the last chapter and the preceding excerpt from the book on reefs in this chapter show, Darwin was rapidly becoming well known in this early period of his life as a capable naturalist and within that broad category rather more as a geologist than as a biologist. That was recognized among other things by his election to the Geological Society of London, of which he was an officer for some time.

During the first few years after the voyage of the *Beagle,* Darwin's personal life-style developed and changed radically, and in addition to the publications already mentioned summarily, he also was engaged in a scientific program kept secret from all but a few of his closest and most trusted friends. Until 1842 he lived in London, briefly with his brother, then in his own lodging, and from early in 1839 until late in 1842 in a house at 12 Upper Gower Street. (That house can still be seen in photographs, but it cannot be visited: it was destroyed by German bombs during Hitler's war.)

In 1837 or 1838 Darwin privately wrote two notes, which he kept and which have been made public in the years since his death. In one he put in parallel columns reasons to marry and in the other reasons not to. In favor of marriage he noted among other things "Children—(if it please God)—constant companion . . . object to be beloved and played with—better than a dog anyhow . . ." As against marriage he included "Freedom to go where one liked—Choice of Society and *little of it* . . . Not forced to visit relatives, and to bend to every trifle . . . *Loss of time* . . .—if many children forced to gain one's bread . . . Perhaps my wife won't like London; then the sentence is banishment and degradation with indolent idle fool—" Not a very romantic approach, but one feels that he wrote with tongue in cheek, aware all the time that his decision would be "Marry—Marry—Marry." Although he did not put this in his notes himself, one feels, too, that he knew whom he wanted to marry. On November 11, 1838, he went to Maer, proposed to his cousin and childhood friend Emma Wedgwood and was accepted. Darwin took the house at 12 Upper Gower Street; they were married at Maer on January 29, 1839, and went the same day to London where Darwin could continue his work. For a year or two he went out a great deal, socially and to learned society meetings, and he became acquainted with the leading scientists and some other noted men of that day. In the summer of 1842 he even made a tour by himself of geological observation in North Wales. His friendship with Lyell became particularly close and lasted until Lyell's death in 1875. In spite of all this activity, and probably in part as a result of it, Darwin's health broke down and he decided to leave London, which he did in September of 1842.

The present book is not formally and consecutively a biography but is primarily devoted to the development of Darwin's thought and works and their results. This must, however, be seen against a background, and at this point two major things in that background, both lasting for the rest of his life, may be briefly discussed: his marriage and his home.

As to Darwin's marriage, none could have been happier. On this we can let Darwin speak for himself. He included the following paragraph in the manuscript autobiography that he wrote for his children. At Emma Darwin's insistence, however, this was among the many parts of that autobiography that were excluded from its publication in *The Life and Letters of Charles Darwin* by his son Francis. After Emma's death, however, it was included in *More Letters of Charles Darwin,* edited by the son Francis Darwin and by A. C. Seward, published in 1903. It was also restored to the autobiography in the unexpurgated edition by Norah Barlow in 1958.

You all know your mother, and what a good mother she has ever been to all of you. She has been my greatest blessing, and I can declare that in my whole life I have never heard her utter one word I would rather have been unsaid. She has never failed in kindest sympathy towards me, and has borne with the utmost patience my frequent complaints of ill-health and discomfort. I do not believe she has ever missed an opportunity of doing a kind action to any one near her. I marvel at my good fortune that she, so infinitely my superior in every single moral quality, consented to be my wife. She has been my wise adviser and cheerful comforter throughout life, which without her would have been during a very long period a miserable one from ill-health. She has earned the love of every soul near her.[2]

The only thing that might have affected this picture of complete, loving conjugality did not in fact do so. Darwin had gone to Cambridge with the intention of entering the ministry and was a Christian, even though one as much by custom as by earnest judgment. By the time he was married, he had doubts about formal religion and was becoming a non- but not clearly an anti-Christian, and on the way through non-Christian theism to a nearly but not completely atheistic agnosticism. When they married and throughout her life, Emma was a devout even if not by English standards a completely orthodox Christian. The children were christened and confirmed in the Church of England, but Emma herself was a Unitarian in belief. There are notes that show her not as complaining or disapproving but just as regretting that Charles did not share her views, and suggesting that what she regretted most was that he did not confidently expect to share an immortal afterlife with her. As Darwin became convinced of the fact of evolution, he did not think of this as inherently antireligious, and although he was bitterly attacked on these grounds, he evaded argument about religion as a subject on which he did not consider himself an authority.

The other aspect of the Darwinian background to be considered in this chapter is the home to which he moved on September 17, 1842, where all but the first two of his ten children were born and reared, and where he died on April 19, 1882. This was (and is) Down House, near the small village of Downe. Darwin described it as: ". . . a good, very ugly house with 18 acres, situated on a chalk flat, 560 feet above the sea. There are peeps of far distant country and the scenery is moderately pretty: its chief merit is its extreme rurality." The house is not architecturally either eye-catching or an eyesore, but it looks, and by Victorian standards was, comfortable, and by the time the Darwins moved in it was large enough for a rapidly growing family and domestic staff. It is an agglomerate starting from a farm house in the mid-seventeenth century. Before the time the Darwins moved there a sturdy four-story brick addition, now the central part of the house, had greatly enlarged it. Within a year the Darwins extended this with a large bow on the garden side. Later, mainly in 1858 and 1877, they extended the house still further by a two-story wing to the right of the central mass as one faces the present front. Darwin's study during most of his life there was on the ground floor in the old main part of the building. When the wing was built, a new and rather larger study was added in 1877 just to the right of the then new, and the present, front door facing the road, but Darwin's work was drawing to a close. His most important and most influential books, through the last revision of *The Origin of Species, The Descent of Man,* and *The Expression of the Emotions in Man and Animals* had all been written in the old study.

The surrounding property was ample and pleasant. There was

room for a greenhouse where some of Darwin's later observations on plants were made. He also took exercise outdoors, especially on the sandwalk, Darwin's "thinking path," at the end of the shaded lawn. It has sometimes been said that Darwin lived in seclusion or even in hiding at Down House, but when his health permitted he often traveled and visited. Every year he made long visits to relatives, especially to his parental family in Shrewsbury. He spent some time in London, but usually only on errands such as overseeing the preparation of illustrations for publication. He had worried lest his wife dislike London, but in fact both he and Emma came to dislike it. He went to various meetings, sometimes including the annual long meetings of the British Association for the Advancement of Science, although for at least nominally health reasons he often missed the annual meeting. He also went to spas for hydropathic treatments, which did little or no good but were persisted in. With Emma and some of the children he also took rather casual trips here and there, oddly including five days at a military camp at Cobham. Longer excursions took him to the Isle of Wight, to Wales and to the Lake District. He did lead a generally quiet and somewhat secluded life, but it was not constantly sedentary and certainly not in any sense a hiding from the world.

After Emma died in 1896 there was much uncertainty about what to do with Down House. There was consideration of somehow making it a memorial to Darwin, but nothing came of this for many years. For a time it was let to tenants, then in 1907 it was taken over by a Miss Olive Willis, who established in it a Downe House School for young ladies ("Downe" so spelled as by the village, not "Down" as for the Darwin house). In 1922 the school had become too large for the house and it was transferred to Cold Ash, near Newbury in Berkshire where, by last accounts, it still flourishes under the retained name of Downe House School. Although the incident has nothing to do with my present topic, I cannot forbear mentioning that for the school in its new quarters an order was sent to Harrods for "three goldfish, all of different sexes." (That suggests some things that the young ladies were not taught.)

After the school's departure Down House remained "empty and rapidly deteriorating" for several years. In 1927 through the mediation of Sir Arthur Keith (1866–1955), an eminent anthropologist, Sir George Buckston Browne, a wealthy and philanthropic physician, bought Down House, endowed it as a Memorial to Charles Darwin and placed it in the care of the British Association. The former furnishings of the house had been scattered, but after diligent search most of those for the ground floor were recovered and placed in the house. The British Association eventually found the expenses of maintenance too great, and the memorial was handed over to the Royal College of Surgeons for a time and finally to the National Trust.

I have gone this far into the later history of Down House because it and its surroundings, still rural despite being near the expansion of London, stand as nearly as possible as they were when *The Origin of Species* was written there in the old study, which is also much as it was in 1859. It is open to the public, must interest any travelers, and is almost a place of pilgrimage for all biologists.

6

On Barnacles and Sub Rosa Evolution

Although this was not mentioned in the *Journal of Researches* or in available notes made on the voyage of the *Beagle,* Darwin's autobiography told how he came upon a new kind of barnacle and what became of it.

In October, 1846, I began to work on 'Cirripedia.' When on the coast of Chile, I found a most curious form, which burrowed into the shells of Concholepas, and which differed so much from all other Cirripedes that I had to form a new sub-order for its sole reception. Lately an allied burrowing genus has been found on the shores of Portugal. To understand the structure of my new Cirripede I had to examine and dissect many of the common forms; and this gradually led me on to take up the whole group. I worked steadily on this subject for the next eight years, and ultimately published two thick volumes describing all the known living species, and two thin quartos on the extinct species. I do not doubt that Sir E. Lytton Bulwer had me in his mind when he introduced in one of his novels a Professor Long, who had written two huge volumes on limpets.

Although I was employed during eight years on this work, yet I record in my diary that about two years out of this time was lost by illness. On this account I went in 1848 for some months to Malvern for hydropathic treatment, which did me much good, so that on my return home I was able to resume work. So much was I out of health that when my dear father died on November 13th, 1848, I was unable to attend his funeral or to act as one of his executors.

My work on the Cirripedia possesses, I think, considerable value, as besides describing several new and remarkable forms, I made out the homologies of the various parts—I discovered the cementing apparatus, though I blundered dreadfully about the cement glands—and lastly I proved the existence in certain genera of minute males complemental to and parasitic on the hermaphrodites. This latter discovery has at last been fully confirmed; though at one time a German writer was pleased to attribute the whole account to my fertile imagination. The Cirripedes form a highly varying and difficult group of species to class; and my work was of considerable use to me, when I had to discuss in the 'Origin of Species' the principles of a natural classification. Nevertheless, I doubt whether the work was worth the consumption of so much time.[1]

The Cirripedia (literally "curl-footed," a characteristic not obvious on casual inspection) are barnacles, familiar in one form or another to everyone who has ever wandered along a coast or sailed a ship. Darwin evinced no special interest in them until after his return when, as related above from the autobiography, he discovered in his collection a uniquely strange tiny parasitic barnacle that had bored into the shell of one of the marine snails he collected in the Chonos while the *Beagle* was mapping that Chilean archipelago. As noted above, at first he intended no more than to describe and name this odd novelty, but his passion for accurate observation and interpretation led him on to description and classification of all the barnacles then known, living and fossil. As a taxonomist—a classifier—he was still somewhat naive when he started work on what turned out to be four volumes. He remarked more than once that he was uncertain how to concoct a scientific name and how to select properly among conflicting usages of names previously given. In the course of his work on barnacles, however, he soon not only mastered the taxonomy current at that time but also added appreciably to its proper practice.

The name that he gave to the tiny barnacle that started all this is *Cryptophialus minutus,* an etymologically and taxonomically impeccable name still validly applied to this species. (*Crypto,* "hidden," and *phialus,* "vial," are correctly combined from Greek roots and put into Neo-Latin form; *"minutus"* is of course Latin and Neo-Latin for "tiny," the combined generic and specific names indicating a tiny flask-shaped creature hidden in the hole it had bored in a snail shell.) Well over a century later (in 1967) two specialists on barnacles, W. A. Newman and V. A. Zullo, wrote that, "It was CHARLES DARWIN who established the morphological nomenclature and systematic concepts upon which subsequent work was based. His two volumes on Recent cirripeds (1851; 1854) are among the finest morphological and systematic publications in zoological literature. Even after a lapse of more than a century, these works are still among the chief sources of reference."

Incidentally, Darwin's genus *Cryptophialus* has since been found also in South Africa, West Africa, New Zealand and Antarctica, and it is the basis (and sole genus) of a distinct family of barnacles, the Cryptophialidae.

Darwin's study of barnacles extended over eight years, 1846 to 1854. In his systematic way of working he generally set aside two and a half hours each day for the barnacles. This became so much a part of the family routine that one of his children assumed that this was what grownup men did and asked the children of another household, "When does your father do his barnacles?" During these eight years there were some lapses due to Darwin's illness, and also as we know now and as will shortly be discussed here, he was busy with quite another, even if not completely unrelated project: that of gathering all possible facts bearing on evolution.

From the end of the preceding extract from the autobiography, it appears that Darwin had some doubts about whether spending so much time on the barnacles had been worth while. Those doubts must have been laid to rest for him by the opinions of Hooker and Huxley as given in the following passages from *The Life and Letters*, edited by Francis Darwin. (Here the first person, when not within quotations from Hooker or Huxley, refers to Francis Darwin himself.)

Writing to Sir J. D. Hooker in 1845, my father says: "I hope this next summer to finish my South American Geology, then to get out a little Zoology, and hurrah for my species work. . . ." This passage serves to show that he had at this time no intention of making an exhaustive study of the Cirripedes. Indeed it would seem that his original intention was, as I learn from Sir J. D. Hooker, merely to work out one special problem. This is quite in keeping with the following passage in the Autobiography: "When on the coast of Chile, I found a most curious form, which burrowed into the shells of Concholepas, and which differed so much from all other Cirripedes that I had to form a new sub-order for its sole reception. . . . To understand the structure of my new Cirripede I had to examine and dissect many of the common forms; and this gradually led me on to take up the whole group." In later years he seems to have felt some doubt as to the value of these eight years of work,—for instance when he wrote in his Autobiography—"My work was of considerable use to me, when I had to discuss in the 'Origin of Species,' the principles of a natural classification. Nevertheless I doubt whether the work was worth the consumption of so much time." Yet I learn from Sir J. D. Hooker that he certainly recognised at the time its value to himself as systematic training. Sir Joseph writes to me: "Your father recognised three stages in his career as a biologist: the mere collector at Cambridge; the collector and observer in the *Beagle,* and for some years afterwards; and the trained naturalist after, and only after the Cirripede work. That he was a thinker all along is true enough, and there is a vast deal in his writings previous to the Cirripedes that a trained naturalist could but emulate. . . . He often alluded to it as a valued discipline, and added that even the 'hateful' work of digging out synonyms, and of describing, not only improved his methods but opened his eyes to the difficulties and merits of the works of the dullest of cataloguers. One result was that he would never allow a depreciatory remark to pass unchallenged on the poorest class of scientific workers, provided that their work was honest, and good of its kind. I have always regarded it as one of the finest traits of his character,—this generous appreciation of the hod-men of science, and of their labours . . . and it was monographing the Barnacles that brought it about."

Professor Huxley allows me to quote his opinion as to the value of the eight years given to the Cirripedes:—

"In my opinion your sagacious father never did a wiser thing than when he devoted himself to the years of patient toil which the Cirripede-book cost him.

"Like the rest of us, he had no proper training in biological science, and it has always struck me as a remarkable instance of his scientific insight, that he saw the necessity of giving himself such training, and of his courage, that he did not shirk the labour of obtaining it.

"The great danger which besets all men of large speculative faculty, is the temptation to deal with the accepted statements of facts in natural science, as if they were not only correct, but exhaustive; as if they might be dealt with deductively, in the same way as propositions in Euclid may be dealt with. In reality, every such statement, however true it may be, is true only relatively to the means of observation and the point of view of those who have enunciated it. So far it may be depended upon. But whether it will bear every speculative conclusion that may be logically deduced from it, is quite another question.

"Your father was building a vast superstructure upon the foundations furnished by the recognised facts of geological and biological science. In Physical Geography, in Geology proper, in Geographical Distribution, and in Palæontology, he had acquired an extensive practical training during the voyage of the *Beagle.* He knew of his own knowledge the way in which the raw materials of these branches of science are acquired, and was therefore a most competent judge of the speculative strain they would bear. That which he needed, after his return to England, was a corresponding acquaintance with Anatomy and Development, and their relation to Taxonomy—and he acquired this by his Cirripede work.

"Thus, in my apprehension, the value of the Cirripede monograph lies not merely in the fact that it is a very admirable piece of work, and constituted a great addition to positive knowledge, but still more in the circumstance that it was a piece of critical self-discipline, the effect of which manifested itself in everything your father wrote afterwards, and saved him from endless errors of detail.

"So far from such work being a loss of time, I believe it would have been well worth his while, had it been practicable, to have supplemented it by a special study of embryology and physiology. His hands would have been greatly strengthened thereby when he came to write out sundry chapters of the 'Origin of Species.' But of course in those days it was almost impossible for him to find facilities for such work."

No one can look at the two volumes on the recent Cirripedes, of 399 and 684 pages respectively (not to speak of the volumes on the fossil species), without being struck by the immense amount of detailed work which they contain. The forty plates, some of them with thirty figures, and the fourteen pages of index in the two volumes together, give some rough idea of the labour spent on the work. The state of knowledge, as regards the Cirripedes, was most unsatisfactory at the time that my father began to work at them. As an illustration of this fact, it may be mentioned that he had even to re-organise the nomenclature of the group, or, as he expressed it, he "unwillingly found it indispensable to give names to several valves, and to some few of the softer parts of Cirripedes." It is interesting to learn from his diary the amount of time which he gave to different genera. Thus the genus Chthamalus, the description of which occupies twenty-two pages, occupied him for thirty-six days; Coronula took nineteen days, and is described in twenty-seven pages. Writing to Fitz-Roy, he speaks of being "for the last half-month daily hard at work in dissecting a little animal about the size of a pin's head, from the Chonos archipelago, and I could spend another month, and daily see more beautiful structure."

Though he became excessively weary of the work before the end of the eight years, he had much keen enjoyment in the course of it. Thus he wrote to Sir J. D. Hooker (1847?): —"As you say, there is an extraordinary pleasure in pure observation; not but what I suspect the pleasure in this case is rather derived from comparisons forming in one's mind with allied structures. After having been so long employed in writing my old geological observations, it is delightful to use one's eyes and fingers again."[2]

Hooker was mentioned in Chapter 2, but should here be more formally introduced. Darwin had met Joseph Dalton Hooker in London after the return of the *Beagle* and before moving to Down House. Sir Joseph Hooker, as he became styled, was an eminent botanist, son of another botanist equally eminent, Sir William Jackson Hooker (1785–1865), whom he followed as Director of

Kew Gardens. Darwin had other close friends who also were
involved in his scientific career, notably Lyell, Henslow and
Huxley, but none were more intimate than Hooker, and this
friendship continued to the day of Darwin's death and in a sense
even thereafter, as Hooker continued his friendship with
Darwin's widow and children. Darwin wrote hundreds of letters
to people all over the world, but his constant correspondence
with Hooker seems to bulk above all the rest. At this stage in his
life, it was only to Hooker that Darwin confided his growing ideas
about evolution and natural selection.

In July 1837 Darwin started the first of what became a considerable series of notebooks on what he usually called "the species
question" and what we call evolution, a word that Darwin did use
but sparingly because at that time it usually had a different sense
than the one later universally given it by friends and foes alike.
Evolution as an English word dates from at least as early as the
seventeenth century and originally meant merely "opening," or
"rolling out," in any way. Later it was commonly used in more
specific application to the development of an embryo and also the
subsequent maturation of a child. That usage continued until late
in the nineteenth century, but in the meantime the word *evolution*
began to be applied also to the suggestion or hypothesis, as it was
at first, that in the course of generations organisms may change
until they differ radically from their ancestors. This gradually
replaced the older application of the term, and it is now almost
exclusively used in this sense.

When Darwin left on the *Beagle* he was undoubtedly a believer
in the orthodox Jewish-Christian Bible. Up to this point he also
seems to have followed simply what everyone thought in his
family and social circle and not to have given the matter much
real thought. On the voyage of the *Beagle* he had to observe
nature in detail and collect specimens of various forms of living
things. It was in the development of his sort of mind, as influenced by such monitors as Henslow, that he also had to think
over all these things, to muse about the relationships among
organisms, to see animals, as a main example, as forms of life that
he should try to explain and not simply to shoot them in sport. In
the *Journal of Researches* there is no quite overt and clear
statement on evolution, but there is evidence that he was beginning to think of this as a possibility, something to be considered
with a more open mind than Fitz-Roy's or than of his own in
younger, less experienced days.

In the first, 1837, notebook Darwin was already an evolutionist, although one who still saw problems in that point of view and difficulties to be faced. He noted the presence of variation within species formerly considered as rigidly fixed in the orthodoxy of that time. He also saw that much of this variation is heritable and, further, that such variation may not have rigid limits and could somehow lead to such changes as occur between different species. He suggested that full "transformation" would be most likely in populations separated by barriers, such as those on each side of the high Andes or on the different islands of the Galápagos. Changes in environment might influence, if not cause, transformations. His fossils suggested that, in notebook style, "in South America parent of all armadillos might be brother to Megatherium uncle now dead." He thought of relationship among organisms as a branching tree, not a ladder of life (the *scala naturae* beloved of earlier naturalists and of Lamarck), with extinction leaving gaps between the surviving branches.

That much is already a simple, testable statement of the scientific generality of "transformation," or of what all of us now call evolution. It is obviously incomplete. It requires more confirmation and complication. And above all, as of the 1830s and indeed even the 1980s, it requires a reasonable and materialistic explanation of the phenomena of adaptation. Every organism that lives is obviously fit and able to live under the always more or less special circumstances in which it does in fact live. The idea of transformation, that is, evolution, had been bandied about since the eighteenth century. It was questioned then and still in the nineteenth century and indeed, but now with neither cogency nor reason, into the twentieth century. Until 1859 the espousing of evolution, whether by Lamarck or by the then anonymous author of the surprisingly popular evolutionary book *Vestiges of the Natural History of Creation* published in 1844, ran headlong into an apparently impossible barrier erected notably by William Paley and by the *Bridgewater Treatises,* published in 1833 to 1840. (The author of *Vestiges* was in fact the publisher, Robert Chambers [1802–71], and the *Bridgewater Treatises* had a number of different authors writing under an endowment from Francis Henry Egerton, the eighth earl of Bridgewater [1756–1829].) The argument intended to be clinching in these works was that an organ, such as the human hand, to which a volume of the *Bridgewater Treatises* was devoted, obviously serves a purpose to which it is intricately adapted. So too (this ridiculous analogy was actually used) does the intricate mechanism of a watch. The watch necessarily has a maker who created it as it stands, and certainly it did not arise by itself in slow accretion over a long span of time. It required a creator, and so does any adaptive organic structure require a Creator. The two accounts of creation in Genesis, chapters 1 and 2, although different in some other respects argue that man (male, like the Creator) was created as such by a God who for the Jews was Jehovah, also known by several other Hebrew names.

For Darwin, then, the "species problem," or "transformation" in the present sense of evolution, could be solved and accepted as essentially true only by some determinable natural process that could indeed transform, for example, the fin of a fish into the hand of a man. As the years of study represented in his mass of notes and their ultimate unveiling in *The Origin of Species* show, Darwin necessarily came to consider this problem and eventually concentrated on it to an extent that seems excessive to some present-day students, who nevertheless regard evolution as a fact and Darwin's consideration of the problem of adaptation as correct up to a point, even if not a complete explanation of evolution. (It may be interpolated here and will become clearer hereafter that Darwin himself did not consider his explanation complete.)

Darwin's notebooks are rather disorganized records of everything possibly bearing on transformation that he encountered mostly in extremely wide reading. They also contain here and there ideas that occurred to him, some later discarded, others hinting, at least, of conclusions to come. In his second journal, written in February–July 1838, he noted an instance of some plants replacing another, a vague forerunner of natural selection, but he also flirted with Lamarckism when he wrote, "All structures either direct effect of habit, or hereditary and combined effect of habit," but immediately thereafter he added that at least one part of Lamarck's theory was absurd and was not applicable to plants. At this point in his accumulation of data he did not really attempt to explain adaptation. He wrote ". . .—the wonderful power of adaptation given to organization—This really perhaps greatest difficulty to whole theory."

Late in 1838 he wrote in the third notebook that ". . . change may be effect of difference of parents, or external circumstances during life," which suggests the ancient (not specifically Lamarckian) view that acquired characters may be inherited. He never entirely abandoned that view, which is now known to be incorrect, but he did relegate it to a minor role in evolution. He added, "(hence every individual is different)" and most significantly, "(All this agrees well with my view of those forms slightly favoured getting the upper hand and forming species.)" Although still inchoate, this presages the most truly Darwinian of evolutionary processes: that of natural selection. The further development of this rudimentary theory occurred rapidly, as is shown in the following excerpt:

From September 1854 I devoted my whole time to arranging my huge pile of notes, to observing, and to experimenting in relation to the transmutation of species. During the voyage of the *Beagle* I had been deeply impressed by discovering in the Pampean formation great fossil animals covered with armour like that on the existing armadillos; secondly, by the manner in which closely allied animals replace one another in proceeding southwards over the Continent; and thirdly, by the South American character of most of the productions of the Galapagos archipelago, and more especially by the manner in which they differ slightly on each island of the group; none of the islands appearing to be very ancient in a geological sense.

It was evident that such facts as these, as well as many others, could only be explained on the supposition that species gradually become modified; and the subject haunted me. But it was equally evident that neither the action of the surrounding conditions, nor the will of the organisms (especially in the case of plants) could account for the innumerable cases in which organisms of every kind are beautifully adapted to their habits of life—for instance, a woodpecker or a tree-frog to climb trees, or a seed for dispersal by hooks or plumes. I had always been much struck by such adaptations, and until these could be explained it seemed to me almost useless to endeavour to prove by indirect evidence that species have been modified.

After my return to England it appeared to me that by following the example of Lyell in Geology, and by collecting all facts which bore in any way on the variation of animals and plants under domestication and nature, some light might perhaps be thrown on the whole subject. My first note-book was opened in July 1837. I worked on true Baconian principles, and without any theory collected facts on a wholesale scale, more especially with respect to domesticated productions, by printed enquiries, by conversation with skilful breeders and gardeners, and by extensive reading. When I see the list of books of all kinds which I read and abstracted, including whole series of Journals and Transactions, I am surprised at my industry. I soon perceived that selection was the keystone of man's success in making useful races of animals and plants. But how selection could be applied to organisms living in a state of nature remained for some time a mystery to me.

In October 1838, that is, fifteen months after I had begun my systematic enquiry, I happened to read for amusement 'Malthus on Population,' and being well prepared to appreciate the struggle for existence which everywhere goes on from long-continued observation of the habits of animals and plants, it at once struck me that under these circumstances favourable variations would tend to be preserved, and unfavourable ones to be destroyed. The result of this would be the formation of new species. Here then I had at last got a theory by which to work; but I was so anxious to avoid prejudice, that I determined not for some time to write even the briefest sketch of it. In June 1842 I first allowed myself the satisfaction of writing a very brief abstract of my theory in pencil in 35 pages; and this was enlarged during the summer of 1844 into one of 230 pages, which I had fairly copied out and still possess.

But at that time I overlooked one problem of great importance; and it is astonishing to me, except on the principle of Columbus and his egg, how I could have overlooked it and its solution. This problem is the tendency in organic beings descended from the same stock to diverge in character as they become modified. That they have diverged greatly is obvious from the manner in which species of all kinds can be classed under genera, genera under families, families under sub-orders and so forth; and I can remember the very spot in the road, whilst in my carriage, when to my joy the solution occurred to me; and this was long after I had come to Down. The solution, as I believe, is that the modified offspring of all dominant and increasing forms tend to become adapted to many and highly diversified places in the economy of nature.

Early in 1856 Lyell advised me to write out my views pretty fully, and I began at once to do so on a scale three or four times as extensive as that which was afterwards followed in my 'Origin of Species;' yet it was only an abstract of the materials which I had collected, and I got through about half the work on this scale. But my plans were overthrown, for early in the summer of 1858 Mr. Wallace, who was then in the Malay archipelago, sent me an essay "On the Tendency of Varieties to depart indefinitely from the Original Type;" and this essay contained exactly the same theory as mine. Mr. Wallace expressed the wish that if I thought well of his essay, I should send it to Lyell for perusal.

The circumstances under which I consented at the request of Lyell and Hooker to allow of an abstract from my MS., together with a letter to Asa Gray, dated September 5, 1857, to be published at the same time with Wallace's Essay, are given in the 'Journal of the Proceedings of the Linnean Society,' 1858, p. 45. I was at first very unwilling to consent, as I thought Mr. Wallace might consider my doing so unjustifiable, for I did not then know how generous and noble was his disposition. The extract from my MS. and the letter to Asa Gray had neither been intended for publication, and were badly written. Mr. Wallace's essay, on the other hand, was admirably expressed and quite clear. Nevertheless, our joint productions excited very little attention, and the only published notice of them which I can remember was by Professor Haughton of Dublin, whose verdict was that all that was new in them was false, and what was true was old.[3]

The date on which Darwin first read Malthus has been given as October 3, 1838. The book was *An Essay on the Principles of Population* by Thomas Robert Malthus (1766–1834), a British cleric, professor and economist. The first edition was published in 1798 and was continuously revised until the last and definitive sixth edition in 1816, which Darwin read. It was not then, and still less is it now, a book most people might find amusing—Julian Huxley (1887–1975) much later noted that "We must be eternally grateful that Darwin had such a peculiar notion of amusement."

Malthus' thesis was that unchecked increase of population increases in a geometric ratio while means of its subsistence increases only in an arithmetic ratio. Therefore the survival of a population depends eventually on some preventive check of increase of the population. Malthus had the human population in mind and at first concluded that its increase had to have such checks as overcrowding, disease, war, poverty and vice. He later added "moral restraint" to the list of checks, and he overlooked the fact that increasing the ratio of subsistence would delay (but still not catch up with) the effects of unchecked population increase. Malthus' sociological thesis has been heavily attacked, but it still requires attention in our present world, which has continued geometric increase of worldwide population and a considerable, but smaller, increase in means of subsistence.

What Darwin seized on, however, was not Malthus' sociology but the Malthusian evidence for intensity of natural selection. In Darwin's third notebook he added after comments on Malthus that, "One may say there is a force like a hundred thousand wedges trying [to] force every kind of adapted structure into the gaps in the economy of nature, or rather forming gaps by thrusting out weaker ones." (This was cut out of his notebook evidently for use in more formal and organized statement of his theory, but it was much later found in a clipping deposited by Sir Robin Darwin in the British Museum [Natural History].)

At this point there was essentially only one important gap in Darwinian theory at the pregenetics level in which he lived and therefore necessarily worked. The element still missing was why and how descendants of the same ancestor could and did become highly diversified among themselves. In the preceding excerpt from Darwin's autobiography, he picturesquely remarks how at a certain spot in the road the solution occurred to him. His solution is still accepted as essentially correct. The phenomenon described has occurred in many groups of organisms and at many times. It is now usually called adaptive radiation.

Now Darwin could sort out all his notes and write summaries of his theory in 1842 and 1844, and then start writing his "big book" in 1856. In Chapter 2 the circumstances that forced him to stop work on the "big book" in 1858 and to publish what he considered a mere summary of it in 1859 were noted. That summary was the book we know as *The Origin of Species*.

7

The Origin of Species

We now come to one of the very few books that have changed the world for us, giving us new insight into ourselves and into the nature and history of all that has led up to us and brought what is now around us into a comprehensible and clear pattern. The full title page of this remarkable work, as first published, was as follows:

ON
THE ORIGIN OF SPECIES
BY MEANS OF NATURAL SELECTION
OR THE
PRESERVATION OF FAVOURED RACES IN THE STRUGGLE
FOR LIFE
BY CHARLES DARWIN, M.A.,
FELLOW OF THE ROYAL, GEOLOGICAL,
LINNÆAN, ETC., SOCIETIES;
AUTHOR OF 'JOURNAL OF RESEARCHES
DURING H.M.S. BEAGLE'S VOYAGE ROUND THE WORLD'
LONDON:
JOHN MURRAY, ALBEMARLE STREET
1859
The right of Translation is reserved.

The printing firm was W. Clowes and Sons, Stamford Street and Charing Cross.

This Victorian title has since then almost always been called just *The Origin of Species*.

Darwin told his friend Hooker that the book would be popular among "scientific, semi-scientific, and non-scientific men," which would seem to cover everyone except women. He was prepared to publish the book at his own expense, but he preferred commercial publication if possible, and he sent John Murray the manuscript of the first three chapters. (This John Murray [1808–92] was the grandson of the John Murray who founded the publishing house, son of the John Murray who continued the business, and father of Sir John Murray who also continued it.) Darwin assured Murray that the book would be "interesting to all (and they are many) who care for the curious problems of the origin of all animal forms." Murray was dubious, but he did undertake to publish a small edition of the book. The first printing was only 2,250 copies of which 1,192 were put on sale, probably on November 26, 1859, although the exact day is somewhat uncertain. (The copies not on sale were sent to reviewers and to some of Darwin's scientific friends.) That printing sold out immediately, in its first day on sale accordng to some accounts. Darwin immediately set about revising the work, and a second edition of 3,000 copies with only slight revision was issued about one month after the first.

Under the circumstances described in Chapter 2, Darwin abandoned his "big book," which was about two-thirds advanced in manuscript. He followed friends' advice to keep *The Origin of Species* in print, and most of the "big book" detail was brought out separately in other books (listed in the Appendix). While writing those more specialized works he kept revising *The Origin of Species*. After the first and second editions, four more were carefully revised by Darwin:

> Third edition, 1861
> Fourth edition, 1866
> Fifth edition, 1869
> Sixth edition, first printing in 1872
>   with frequent reprintings up to 1890
> Sixth edition with minor corrections, 1878

Present-day writers will be astonished and envious to learn that payments to Murray as publisher were divided giving two-thirds to Darwin. The book has never been out of print, and several editions in English are now available. Most of these are from the 1878 version, the sixth edition with minor corrections. There is a modern reprint and a facsimile of the first edition, and for students of Darwin there is also a variorum which indicates all the changes made in the revisions and in the corrected sixth edition of 1878. The first edition and later ones were widely pirated, especially in the United States. The copyright ran out long ago, and permission to republish any edition in English or to translate into any other language then became unnecessary. There have been translations into every literary language. It is impossible to estimate how many copies have been published throughout the world, but the number certainly has been in the hundreds of thousands and probably in the millions. Nevertheless some of the religious attacks on "Darwinism," which continue even in this period when more enlightenment might be expected, lead one to suspect, or often to be certain, that the authors of such attacks have never read *The Origin of Species* in any edition.

There has been much discussion of why Darwin delayed publication so long, and would have delayed it even longer if possible. Darwin certainly knew that his views on evolution would cause a furor when they were published. It has been suggested that Darwin so dreaded this that he put off revealing his ideas from simple funk, or one might say "cowardice." There is nothing in his work or in his known character to support that view. Darwin was not wasting time or evading the topic of evolution. He knew that earlier treatments of the idea of evolution, which had been fairly numerous, were unconvincing and inadequate when not flatly wrong. He therefore devoted those many years to gathering every available fact bearing on the subject and developing an interpretation consonant with those facts. The years spent on barnacles were not wasted, and Darwin was not being entirely true to himself when he expressed some doubts on that point. It is unfortunate that some present-day generalizers and theorizers in biology, both paleobiology and neo-biology, have not put themselves first through a rigorous examination of some group of organisms—that they have not "done their barnacles" before speaking out on broader subjects. *The Origin of Species* has no footnotes or direct references, but what Darwin had completed of his "big book" cited nearly 750 relevant publications in addition to his own observations.

Darwin's first two editions of *The Origin of Species* were criticized for not having given credit to previous writers who had in one way or another considered the possibility of evolution. In his third edition (1861) he therefore prefaced the book with "An Historical Sketch of the Progress of Opinion on the Origin of Species." This was retained, with revision, through all subsequent editions. I do not quote from this sketch, because the fact is that no previous work convinced biologists in general of the truth of evolution. Darwin's work was completely original and did not derive from any earlier one although utilizing such strictly factual, observational material as some earlier works contained.

In the first and all later editions, Darwin inserted before the title page the following quotation from William Whewell (1794–1866) in the first of the *Bridgewater Treatises,* which were by intention religious and nonevolutionary. (Whewell's treatise in this series, published in 1833, was nominally on astronomy but ranged widely into the history and philosophy of science.)

But with regard to the material world, we can at least go so far as this—we can perceive that events are brought about not by—insulated—interpositions of Divine power, exerted in each particular case, but by the establishment of general laws.

This pre-Darwinian statement is one to which any evolutionist can subscribe. As scientists we can investigate the history, properties and processes of the observable universe. Evolution is the key to that history, those properties and those processes. It is a "general law" in Whewell's sense. We do not know and cannot scientifically investigate the origin of those "general laws," and that is where rational religion takes over and science stops.

The reader is urged to read the whole of *The Origin of Species.* Here obviously it can only be sampled and some idea of its contents conveyed. This is now first done by an extract from the introduction.

In considering the origin of species, it is quite conceivable that a naturalist, reflecting on the mutual affinities of organic beings, on their embryological relations, their geographical distribution, geological succession, and other such facts, might come to the conclusion that species had not been independently created, but had descended, like varieties, from other species. Nevertheless, such a conclusion, even if well founded, would be unsatisfactory, until it could be shown how the innumerable species, inhabiting this world have been modified, so as to acquire that perfection of structure and coadaptation which justly excites our admiration. Naturalists continually refer to external conditions, such as climate, food, etc., as the only possible cause of variation. In one limited sense, as we shall hereafter see, this may be true; but it is preposterous to attribute to mere external conditions, the structure, for instance, of the woodpecker, with its feet, tail, beak and tongue, so admirably adapted to catch insects under the bark of trees. In the case of the mistletoe, which draws its nourishment from certain trees, which has seeds that must be transported by certain birds, and which has flowers with separate sexes absolutely requiring the agency of certain insects to bring pollen from one flower to the other, it is equally preposterous to account for the structure of this parasite, with its relations to several distinct organic beings, by the effects of external conditions, or of habit, or of the volition of the plant itself.

It is, therefore, of the highest importance to gain a clear insight into the means of modification and coadaptation. At the commencement of my observations it seemed to me probable that a careful study of domesticated animals and of cultivated plants would offer the best chance of making out this obscure problem. Nor have I been disappointed; in this and in all other perplexing cases I have invariably found that our knowledge, imperfect though it be, of variation under domestication, afforded the best and safest clue. I may venture to express my conviction of the high value of such studies, although they have been very commonly neglected by naturalists.

From these considerations, I shall devote the first chapter of this abstract to variation under domestication. We shall thus see that a large amount of hereditary modification is at least possible; and, what is equally or more important, we shall see how great is the power of man in accumulating by his selection successive slight variations. I will then pass on to the variability of species in a state of nature; but I shall, unfortunately, be compelled to treat this subject far too briefly, as it can be treated properly only by giving long catalogues of facts. We shall, however, be enabled to discuss what circumstances are most favorable to variation. In the next chapter the struggle for existence among all organic beings throughout the world, which inevitably follows from the high geometrical ratio of their increase, will be considered. This is the doctrine of Malthus, applied to the whole animal and vegetable kingdoms. As many more individuals of each species are born than can possibly survive; and as, consequently, there is a frequently recurring struggle for existence, it follows that any being, if it vary however slightly in any manner profitable to itself, under the complex and sometimes varying conditions of life, will have a better chance of surviving, and thus be *naturally selected*. From the strong principle of inheritance, any selected variety will tend to propagate its new and modified form.

This fundamental subject of natural selection will be treated at some length in the fourth chapter; and we shall then see how natural selection almost inevitably causes much extinction of the less improved forms of life, and leads to what I have called divergence of character. In the next chapter I shall discuss the complex and little known laws of variation. In the five succeeding chapters, the most apparent and gravest difficulties in accepting the theory will be given: namely, first, the difficulties of transitions, or how a simple being or a simple organ can be changed and perfected into a highly developed being or into an elaborately constructed organ; secondly, the subject of instinct, or the mental powers of animals; thirdly, hybridism, or the infertility of species and the fertility of varieties when intercrossed; and fourthly, the imperfection of the geological record. In the next chapter I shall consider the geological succession of organic beings throughout time; in the twelfth and thirteenth, their geographical distribution throughout space; in the fourteenth, their classification or mutual affinities, both when mature and in an embryonic condition. In the last chapter I shall give a brief recapitulation of the whole work, and a few concluding remarks.

No one ought to feel surprise at much remaining as yet unexplained in regard to the origin of species and varieties, if he make due allowance for our profound ignorance in regard to the mutual relations of the many beings which live around us. Who can explain why one species ranges widely and is very numerous, and why another allied species has a narrow range and is rare? Yet these relations are of the highest importance, for they determine the present welfare and, as I believe, the future success and modification of every inhabitant of this world. Still less do we know of the mutual relations of the innumerable inhabitants of the world during the many past geological epochs in its history. Although much remains obscure, and will long remain obscure, I can entertain no doubt, after the most deliberate study and dispassionate judgment of which I am capable, that the view which most naturalists until recently entertained, and which I formerly entertained—namely, that each species has been independently created—is erroneous. I am fully convinced that species are not immutable; but that those belonging to what are called the same genera are lineal descendants of some other and generally extinct species, in the same manner as the acknowledged varieties of any one species are the descendants of that species. Furthermore, I am convinced that natural selection has been the most important, but not the exclusive, means of modification.[1]

As noted in the introduction, the following first chapter is devoted to variation under domestication. It treats at length the selection by man of different breeds of animals, with breeds of pigeons as a special example. Darwin's own work with these birds convinced him that human selection has produced true-breeding varieties that would be considered distinct species or genera if they occurred wild.

Believing that it is always best to study some special group, I have, after deliberation, taken up domestic pigeons. I have kept every breed which I could purchase or obtain, and have been most kindly favored with skins from several quarters of the world, more especially by the Hon. W. Elliot, from India, and by the Hon. C. Murray, from Persia. Many treatises in different languages have been published on pigeons, and some of them are very important as being of considerable antiquity. I have associated with several eminent fanciers and have been permitted to join two of the London Pigeon Clubs. The diversity of the breeds is something astonishing. Compare the English carrier and the short-faced tumbler, and see the wonderful difference in their beaks, entailing corresponding differences in their skulls. The carrier, more especially the male bird, is also remarkable from the wonderful development of the carunculated skin about the head; and this is accompanied by greatly elongated eyelids, very large external orifices to the nostrils, and a wide gape of mouth. The short-faced tumbler has a beak in outline almost like that of a finch; and the common tumbler has the singular inherited habit of flying at a great height in a compact flock and tumbling in the air head over heels. The runt is a bird of great size, with long massive beak and large feet; some of the sub-breeds of runts have very long necks, others very long wings and tails, others singularly short tails. The barb is allied to the carrier, but, instead of a large beak, has a very short and broad one. The pouter has a much elongated body, wings and legs; and its enormously developed crop, which it glories in inflating, may well excite astonishment and even laughter. The turbit has a short and conical beak with a line of reversed feathers down the breast; and it has the habit of continually expanding, slightly, the upper part of the esophagus. The Jacobin has the feathers so much reversed along the back of the neck that they form a hood; and it has, proportionally to its size, elongated wing and tail feathers. The trumpeter and laugher, as their names express, utter a very different coo from the other breeds. The fantail has thirty or even forty tail-feathers, instead of twelve or fourteen—the normal number in all the members of the great pigeon family: these feathers are kept expanded and are carried so erect that in good birds the head and tail touch: the oil gland is quite aborted. Several other less distinct breeds might be specified.

In the skeletons of the several breeds, the development of the bones of the face, in length and breadth and curvature, differs enormously. The shape, as well as the breadth and length of the ramus of the lower jaw, varies in a highly remarkable manner. The caudal and sacral vertebra vary in number; as does the number of the ribs, together with their relative breadth and the presence of processes. The size and shape of the apertures in the sternum are highly variable; so is the degree of divergence and relative size of the two arms of the furcula. The proportional width of the gape of mouth, the proportional length of the eyelids, of the orifice of the nostrils, of the tongue (not always in strict correlation with the length of beak), the size of the crop and of the upper part of the esophagus; the development and abortion of the oil-gland; the number of the primary wing and caudal feathers; the relative length of the wing and tail to each other and to the body; the relative length of the leg and foot;

the number of scutellæ on the toes, are all points of structure which are variable. The period at which the perfect plumage is acquired varies, as does the state of the down with which the nestling birds are clothed when hatched. The shape and size of the eggs vary. The manner of flight, and in some breeds the voice and disposition, differ remarkably. Lastly, in certain breeds, the males and females have come to differ in a slight degree from each other.

Altogether at least a score of pigeons might be chosen which, if shown to an ornithologist, and he were told that they were wild birds, would certainly be ranked by him as well-defined species. Moreover, I do not believe that any ornithologist would in this case place the English carrier, the short-faced tumbler, the runt, the barb, pouter, and fantail in the same genus; more especially as in each of these breeds several truly-inherited sub-breeds, or species, as he would call them, could be shown him.

Great as are the differences between the breeds of the pigeon, I am fully convinced that the common opinion of naturalists is correct, namely, that all are descended from the rock-pigeon (Columbia livia), including under this term several geographical races or sub-species, which differ from each other in the most trifling respects.[2]

Beyond the excerpt given above, Darwin went on to detail the convincing evidence that all the domestic breeds of pigeons were indeed formed by human selection from a single wild species. Elsewhere in this chapter he indicated that many other domesticated animals likewise have been developed from single wild species into distinct breeds by human selection. This depends on the occurrence of variation within populations of originally wild and eventually domesticated animals. If selection is to be related to the diversity of organisms in nature, it must first be established that variation does occur in wild populations. That is indeed a fact that has been observed by naturalists from antiquity onward. Darwin might have taken this for granted, but his line of thought required that such variation be more related to the further development in later chapters. This was done in the next chapter, which was summarized in the following excerpt:

SUMMARY

Finally, varieties cannot be distinguished from species,—except, first, by the discovery of intermediate linking forms; and, secondly, by a certain indefinite amount of difference between them; for two forms, if differing very little, are generally ranked as varieties, notwithstanding that they cannot be closely connected; but the amount of difference considered necessary to give to any two forms the rank of species cannot be defined. In genera having more than the average number of species in any country, the species of these genera have more than the average number of varieties. In large genera the species are apt to be closely but unequally allied together, forming little clusters round other species. Species very closely allied to other species apparently have restricted ranges. In all these respects the species of large genera present a strong analogy with varieties. And we can clearly understand these analogies, if species once existed as varieties, and thus originated; whereas, these analogies are utterly inexplicable if species are independent creations.

We have also seen that it is the most flourishing or dominant species of the larger genera within each class which on an average yield the greatest number of varieties; and varieties, as we shall hereafter see, tend to become converted into new and distinct species. Thus the larger genera tend to become larger; and throughout nature the forms of life which are now dominant tend to become still more dominant by leaving many modified and dominant descendants. But, by steps hereafter to be explained, the larger genera also tend to break up into smaller genera. And thus, the forms of life throughout the universe become divided into groups subordinate to groups.[3]

Evolution demands some diversity in an ancestral population of species, and selection by man has shown that such diversity can be maintained and increased by human selection. It is, however, obvious that if evolution has occurred, such selection in nature cannot have been caused by human selection. The next step in Darwin's logical progression then had to move on to some facts and principles existing in nature that have an analogous effect. He found these principles in what he unfortunately called "the struggle for existence" and in a new application of the Malthusian doctrine to the history of organisms. This is introduced in the following excerpt from the next chapter of *The Origin of Species:*

Before entering on the subject of this chapter I must make a few preliminary remarks to show how the struggle for existence bears on natural selection. It has been seen in the last chapter that among organic beings in a state of nature there is some individual variability: indeed I am not aware that this has ever been disputed. It is immaterial for us whether a multitude of doubtful forms be called species or sub-species or varieties; what rank, for instance, the two or three hundred doubtful forms of British plants are entitled to hold, if the existence of any well-marked varieties be admitted. But the mere existence of individual variability and of some few well-marked varieties, though necessary as the foundation for the work, helps us but little in understanding how species arise in nature. How have all those exquisite adaptations of one part of the organization to another part, and to the conditions of life and of one organic being to another being, been perfected? We see these beautiful co-adaptations most plainly in the woodpecker and the mistletoe; and only a little less plainly in the humblest parasite which clings to the hairs of a quadruped or feathers of a bird; in the structure of the beetle which dives through the water; in the plumed seed which is wafted by the gentlest breeze; in short, we see beautiful adaptations everywhere and in every part of the organic world.

Again, it may be asked, how is it that varieties, which I have called incipient species, become ultimately converted into good and distinct species, which in most cases obviously differ from each other far more than do the varieties of the same species? How do those groups of species, which constitute what are called distinct genera and which differ from each other more than do the species of the same genus, arise? All these results, as we shall more fully see in the next chapter, follow from the struggle for life. Owing to this struggle, variations, however slight and from whatever cause proceeding, if they be in any degree profitable to the individuals of a species, in their infinitely complex relations to other organic beings and to their physical conditions of life, will tend to the preservation of such individuals, and will generally be inherited by the offspring. The offspring, also, will thus have a better chance of surviving, for, of the many individuals of any species which are periodically born, but a small number can survive. I have called this principle, by which each slight variation, if useful, is preserved, by the term natural selection, in order to mark its relation to man's power of selection. But the expression often used by Mr. Herbert Spencer, of the Survival of the Fittest, is more accurate, and is sometimes equally convenient. We have seen that man by selection can certainly produce great results, and can adapt organic beings to his own uses, through the accumulation of slight but useful variations, given to him by the hand of Nature. But Natural Selection, we shall hereafter see, is a power incessantly ready for action, and is as immeasurably superior to man's feeble efforts as the works of Nature are to those of Art.

We will now discuss in a little more detail the struggle for existence. In my future work this subject will be treated, as it well deserves, at greater length. The elder De Candolle and Lyell have largely and philosophically shown that all organic beings are exposed to severe competition. In regard to plants, no one has treated this subject with more spirit and ability than W. Herbert, Dean of Manchester, evidently the result of his great horticultural knowledge. Nothing is easier than to admit in words the truth of the universal struggle for life, or more difficult—at least I found it so—than constantly to bear this conclusion in mind. Yet unless it be thoroughly engrained in the mind, the whole economy of nature, with every fact on distribution, rarity, abundance, extinction, and variation, will be dimly seen or quite misunderstood. We behold the face of nature bright with gladness, we often see superabundance of food; we do not see or we forget that the birds which are idly singing round us mostly live on insects or seeds, and are thus constantly destroying life; or we forget how largely these songsters, or their eggs, or their nestlings, are destroyed by birds and beasts of prey; we do not always bear in mind, that, though food may be now superabundant, it is not so at all seasons of each recurring year.

THE TERM, STRUGGLE FOR EXISTENCE, USED IN A LARGE SENSE

I should premise that I use this term in a large and metaphorical sense, including dependence of one being on another, and including (which is more important) not only the life of the individual, but success in leaving progeny. Two canine animals, in a time of dearth, may be truly said to struggle with each other which shall get food and live. But a plant on the edge of a desert is said to struggle for life against the drought, though more properly it should be said to be dependent on the moisture. A plant which annually produces a thousand seeds, of which only one of an average comes to maturity, may be more truly said to struggle with the plants of the same and other kinds which already clothe the ground. The mistletoe is dependent on the apple and a few other trees, but can only in a far-fetched sense be said to struggle with these trees, for, if too many of these parasites grow on the same tree, it languishes and dies. But several seedling mistletoes, growing close together on the same branch, may more truly be said to struggle with each other. As the mistletoe is disseminated by birds, its existence depends on them; and it may metaphorically be said to struggle with other fruit-bearing plants, in tempting the birds to devour and thus disseminate its seeds. In these several senses, which pass into each other, I use for convenience sake the general term of Struggle for Existence.

GEOMETRICAL RATIO OF INCREASE

A struggle for existence inevitably follows from the high rate at which all organic beings tend to increase. Every being, which during its natural lifetime produces several eggs or seeds, must suffer destruction during some period of its life, and during some season or occasional year, otherwise, on the principle of geometrical increase, its numbers would quickly become so inordinately great that no country could support the product. Hence, as more individuals are produced than can possibly survive, there must in every case be a struggle for existence, either one individual with another of the same species, or with the individuals of distinct species, or with the physical conditions of life. It is the doctrine of Malthus applied with manifold force to the whole animal and vegetable kingdoms; for in this case there can be no artificial increase of food, and no prudential restraint from marriage. Although some species may be now increasing, more or less rapidly, in numbers, all can not do so, for the world would not hold them.

There is no exception to the rule that every organic being naturally increases at so high a rate, that, if not destroyed, the earth would soon be covered by the progeny of a single pair. Even slow-breeding man has doubled in twenty-five years, and at this rate, in less than a thousand years, there would literally not be standing-room for his progeny. Linnæus has calculated that if an annual plant produced only two seeds—and there is no plant so unproductive as this—and their seedlings next year produced two, and so on, then in twenty years there would be a million plants.[4]

I have called Darwin's term *struggle for existence* an unfortunate choice because it has so often been taken in the sense of a physical struggle or combat, "nature red in tooth and claw." Darwin did not mean it in that sense. As he showed in the excerpt here preceding, his concept of the "struggle" was much broader than that and did not exclusively or even primarily refer to combat. He also makes clear that the most important point is not the survival of individuals, as can be an interpretation of Spencer's term "the Survival of the Fittest," but is "success in leaving progeny." This has often been and still sometimes is misunderstood by critics of Darwin and of natural selection.

As mentioned earlier, Darwin first read Malthus in 1838. Although Malthus applied his principle that "population increases in a geometrical, food in an arithmetical ratio" and that for the long-term good of mankind there must therefore be checks on increase of human population, only to the human species, Darwin's inspiration was that the principle also applies to most or to all other species of organisms throughout geological time. One of the examples given by Darwin in *The Origin of Species* was that if all offspring of elephants, among the slowest breeders, were to survive through a time of only 740 to 750 years— incidentally a period usually imperceptible in the fossil record— "there would be nearly nineteen million elephants alive descended from the first pair." In this instance Darwin's calculation somehow went astray, but his point was correct: for any species over a considerable span of time survival of the species does demand limits on the number of individuals in it. This then is a way in which selection not only may but also inevitably does affect species in nature. It is interesting that it was also the recollection of Malthus' *Essay on the Principles of Population*, which he had read years earlier, that led in 1858 to Wallace's independent statement of natural selection, which had occurred to Darwin, but not been published, twenty years earlier.

The following excerpt from Chater IV of *The Origin of Species* logically brings together the sequence of statements in the previous three chapters:

How will the struggle for existence, briefly discussed in the last chapter, act in regard to variation? Can the principle of selection, which we have seen is so potent in the hands of man, apply under nature? I think we shall see that it can act most efficiently. Let the endless number of slight variations and individual differences occurring in our domestic productions, and, in a lesser degree, in those under nature, be borne in mind; as well as the strength of the hereditary tendency. Under domestication, it may truly be said that the whole organization becomes in some degree plastic. But the variability, which we almost universally meet with in our domestic productions is not directly produced, as Hooker and Asa Gray have well remarked, by man; he can neither originate varieties nor prevent their occurrence; he can only preserve and accumulate such as do occur. Unintentionally he exposes organic beings to new and changing conditions of life, and variability ensues; but similar changes of conditions might and do occur under nature. Let it also be borne in mind how infinitely complex and close-fitting are the mutual relations of all organic beings to each other and to their physical conditions of life; and consequently what infinitely varied diversities of structure might be of use to each being under changing conditions of life. Can it then be thought improbable, seeing that variations useful to man have undoubtedly occurred, that other variations useful in some way to each being in the great and complex battle of life, should occur in the course of many successive generations? If such do occur, can we doubt (remembering that many more individuals are born than can possibly survive) that individuals having any advantage, however slight, over others, would have the best chance of surviving and procreating their kind? On the other hand, we may feel sure that any variation in the least degree injurious would be rigidly destroyed. This preservation of favorable individual differences and variations, and the destruction of those which are injurious, I have called Natural Selection, or the Survival of the Fittest. Variations neither useful nor injurious would not be affected by natural selection, and would be left either a fluctuating element, as perhaps we see in certain polymorphic species, or would ultimately become fixed, owing to the nature of the organism and the nature of the conditions.

Several writers have misapprehended or objected to the term Natural Selection. Some have even imagined that natural selection induces variability, whereas it implies only the preservation of such variations as arise and are beneficial to the being under its conditions of life. No one objects to agriculturists speaking of the potent effects of man's selection; and in this case the individual differences given by nature, which man for some object selects, must of necessity first occur. Others have objected that the term selection implies conscious choice in the animals which become modified; and it has even been urged that, as plants have no volition, natural selection is not applicable to them! In the literal sense of the word, no doubt, natural selection is a false term; but who ever objected to chemists speaking of the elective affinities of the various elements? —and yet an acid cannot strictly be said to elect the base with which it in preference combines. It has been said that I speak of natural selection as an active power or Deity; but who objects to an author speaking of the attraction of gravity as ruling the movements of the planets? Every one knows what is meant and is implied by such metaphorical expressions; and they are almost necessary for brevity. So again it is difficult to avoid personifying the word Nature; but I mean by nature, only the aggregate action and product of many natural laws, and by laws the sequence of events as ascertained by us. With a little familiarity such superficial objections will be forgotten.[5]

The second paragraph of the preceding excerpt was inserted in the third (1861) edition of *The Origin of Species* and thereafter only slightly revised. Criticism of the term *natural selection* of course did not arise until the term had been published in 1859.

The following longer excerpt is headed as "Circumstances Favorable for the Production of New Forms through Natural Selection" and gives an example of the complexity of Darwin's investigations and of the application of the original Darwinian concept of natural selection to a variety of evolutionary events:

This is an extremely intricate subject. A great amount of variability, under which term individual differences are always included, will evidently be favorable. A large number of individuals, by giving a better chance within any given period for the appearance of profitable variations, will compensate for a lesser amount of variability in each individual, and is, I believe, a highly important element of success. Though nature grants long periods of time for the work of natural selection, she does not grant an indefinite period, for as all organic beings are striving to seize on each place in the economy of nature, if any one species does not become modified and improved in a corresponding degree with its competitors it will be exterminated. Unless favorable variations be inherited by some at least of the offspring, nothing can be effected by natural selection. The tendency to reversion may often check or prevent the work; but as this tendency has not prevented man from forming by selection numerous domestic races, why should it prevail against natural selection?

In the case of methodical selection, a breeder selects for some definite object, and if the individuals be allowed freely to intercross, his work will completely fail. But when many men, without intending to alter the breed, have a nearly common standard of perfection, and all try to procure and breed from the best animals, improvement surely but slowly follows from this unconscious process of selection, notwithstanding that there is no separation of selected individuals. Thus it will be under nature; for within a confined area, with some place in the natural polity not perfectly occupied, all the individuals varying in the right direction, though in different degrees, will tend to be preserved. But if the area be large, its several districts will almost certainly present different conditions of life; and then, if the same species undergoes modification in different districts, the newly formed varieties will intercross on the confines of each. But we shall see in the sixth chapter that intermediate varieties, inhabiting intermediate districts, will in the long run generally be supplanted by one of the adjoining varieties. Intercrossing will chiefly affect those animals which unite for each birth and wander much, and which do not breed at a very quick rate. Hence with animals of this nature, for instance birds, varieties will generally be confined to separated countries; and this I find to be the case. With hermaphrodite organisms which cross only occasionally, and likewise with animals which unite for each birth, but which wander little and can increase at a rapid rate, a new and improved variety might be quickly formed on any one spot, and might there maintain itself in a body and afterward spread, so that the individuals of the new variety would chiefly cross together. On this principle nurserymen always prefer saving seed from a large body of plants, as the chance of intercrossing is thus lessened.

Even with animals which unite for each birth, and which do not propagate rapidly, we must not assume that free intercrossing would always eliminate the effects of natural selection; for I can bring forward a considerable body of facts showing that within the same area two varieties of the same animal may long remain distinct, from haunting different stations, from breeding at slightly different seasons, or from the individuals of each variety preferring to pair together.

Intercrossing plays a very important part in nature by keeping the individuals of the same species, or of the same variety, true and uniform in character. It will obviously thus act far more efficiently with those animals which unite for each birth; but, as already stated, we have reason to believe that occesional intercrosses take place with all animals and plants. Even if these take place only at long intervals of time, the young thus produced will gain so much in vigor and fertility over the offspring from long-continued self-fertilization, that they will have a better chance of surviving and propagating their kind; and thus in the long-run the influence of crosses, even at rare intervals, will be great. With respect to organic beings extremely low in the scale, which do not propagate sexually, nor conjugate, and which cannot possibly intercross, uniformity of character can be retained by them under the same conditions of life, only through the principle of inheritance, and through natural selection which will destroy any individuals departing from the proper type. If the conditions of life change and the form undergoes modification, uniformity of character can be given to the modified offspring, solely by natural selection preserving similar favorable variations.

Isolation also is an important element in the modification of species through natural selection. In a confined or isolated area, if not very large, the organic and inorganic conditions of life will generally be almost uniform; so that natural selection will tend to modify all the varying individuals of the same species in the same manner. Intercrossing with the inhabitants of the surrounding districts, will also be thus prevented. Moritz Wagner has lately published an interesting essay on this subject, and has shown that the service rendered by isolation in preventing crosses between newly-formed varieties is probably greater even than I supposed. But from reasons already assigned I can by no means agree with this naturalist, that migration and isolation are necessary elements for the formation of new species. The importance of isolation is likewise great in preventing, after any physical change in the conditions, such as of climate, elevation of the land, etc., the immigration of better adapted organisms; and thus new places in the natural economy of the district will be left open to be filled up by the modification of the old inhabitants. Lastly, isolation will give time for a new variety to be improved at a slow rate; and this may sometimes be of much importance. If, however, an isolated area be very small, either from being surrounded by barriers, or from having very peculiar physical conditions, the total number of the inhabitants will be small; and this will retard the production of new species through natural selection, by decreasing the chances of favorable variations arising.

The mere lapse of time by itself does nothing, either for or against natural selection. I state this because it has been erroneously asserted that the element of time has been assumed by me to play an all-important part in modifying species, as if all the forms of life were necessarily undergoing change through some innate law. Lapse of time is only so far important, and its importance in this respect is great, that it gives a better chance of beneficial variations arising and of their being selected, accumulated, and fixed. It likewise tends to increase the direct action of the physical conditions of life, in relation to the constitution of each organism.

If we turn to nature to test the truth of these remarks, and look at any small isolated area, such as an oceanic island, although the number of species inhabiting it is small, as we shall see in our chapter on Geographical Distribution; yet of these species a very large proportion are endemic,—that is, have been produced there and nowhere else in the world. Hence an oceanic island at first sight seems to have been highly favorable for the production of new species. But we may thus deceive ourselves, for to ascertain whether a small isolated area, or a large open area like a continent, has been most favorable for the production of new organic forms, we ought to make the comparison within equal times; and this we are incapable of doing.

Although isolation is of great importance in the production of new species, on the whole I am inclined to believe that largeness of area is still more important, especially for the production of species which shall prove capable of enduring for a long period, and of spreading widely. Throughout a great and open area, not only will there be a better chance of favorable variations, arising from the large number of individuals of the same species there supported, but the conditions of life are much more complex from the large number of already existing species; and if some of these many species become modified and improved, others will have to be improved in a corresponding degree, or they will be exterminated. Each new form, also, as soon as it has been much improved, will be able to spread over the open and continuous area, and will thus come into competition with many other forms. Moreover, great areas, though now continuous, will often, owing to former oscillations of level, have existed in a broken condition; so that the good effects of isolation will generally, to a certain extent, have concurred. Finally, I conclude that, although small isolated areas have been in some respects highly favorable for the production of new species, yet that the course of modification will generally have been more rapid on large areas; and what is more important, that the new forms produced on large areas, which already have been victorious over many competitors, will be those that will spread most widely, and will give rise to the greatest number of new varieties and species. They will thus play a more important part in the changing history of the organic world.

In accordance with this view, we can, perhaps, understand some facts which will be again alluded to in our chapter on Geographical Distribution; for instance, the fact of the productions of the smaller continent of Australia now yielding before those of the larger Europaeo-Asiatic area. Thus, also, it is that continental productions have everywhere become so largely naturalized on islands. On a small island, the race for life will have been less severe, and there will have been less modification and less extermination. Hence, we can understand how it is that the flora of Maderia, according to Oswald Heer, resembles to a certain extent the extinct tertiary flora of Europe. All fresh water basins, taken together, make a small area compared with that of the sea or of the land. Consequently, the competition between fresh water productions will have been less severe than elsewhere, new forms will have been then more slowly produced, and old forms more slowly exterminated. And it is in fresh water basins that we find seven genera of Ganoid fishes, remnants of a once preponderant order: and in fresh water we find some of the most anomalous forms now known in the world as the Ornithorhynchus and Lepidosiren, which, like fossils, connect to a certain extent orders at present widely sundered in the natural scale. These anomalous forms may be called living fossils; they have endured to the present day, from having inhabited a confined area, and from having been exposed to less varied, and therefore less severe, competition.

To sum up, as far as the extreme intricacy of the subject permits, the circumstances favorable and unfavorable for the production of new species through natural selection. I conclude that for terrestrial productions a large continental area, which has undergone many oscillations of level, will have been the most favorable for the production of many new forms of life, fitted to endure for a long time and to spread widely. While the area existed as a continent the inhabitants will have been numerous in individuals and kinds, and will have been subjected to severe competition. When converted by subsistance into large separate islands there will still have existed many individuals of the same species on each island: intercrossing on the confines of the range of each new species will have been checked: after physical changes of any kind immigration will have been prevented, so that new places in the polity of each island will have had to be filled up by the modification of the old inhabitants; and time will have been allowed for the varieties in each to become well modified and perfected. When, by renewed elevation, the islands were reconverted into a continental area, there will again have been very severe competition; the most favored or improved varieties will have been enabled to spread; there will have been much extinction of the less improved forms, and the relative proportional numbers of the various inhabitants of the reunited continent will again have been changed; and again there will have been a fair field for natural selection to improve still further the inhabitants, and thus to produce new species.

That natural selection generally acts with extreme slowness I fully admit. It can act only when there are places in the natural polity of a district which can be better occupied by the modification of some of its existing inhabitants. The occurrence of such places will often depend on physical changes, which generally take place very slowly, and on the immigration of better adapted forms being prevented. As some few of the old inhabitants become modified the mutual relations of others will often be disturbed; and this will create new places, ready to be filled up by better adapted forms; but all this will take place very slowly. Although all the individuals of the same species differ in some slight degree from each other, it would often be long before differences of the right nature in various parts of the organization might occur. The result would often be greatly retarded by free intercrossing. Many will exclaim that these several causes are amply sufficient to neutralize the power of natural selection. I do not believe so. But I do believe that natural selection will generally act very slowly, only at long intervals of time, and only on a few of the inhabitants of the same region. I further believe that these slow, intermittant results accord well with what geology tells us of the rate and manner at which the inhabitants of the world have changed.

Slow though the process of selection may be, if feeble man can do much by artificial selection, I can see no limit to the amount of change, to the beauty and complexity of the coadaptations between all organic beings, one with another and with their physical conditions of life, which may have been affected in the long course of time through nature's power of selection, that is by the survival of the fittest.[6]

From the first edition through the last (sixth) *The Origin of Species* has a single, large figure. This figure and the relevant text, still in Chapter IV, add essentially to comprehension of the strictly Darwinian concept of evolution. The excerpt is taken from the first edition (1859). Darwin found little need for revision of this section of the book, and the changes that he did make are almost all trivial.

After the foregoing discussion, which ought to have been much amplified, we may, I think, assume that the modified descendants of any one species will succeed by so much the better as they become more diversified in structure, and are thus enabled to encroach on places occupied by other beings. Now let us see how this principle of great benefit being derived from divergence of character, combined with the principles of natural selection and of extinction, will tend to act.

The accompanying diagram will aid us in understanding this rather perplexing subject. Let A to L represent the species of a genus large in its own country; these species of a genus large in its own country; these species are supposed to resemble each other in unequal degrees, as is so generally the case in nature, and as is represented in the diagram by the letters standing at unequal distances. I have said a large genus, because we have seen in the second chapter, that on an average more of the species of large genera vary than of small genera; and the varying species of the large genera present a greater number of varieties. We have, also, seen that the species, which are the commonest and the most widely-diffused, vary more than rare species with restricted ranges. Let (A) be a common, widely-diffused, and varying species, belonging to a genus large in its own country. The little fan of diverging dotted lines of unequal lengths proceeding from (A), may represent its varying offspring. The variations are supposed to be extremely slight, but of the most diversified nature; they are not supposed all to appear simultaneously, but often after long intervals of time; nor are they all supposed to endure for equal periods. Only those variations which are in some way profitable will be preserved or naturally selected. And here the importance of the principle of benefit being derived from divergence of character comes in; for this will generally lead to the most different or divergent variations (represented by the outer dotted lines) being preserved and accumulated by natural selection. When a dotted line reaches one of the horizontal lines, and is there marked by a small numbered letter, a sufficient amount of variation is supposed to have been accumulated to have formed a fairly well-marked variety, such as would be thought worthy of record in a systematic work.

The intervals between the horizontal lines in the diagram, may represent each a thousand generations; but it would have been better if each had represented ten thousand generations. After a thousand generations, species (A) is supposed to have produced two fairly well-marked va-

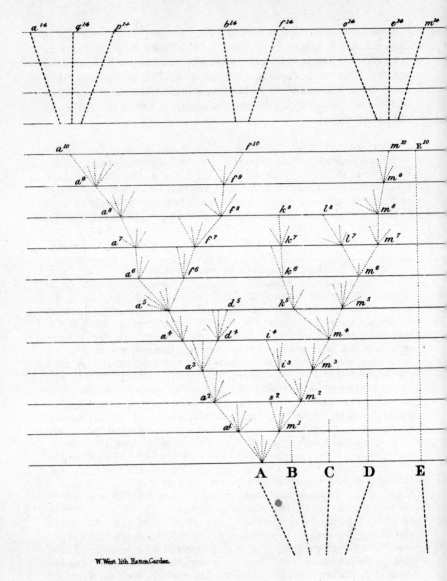

W. West lith. Hatton Garden.

This diagram appeared as a fold-in in lithograph in the first and all editions of *The Origin of Species*, although after Darwin's sixth edition sometimes reduced to a single page. It is the only figure in that work. In Darwin's book it had no legend but was explained in the accompanying text, the significant part of which is reprinted here.

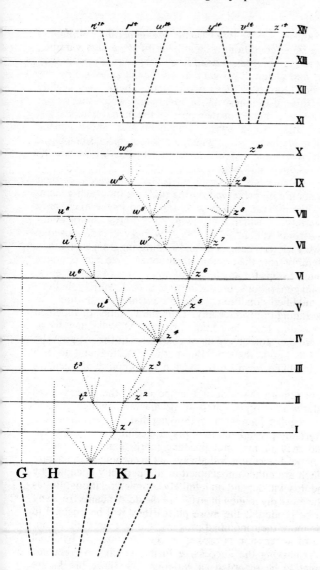

rieties, namely a^l and m^l. These two varieties will generally continue to be exposed to the same conditions which made their parents variable, and the tendency to variability is in itself hereditary, consequently they will tend to vary, and generally to vary in nearly the same manner as their parents varied. Moreover, these two varieties, being only slightly modified forms, will tend to inherit those advantages which made their common parent (A) more numerous than most of the other inhabitants of the same country; they will likewise partake of those more general advantages which made the genus to which the parent-species belonged, a large genus in its own country. And these circumstances we know to be favourable to the production of new varieties.

If, then, these two varieties be variable, the most divergent of their variations will generally be preserved during the next thousand generations. And after this interval, variety a^l is supposed in the diagram to have produced variety a^2, which will, owing to the principle of divergence, differ more from (A) than did variety a^l. Variety m^l is supposed to have produced two varieties, namely m^2 and s^2, differing from each other, and more considerably from their common parent (A). We may continue the process by similar steps for any length of time; some of the varieties, after each thousand generations, producing only a single variety, but in a more and more modified condition, some producing two or three varieties, and some failing to produce any. Thus the varieties or modified descendants, proceeding from the common parent (A), will generally go on increasing in number and diverging in character. In the diagram the process is represented up to the ten-thousandth generation, and under a condensed and simplified form up to the fourteen-thousandth generation.

But I must here remark that I do not suppose that the process ever goes on so regularly as is represented in the diagram, though in itself made somewhat irregular. I am far from thinking that the most divergent varieties will invariably prevail and multiply: a medium form may often long endure, and may or may not produce more than one modified descendant; for natural selection will always act according to the nature of the places which are either unoccupied or not perfectly occupied by other beings; and this will depend on infinitely complex relations. But as a general rule, the more diversified in structure the descendants from any one species can be rendered, the more places they will be enabled to seize on, and the more their modified progeny will be increased. In our diagram the line of succession is broken at regular intervals by small numbered letters marking the successive forms which have become sufficiently distinct to be recorded as varieties. But these breaks are imaginary, and might have been inserted anywhere, after intervals long enough to have allowed the accumulation of a considerable amount of divergent variation.

As all the modified descendants from a common and widely-diffused species, belonging to a large genus, will tend to partake of the same advantages which made their parent successful in life, they will generally go on multiplying in number as well as diverging in character: this is represented in the diagram by the several divergent branches proceeding from (A). The modified offspring from the later and more highly improved branches in the lines of descent, will, it is probable, often take the place of, and so destroy, the earlier and less improved branches: this is represented in the diagram by some of the lower branches not reaching to the upper horizontal lines. In some cases I do not doubt that the process of modification will be confined to a single line of descent, and the number of the descendants will not be increased; although the amount of divergent modification may have been increased in the successive generations. This case would be represented in the diagram, if all the lines proceeding from (A) were removed, excepting that from a^l to a^{10}. In the same way, for instance, the English race-horse and English pointer have apparently both gone on slowly diverging in character from their original stocks, without either having given off any fresh branches or races.

After ten thousand generations, species (A) is supposed to have produced three forms, a^{10}, f^{10}, and m^{10}, which, from having diverged in character during the successive generations, will have come to differ largely, but perhaps unequally, from each other and from their common parent. If we suppose the amount of change between each horizontal line in our diagram to be excessively small, these three forms may still be only well-marked varieties; or they may have arrived at the doubtful category of sub-species; but we have only to suppose the steps in the process of modification to be more numerous or greater in amount, to convert these three forms into well-defined species: thus the diagram illustrates the steps by which the small differences distinguishing varieties are increased into the larger differences distinguishing species. By continuing the same process for a greater number of generations (as shown in the diagram in a condensed and simplified manner), we get eight species, marked by the letters between a^{14} and m^{14}, all descended from (A). Thus, as I believe, species are multiplied and genera are formed.

In a large genus it is probable that more than one species would vary. In the diagram I have assumed that a second species (I) has produced, by analogous steps, after ten thousand generations, either two well-marked varieties (w^{10} and z^{10}) or two species, according to the amount of change supposed to be represented between the horizontal lines. After fourteen thousand generations, six new species, marked by the letters n^{14} to z^{14}, are supposed to have been produced. In each genus, the species, which are already extremely different in character, will generally tend to produce the greatest number of modified descendants; for these will have the best chance of filling new and widely different places in the polity of nature: hence in the diagram I have chosen the extreme species (A), and the nearly extreme species (I), as those which have largely varied, and have given rise to new varieties and species. The other nine species (marked by capital letters) of our original genus, may for a long period continue transmitting unaltered descendants; and this is shown in the diagram by the dotted lines not prolonged far upwards from want of space.

But during the process of modification, represented in the diagram, another of our principles, namely that of extinction, will have played an important part. As in each fully stocked country natural selection necessarily acts by the selected form having some advantage in the struggle for life over other forms, there will be a constant tendency in the improved descendants of any one species to supplant and exterminate in each stage of descent their predecessors and their original parent. For it should be remembered that the competition will generally be most severe between those forms which are most nearly related to each other in habits, constitution, and structure. Hence all the intermediate forms between the earlier and later states, that is between the less and more improved state of a species, as well as the original parent-species itself, will generally tend to become extinct. So it probably will be with many whole collateral lines of descent, which will be conquered by later and improved lines of descent. If, however, the modified offspring of a species get into some distinct country, or become quickly adapted to some quite new station, in which child and parent do not come into competition, both may continue to exist.

If then our diagram be assumed to represent a considerable amount of modification, species (A) and all the earlier varieties will have become extinct, having been replaced by eight new species (a^{14} to m^{14}); and (I) will have been replaced by six (n^{14} to z^{14}) new species.

But we may go further than this. The original species of our genus were supposed to resemble each other in unequal degrees, as is so generally the case in nature; species (A) being more nearly related to B, C, and D, than to the other species; and species (I) more to G, H, K, L, than to the others. These two species (A) and (I), were also supposed to be very common and widely diffused species, so that they must originally have had some advantage over most of the other species of the genus. Their modified descendants, fourteen in number at the fourteen-thousandth generation, will probably have inherited some of the same advantages: they have also been modified and improved in a diversified manner at each stage of descent, so as to have become adapted to many related places in the natural economy of their country. It seems, therefore, to me extremely probable that they will have taken the places of, and thus exterminated, not only their parents (A) and (I), but likewise some of the original species which were most nearly related to their parents. Hence very few of the original species will have transmitted offspring to the fourteen-thousandth generation. We may suppose that only one (F), of the two species which were least closely related to the other nine original species, has transmitted descendants to this late stage of descent.

The new species in our diagram descended from the original eleven species, will now be fifteen in number. Owing to the divergent tendency of natural selection, the extreme amount of difference in character between species a^{14} and z^{14} will be much greater than that between the most different of the original eleven species. The new species, moreover, will be allied to each other in a widely different manner. Of the eight descendants from (A) the three marked a^{14}, q^{14}, p^{14}, will be nearly related from having recently branched off from a^{10}; b^{14} and f^{14}, from having diverged at an earlier period from a^5, will be in some degree distinct from the three first-named species; and lastly, o^{14}, e^{14}, and m^{14}, will be nearly related one to the other, but from having diverged at the first commencement of the process of modification, will be widely different from the other five species, and may constitute a sub-genus or even a distinct genus.

The six descendants from (I) will form two sub-genera or even genera. But as the original species (I) differed largely from (A), standing nearly at the extreme points of the original genus, the six descendants from (I) will, owing to inheritance, differ considerably from the eight descendants from (A); the two groups, moreover, are supposed to have gone on diverging in different directions. The intermediate species, also (and this is a very important consideration), which connected the original species (A) and (I), have all become, excepting (F), extinct, and have left no descendants. Hence the six new species descended from (I), and the eight descended from (A), will have to be ranked as very distinct genera, or even as distinct sub-families.

Thus it is, as I believe, that two or more genera are produced by descent, with modification, from two or more species of the same genus. And the two or more parent-species are supposed to have descended from some one species of an earlier genus. In our diagram, this is indicated by the broken lines, beneath the capital letters, converging in sub-branches downwards towards a single point; this point representing a single species, the supposed single parent of our several new sub-genera and genera.

It is worth while to reflect for a moment on the character of the new species F^{14}, which is supposed not to have diverged much in character, but to have retained the form of (F), either unaltered or altered only in a slight degree. In this case, its affinities to the other fourteen new species will be of a curious and circuitous nature. Having descended from a form which stood between the two parent-species (A) and (I), now supposed to be extinct and unknown, it will be in some degree intermediate in character between the two groups descended from these species. But as these two groups have gone on diverging in character from the type of their parents, the new species (F^{14}) will not be directly intermediate between them, but rather between types of the two groups; and every naturalist will be able to bring some such case before his mind.

In the diagram, each horizontal line has hitherto been supposed to represent a thousand generations, but each may represent a million or hundred million generations, and likewise a section of the successive strata of the earth's crust including extinct remains. We shall, when we come to our chapter on Geology, have to refer again to this subject, and I think we shall then see that the diagram throws light on the affinities of extinct beings, which, though generally belonging to the same orders, or families, or genera, with those now living, yet are often, in some degree, intermediate in character between existing groups; and we can understand this fact, for the extinct species lived at very ancient epochs when the branching lines of descent had diverged less.

I see no reason to limit the process of modification, as now explained, to the formation of genera alone. if, in our diagram, we suppose the amount of change represented by each successive group of diverging dotted lines to be very great, the forms marked a^{14} to p^{14}, those marked b^{14} and f^{14}, and those marked o^{14} to m^{14}, will form three very distinct genera. We shall also have two very distinct genera descended from (I); and as these latter two genera, both from continued divergence of character and from inheritance from a different parent, will differ widely from the three genera descended from (A), the two little groups of genera will form two distinct families, or even orders, according to the amount of divergent modification supposed to be represented in the diagram. And the two new families, or orders, will have descended from two species of the original genus; and these two species are supposed to have descended from one species of a still more ancient and unknown genus.[7]

The excerpts given up to this point show the progress of Darwin's exposition and argument up to his major conclusion. As space here does not permit even an adequate summary of Chapters V–XV I append only a list of the chapter headings and then give as a final excerpt the conclusions from the end of the last chapter.

I have now recapitulated the facts and considerations which have thoroughly convinced me that species have been modified, during a long course of descent. This has been effected chiefly through the natural selection of numerous successive, slight, favorable variations; aided in an important manner by the inherited effects of the use and disuse of parts; and in an unimportant manner, that is, in relation to adaptive structures, whether past or present, by the direct action of external conditions, and by variations which seem to us in our ignorance to arise spontaneously. It appears that I formerly underrated the frequency and value of these latter forms of variation, as leading to permanent modifications of structure independently of natural selection. But as my conclusions have lately been much misrepresented, and it has been stated that I attribute the modification of species exclusively to natural selection, I may be permitted to remark that in the first edition of this work, and subsequently, I placed in a most conspicuous position—namely, at the close of the Introduction—the following words: "I am convinced that natural selection has been the main but not the exclusive means of modification." This has been of no avail. Great is the power of steady misrepresentation; but the history of science shows that fortunately this power does not long endure.

It can hardly be supposed that a false theory would explain, in so satisfactory a manner as does the theory of natural selection, the several large classes of facts above specified. It has recently been objected that this is an unsafe method of arguing; but it is a method used in judging of the common events of life, and has often been used by the greatest natural philosophers. The undulatory theory of light has thus been arrived at; and the belief in the revolution of the earth on its own axis was until lately supported by hardly any direct evidence. It is no valid objection that science as yet throws no light on the far higher problem of the essence or origin of life. Who can explain what is the essence of the attraction of gravity? No one now objects to following out the results consequent on this unknown element of attraction; notwithstanding that Leibnitz formerly accused Newton of introducing "occult qualities and miracles into philosophy."

I see no good reasons why the views given in this volume should shock the religious feelings of any one. It is satisfactory, as showing how transient such impressions are, to remember that the greatest discovery ever made by man, namely, the law of the attraction of gravity, was also attacked by Leibnitz, "as subversive of natural, and inferentially of revealed, religion." A celebrated author and divine has written to me that "he has gradually learned to see that it is just as noble a conception of the Deity to believe that He created a few original forms capable of self-development into other and needful forms, as to believe that He required a fresh act of creation to supply the voids caused by the action of His laws."

Why, it may be asked, until recently did nearly all the most eminent living naturalists and geologists disbelieve in the mutability of species? It cannot be asserted that organic beings in a state of nature are subject to no variation; it cannot be proved that the amount of variation in the course of long ages is a limited quantity; no clear distinction has been, or can be, drawn between species and well-marked varieties. It cannot be maintained that species when intercrossed are invariably sterile and varieties invariably fertile; or that sterility is a special endowment and sign of creation. The belief that species were immutable productions was almost unavoidable as long as the history of the world was thought to be of short duration; and now that we have acquired some idea of the lapse of time, we are too apt to assume, without proof, that the geological record is so perfect that it would have afforded us plain evidence of the mutation of species, if they had undergone mutation.

But the chief cause of our natural unwillingness to admit that one species has given birth to other and distinct species, is that we are always slow in admitting great changes of which we do not see the steps. The difficulty is the same as that felt by so many geologists, when Lyell first insisted that long lines of inland cliffs had been formed, and great valleys excavated, by the agencies which we still see at work. The mind cannot possibly grasp the full meaning of the term of even a million years; it cannot add up and perceive the full effects of many slight variations, accumulated during an almost infinite number of generations.

Although I am fully convinced of the truth of the views given in this volume under the form of an abstract, I by no means expect to convince experienced naturalists whose minds are stocked with a multitude of facts all viewed, during a long course of years, from a point of view directly opposite to mine. It is so easy to hide our ignorance under such expressions as the "plan of creation," "unity of design," etc., and to think that we give an explanation when we only restate a fact. Any one whose disposition leads him to attach more weight to unexplained difficulties than to the explanation of a certain number of facts will certainly reject the theory. A few naturalists, endowed with much flexibility of mind, and who have already begun to doubt the immutability of species, may be influenced by this volume; but I look with confidence to the future, to young and rising naturalists, who will be able to view both sides of the question with impartiality. Whoever is led to believe that species are mutable will do good service by conscientiously expressing his conviction; for thus only can the load of prejudice by which this subject is overwhelmed be removed.

Several eminent naturalists have of late published their belief that a multitude of reputed species in each genus are not real species; but that other species are real, that is, have been independently created. This seems to me a strange conclusion to arrive at. They admit that a multitude of forms, which till lately they themselves thought were special creations, and which are still thus looked at by the majority of naturalists, and which consequently have all the external characteristic features of true species—they admit that these have been produced by variation, but they refuse to extend the same view to other and slightly different forms. Nevertheless, they do not pretend that they can define, or even conjecture, which are the created forms of life, and which are those produced by secondary laws. They admit variation as a *vera causa* in one case, they arbitrarily reject it in another, without assigning any distinction in the two cases. The day will come when this will be given as a curious illustration of the blindness of preconceived opinion. These authors seem no more startled at a miraculous act of creation than at an ordinary birth. But do they really believe that at innumerable periods in the earth's history certain elemental atoms have been commanded suddenly to flash into living tissues? Do they believe that at each supposed act of creation one individual or many were produced? Were all the infinitely numerous kinds of animals and plants created as eggs or seed, or as full grown? and in the case of mammals, were they created bearing the false marks of nourishment from the mother's womb? Undoubtedly some of these same questions cannot be answered by those who believe in the appearance or creation of only a few forms of life or of some one form alone. It has been maintained by several authors that it is as easy to believe in the creation of a million beings as of one; but Maupertuis' philosophical axiom "of least action" leads the mind more willingly to admit the smaller number; and certainly we ought not to believe that innumerable beings within each great class have been created with plain, but deceptive, marks of descent from a single parent.

As a record of a former state of things, I have retained in the foregoing paragraphs, and elsewhere, several sentences which imply that naturalists believe in the separate creation of each species; and I have been much censured for having thus expressed myself. But undoubtedly this was the general belief when the first edition of the present work appeared. I formerly spoke to very many naturalists on the subject of evolution, and never once met with any sympathetic agreement. It is probable that some did then believe in evolution, but they were either silent or expressed themselves so ambiguously that it was not easy to understand their meaning. Now, things are wholly changed, and almost every naturalist admits the great principle of evolution. There are, however, some who still think that species have suddenly given birth, through quite unexplained means, to new and totally different forms. But, as I have attempted to show, weighty evidence can be opposed to the admission of great and abrupt modifications. Under a scientific point of view, and as leading to further investigation, but little advantage is gained by believing that new forms are suddenly developed in an inexplicable manner from old and widely different forms, over the old belief in the creation of species from the dust of the earth.

It may be asked how far I extend the doctrine of the modification of species. The question is difficult to answer, because the more distinct the forms are which we consider, by so much the arguments in favor of community of descent become fewer in number and less in force. But some arguments of the greatest weight extend very far. All the members of whole classes are connected together by a chain of affinities, and all can be classed on the same principle, in groups subordinate to groups. Fossil remains sometimes tend to fill up very wide intervals between existing orders.

Organs in a rudimentary condition plainly show that an early progenitor had the organ in a fully developed condition, and this in some cases implies an enormous amount of modification in the descendants. Throughout whole classes various structures are formed on the same pattern, and at a very early age the embryos closely resemble each other. Therefore I cannot doubt that the theory of descent with modification embraces all the members of the same great class or kingdom. I believe that animals are descended from at most only four or five progenitors, and plants from an equal or lesser number.

Analogy would lead me one step further, namely, to the belief that all animals and plants are descended from some one prototype. But analogy may be a deceitful guide. Nevertheless all living things have much in common, in their chemical composition, their cellular structure, their laws of growth, and their liability to injurious influences. We see this even in so trifling a fact as that the same poison often similarly affects plants and animals; or that the poison secreted by the gall-fly produces monstrous growths on the wild rose or oak tree. With all organic beings, excepting perhaps some of the very lowest, sexual reproduction seems to be essentially similar. With all, as far as is at present known, the germinal vesicle is the same; so that all organisms start from a common origin. If we look even to the two main divisions—namely, to the animal and vegetable kingdoms—certain low forms are so far intermediate in character that naturalists have disputed to which kingdom they should be referred. As Professor Asa Gray has remarked, "the spores and other reproductive bodies of many of the lower algae may claim to have first a characteristically animal, and then an unequivocally vegetable existence." Therefore, on the principle of natural selection with divergence of character, it does not seem incredible that, from some such low and intermediate form, both animals and plants may have been developed; and if we admit this, we must likewise admit that all the organic beings which have ever lived on this earth may be descended from some one primordial form. But this inference is chiefly grounded on analogy, and it is immaterial whether or not it be accepted. No doubt it is possible, as Mr. G. H. Lewes has urged, that at the first commencement of life many different forms were evolved; but if so, we may conclude that only a very few have left modified descendants. For, as I have recently remarked in regard to the members of each great kingdom, such as the Vertebrata, Articulata, etc., we have distinct evidence in their embryological, homologous, and rudimentary structures, that within each kingdom all the members are descended from a single progenitor.

When the views advanced by me in this volume, and by Mr. Wallace or when analogous views on the origin of species are generally admitted, we can dimly foresee that there will be a considerable revolution in natural history. Systematists will be able to pursue their labors as at present; but they will not be incessantly haunted by the shadowy doubt whether this or that form be a true species. This, I feel sure and I speak after experience, will be no slight relief. The endless disputes whether or not some fifty species of British brambles are good species will cease. Systematists will have only to decide (not that this will be easy) whether any form be sufficiently constant and distinct from other forms, to be capable of definition; and if definable, whether the differences be sufficiently important to deserve a specific name. This latter point will become a far more essential consideration than it is at present; for differences, however slight, between any two forms, if not blended by intermediate gradations, are looked at by most naturalists as sufficient to raise both forms to the rank of species.

Hereafter we shall be compelled to acknowledge that the only distinction between species and well-marked varieties is, that the latter are known, or believed to be connected at the present day by intermediate gradations, whereas species were formerly thus connected. Hence, without rejecting the consideration of the present existence of intermediate gradations between any two forms, we shall be led to weigh more carefully and to value higher the actual amount of difference between them. It is quite possible that forms now generally acknowledged to be merely varieties may hereafter be thought worthy of specific names; and in this case scientific and common language will come into accordance. In short, we shall have to treat species in the same manner as those naturalists treat genera, who admit that genera are merely artificial combinations made for convenience. This may not be a cheering prospect; but we shall at least be freed from the vain search for the undiscovered and undiscoverable essence of the term species.

The other and more general departments of natural history will rise greatly in interest. The terms used by naturalists, of affinity, relationship, community of type, paternity, morphology, adaptive characters, rudimentary and aborted organs, etc., will cease to be metaphorical and will have a plain signification. When we no longer look at an organic being as a savage looks at a ship, as something wholly beyond his comprehension; when we regard every production of nature as one which has had a long history; when we contemplate every complex structure and instinct as the summing up of many contrivances, each useful to the possessor, in the same way as any great mechanical invention is the summing up of the labor, the experience, the reason, and even the blunders of numerous workmen; when we thus view each organic being, how far more interesting—I speak from experience—does the study of natural history become!

A grand and almost untrodden field of inquiry will be opened, on the causes and laws of variation, on correlation, on the effects of use and disuse, on the direct action of external conditions, and so forth. The study of domestic productions will rise immensely in value. A new variety raised by man will be a more important and interesting subject for study than one more species added to the infinitude of already recorded species. Our classifications will come to be, as far as they can be so made, genealogies; and will then truly give what may be called the plan of creation. The rules for classifying will no doubt become simpler when we have a definite object in view. We possess no pedigree or armorial bearings; and we have to discover and trace the many diverging lines of descent in our natural genealogies, by characters of any kind which have long been inherited. Rudimentary organs will speak infallibly with respect to the nature of long-lost structures. Species and groups of species which are called aberrant, and which may fancifully be called living fossils, will aid us in forming a picture of the ancient forms of life. Embryology will often reveal to us the structure, in some degree obscured, of the prototypes of each great class.

When we can feel assured that all the individuals of the same species, and all the closely allied species of most genera, have, within a not very remote period descended from one parent, and have migrated from some one birth-place; and when we better know the many means of migration, then, by the light which geology now throws, and will continue to throw, on former changes of climate and of the level of the land, we shall surely be enabled to trace in an admirable manner the former migrations of the inhabitants of the whole world. Even at present, by comparing the differences between the inhabitants of the sea on the opposite sides of a continent, and the nature of the various inhabitants on that continent in relation to their apparent means of immigration, some light can be thrown on ancient geography.

The noble science of geology loses glory from the extreme imperfection of the record. The crust of the earth, with its imbedded remains, must not be looked at as a well-filled museum, but as a poor collection made at hazard and at rare intervals. The accumulation of each great fossiliferous formation will be recognized as having depended on an unusual occurrence of favorable circumstances, and the blank intervals between the successive stages as having been of vast duration. But we shall be able to gauge with some security the duration of these intervals by a comparison of the preceding and succeeding organic forms. We must be cautious in attempting to correlate as strictly contemporaneous two formations, which do not include many identical species, by the general succession of the forms of life. As species are produced and exterminated by slowly acting and still existing causes, and not by miraculous acts of creation; and as the most important of all causes of organic change is one which is almost independent of altered and perhaps suddenly altered physical conditions, namely, the mutual relation of organism to organism—the improvement of one organism entailing the improvement or the extermination of others; it follows, that the amount of organic change in the fossils of consecutive formations probably serves as a fair measure of the relative, though not actual lapse of time. A number of species, however, keeping in a body might remain for a long period unchanged, while within the same period, several of these species, by migrating into new countries and coming into competition with foreign associates, might become modified; so that we must not overrate the accuracy of organic change as a measure of time.

In the future I see open fields for far more important researches.

Psychology will be securely based on the foundation already well laid by Mr. Herbert Spencer, that of the necessary acquirement of each mental power and capacity by gradation. Much light will be thrown on the origin of man and his history.

Authors of the highest eminence seem to be fully satisfied with the view that each species has been independently created. To my mind it accords better with what we know of the laws impressed on matter by the Creator, that the production and extinction of the past and present inhabitants of the world should have been due to secondary causes, like those determining the birth and death of the individual. When I view all beings not as special creations, but as the lineal descendants of some few beings which lived long before the first bed of the Cambrian system was deposited, they seem to me to become ennobled. Judging from the past, we may safely infer that not one living species will transmit its unaltered likeness to a distinct futurity. And of the species now living very few will transmit progeny of any kind to a far distant futurity; for the manner in which all organic beings are grouped, shows that the greater number of species in each genus, and all the species in many genera, have left no descendants, but have become utterly extinct. We can so far take a prophetic glance into futurity as to foretell that it will be the common and widely spread species, belonging to the larger and dominant groups within each class, which will ultimately prevail and procreate new and dominant species. As all the living forms of life are the lineal descendants of those which lived long before the Cambrian epoch, we may feel certain that the ordinary succession by generation has never once been broken, and that no cataclysm has desolated the whole world. Hence, we may look with some confidence to a secure future of great length. And as natural selection works solely by and for the good of each being, all corporeal and mental endowments will tend to progress toward perfection.

It is interesting to contemplate a tangled bank, clothed with many plants of many kinds, with birds singing on the bushes, with various insects flitting about, and with worms crawling through the damp earth, and to reflect that these elaborately constructed forms, so different from each other, and dependent upon each other in so complex a manner, have all been produced by laws acting around us. These laws, taken in the largest sense, being Growth with reproduction; Inheritance which is almost implied by reproduction; Variability from the indirect and direct action of the conditions of life, and from use and disuse: a Ratio of Increase so high as to lead to a Struggle for Life, and as a consequence to Natural Selection, entailing Divergence of Character and the Extinction of less improved forms. Thus, from the war of nature, from famine and death, the most exalted object which we are capable of conceiving, namely, the production of the higher animals, directly follows. There is grandeur in this view of life, with its several powers, having been originally breathed by the Creator into a few forms or into one; and that, while this planet has gone circling on according to the fixed law of gravity, from so simple a beginning endless forms most beautiful and most wonderful have been, and are being evolved.[8]

There are many things in this "conclusion" that call for consideration. They had a great influence on Darwin's contemporaries and still have on biologists today.

In retrospect there are several points that are of special interest. One is that Darwin did not here deal even by speculation with the origin of life. Although in then private correspondence Darwin did consider the possibility that life originated by natural means from inorganic matter, here he has life "originally breathed by the Creator into a few forms of life or into one." It is interesting that the first printing did not have the words "by the Creator" in this sentence. That was one of the relatively few important changes between the first and second editions. However, even in the first edition Darwin did refer to evolutionary genealogies as "what may be called the plan of creation."

The origin of man is not discussed in *The Origin of Species*, which only says that "Light will be thrown on the origin of man and his history." (This was not changed to "Much light" until the sixth edition.) Here one cannot avoid thinking that Darwin was being purposely evasive. He was already convinced that mankind evolved from "lower" forms of life, and he must have known that this would be generally deduced, both by evolutionists and anti-evolutionists, from what he did write. Such was indeed the case. Darwin's evasion was certainly meant to evade prejudice against his views on evolution as a general "law" of nature. Other naturalists who were converted to the Darwinian view of evolution quickly brought man into the picture. Most noteworthy in this respect was Thomas Henry Huxley, Darwin's convert and defender, who in 1863 published *Evidence of Man's Place in Nature*, which gave thoroughly convincing evidence of man's kinship with the apes. Darwin himself finally abandoned all subterfuge and in 1871 published *The Descent or Origin of Man*. (See Chapter 9 of the present book.) In this connection it is noteworthy that Wallace, who had independently proposed the process of natural selection and who ever after considered himself a disciple of Darwin nevertheless made mankind the one exception to the origin of species by natural selection.

Even today those who attack evolution on religious grounds consider "Darwinism" to be the theory that mankind descended from an ape, which is rejected more for emotional than for any rational reasons. Darwin did assert that among living animals the apes most resemble humans and that apes and humans did have a common ancestry among ancient Old World monkeys, which is not the same as saying that man descended from apes. That is only one detail, although a particularly interesting one, in the overall Darwinian discussion of evolution.

The Origin of Species, which is definitive of Darwinism in a strict sense, has three interrelated but distinct levels. First is an axiom or definition of science: that the scientific investigation and explanation of observed phenomena eschews reference to anything supernatural. In that sense the Darwinian canon as represented by *The Origin of Species* is definitely materialistic, although Darwin found "no good reason" why this "should shock the religious feelings of anyone." As a matter of fact, it did shock the religious feelings of a good many people when first propounded, and it still does so for some people who do not understand the necessary basis for scientific investigation. In this connection the debate at the Oxford meeting of the British Association for the Advancement of Science in 1860 was especially significant. Bishop Samuel Wilberforce (1805–73) was scheduled to speak about evolution and *The Origin of Species*. The Bishop attacked Darwin's views with brilliant oratory but little logic. Darwin, ill as so often, was not at the meeting but his friend T. H. Huxley was. The Bishop ended his performance by asking Huxley whether it was through his grandfather or his grandmother that he claimed descent from a monkey. Huxley then spoke, first demolishing the Bishop's thesis on firmly based scientific grounds. He ended by saying more or less (no exact record was made) as follows: "If I had to choose between an ape for an ancestor and a man highly endowed by nature and of great influence, who used those gifts to introduce ridicule into a scientific discussion and to discredit seekers after truth, I would prefer the ape." Wilberforce did not reply.

The second and more obvious major level of *The Origin of Species* is demonstration that evolution is a fact, a "general law" of nature in Whewell's sense. This was done by demonstration that there are a great many observed, material phenomena that can be scientifically explained only by evolution and that there are no contradictory phenomena established as factual. Darwin realistically recognized that some experienced naturalists would not accept this conclusion, but he anticipated that naturalists with more flexible minds and especially those young and still open-minded would become convinced of its truth. This did occur. Darwin's old and firm friend Lyell, who had been a confirmed nonevolutionist, was sixty-two years old when *The Origin of Species* was published but his mind was still flexible, and he did accept the reality of evolution. Owen, although only fifty-five at that time, did not. Within a generation virtually all biologists were convinced evolutionists, and that is true today of all scientists competent to judge this issue.

The third major level of Darwin's text was devoted to the demonstration that adaptation, previously the mainstay of the supernatural creationist argument, could be explained as well or better by natural evolutionary processes. In this respect he considered natural selection, as defined by him, the most important but not the only evolutionary process. As noted in the previous quotation of his conclusions, he specified four factors:

Major factor: 1. Natural Selection.
Subsidiary factors: 2. Inheritance of effects of use and disuse of parts.
                     3. Direct action of external conditions.
                     4. "Spontaneous" variation.

The second (subsidiary) factor implies the inheritance of acquired characters, which is generally considered Lamarckian. However belief in it long antedated Lamarck and was general in both Lamarck's day and Darwin's. Moreover Lamarck himself believed that evolution was essentially linear, for completely unexplained reasons, and that the inheritance of acquired characters interfered with rather than caused the advance of evolution. The third of Darwin's factors has also been called Lamarckian but Lamarck himself explicitly repudiated it. It was added to the so-called Neo-Lamarckian tenets that developed in the latter part of the nineteenth century. The term applied to Darwin's fourth factor might be equated with what are now called genetic mutations, but that cannot be accepted as consonant with Darwin's own usage. He thought of spontaneous variation as the abrupt appearance of individuals markedly different from their parents, outside the normal range of variation in a population and not the usual basis for natural selection. Darwin did sometimes use the word *mutation,* but in the sense, which dates back to Chaucer if not earlier, simply of any change, without understood connection with the cause or nature of the change.

As I write these words it is 110 years since the definitive sixth edition of *The Origin of Species* was published. It was that book that revolutionized the science of biology and set it on the track that it still follows. In a foreword to a modern reprint of the sixth edition I said of this book:

Any student of biology can still learn from it and profit not only from its information but also and especially from its spirit and method. Of course it is deficient as regards discoveries made since its last revision. Just as inevitably, it does contain errors that have since been corrected. There is probably no other scientific classic on which the hand of time rests so lightly, but the present-day reader must make some allowance for the later progress of knowledge.

The most important change is that Darwin's second and third factors, considered by him real but subsidiary, are now known not to occur. After long debate, it is fully established that acquired characters, in the sense properly given those words, are not genetically heritable. Darwin was greatly puzzled by heredity and he noted that it simply was not understood in his day. He stated a hypothesis, carefully labeled as such and considered as falsifiable, that has in fact been falsified. Heredity began to be truly understood only with the rise and subsequent development of the modern science of genetics. The beginning of this understanding of heredity is usually dated from the publication in 1866 of a paper by the Austrian Augustinian monk Gregor Johann Mendel (1822–84). Darwin twice revised *The Origin of Species* after 1866, and it would have been possible for him to have read Mendel's paper, but there is no evidence that he did, and that is unlikely. Mendel's publication was more widely distributed than has sometimes been realized, but it should be noted and emphasized that neither Mendel nor anyone who read his paper saw any connection between it and evolution. There was no reason why anyone would call Darwin's attention to it, and it is probable that even he would not have seen its ultimate connection with evolutionary theory. (It is not wholly irrelevant that later analyses of Mendel's statistics strongly suggest that he manipulated some of the figures to make them better support his hypothesis.)

Modern genetics really dates from around 1900, years after the deaths of both Darwin and Mendel, when several biologists almost simultaneously began experimentation and statistical studies of heredity. As this developed it was plainly in accord with evolution, but for some time it seemed to fail to support or even was taken to contradict the Darwinian theory of natural selection.

As previously noted *The Origin of Species* did soon convince naturalists and biologists that evolution is a fact. Acceptance of Darwinian natural selection was slower and more limited. That was in part outdated reluctance to abandon the concept of inherent and linear progress in evolution, in part ignorance on the genetic nature and import of the variations on which natural selection must operate, and, among other things, also in part misunderstanding of the limitations of natural selection of which Darwin was aware but which did require stronger clarification. Thus it was noted that not all characteristics of organisms are plainly adaptive and some seem to be nonadaptive. But Darwin was well aware of this problem and made it clear that not all characteristics are subject to natural selection, and also that selection works on the whole complex of organisms and populations and not necessarily on separate and unitary characteristics. He stated that characteristics that are definitely adaptive will be favored by natural selection, those definitely inadaptive or antiadaptive will tend to be eliminated, and those not definitely one or the other would not be acted on by natural selection. It may also be added that more sophisticated study of supposedly nonadaptive or inadaptive characters has often shown them to be in fact adaptive.

Not until the 1930s and early 1940s was there a concerted synthesis of genetics, now on an increasingly firm and detailed basis, of systematics as the study of relationships among populations, of the fossil record as demonstrative of much of the evolutionary history of organisms, and indeed of all aspects of and approaches to the study of evolution. This has brought a strong consensus that natural selection is indeed the principal causative principle in nonrandom evolution. There does continue some healthily productive discussion of the intensity and effectiveness of natural selection in particular examples or in general.

Another point about advancing knowledge of evolution since Darwin concerns his repeated statement that local variations within populations are incipient species. He sometimes did not clearly distinguish the essential difference between variant individuals in populations and variant populations within species. Although he recognized isolation and barriers as factors for speciation in the sense of separation of an ancestral species into two or more descendant species, he was not entirely clear about the factors that cause interbreeding of the descendants to cease. Here, as in so many instances, the extensive later studies of isolating mechanisms supplement Darwin rather than contradicting him.

Another argument now current has to do with the levels at which natural selection acts. Some students speak of "decoupling" evolution at and within the species level, "microevolution," and that above that level, "macroevolution." They seem to have overlooked or misunderstood Darwin's statements that natural selection is the same process not just within but also between species and at higher levels.

The Origin of Species is not only the basic work on evolution and natural selection but also on the fossil record, biogeography, morphology, classification, and much else in the life sciences. In all of these there have been important advances and discoveries in the century since Darwin's death, but all have their historical antecedents in this great book.

8

Some New Slants on Botany

It has already been noted that Darwin's "big book," simply entitled *Natural Selection,* never was completed or published as such. By 1858 he had essentially completed drafts of eleven chapters. The purport of these was given in much abbreviated and more readable form in Chapters I–VIII and XI in the first edition of *The Origin of Species* (1–6, 8, 9 and 12 in later editions). From 1860 to 1867 besides twice revising *The Origin of Species,* Darwin undertook revising and expanding the first two chapters of the "big book," both of these being devoted to variation under domestication, the subject of just the first chapter of *The Origin of Species.* Darwin figured that he devoted four years and two months to this project. The result was an enormous manuscript entitled *The Variation of Animals and Plants under Domestication.* After submitting this to Murray for publication Darwin wrote to Hooker, "I have been these last few days vexed and annoyed to a foolish degree by hearing that my MS. on Dom. An. and Cult. Plants will make 2 vols., both bigger than the 'Origin.' " The weighty volumes, in "full-sized octavo," were nominally published in January 1868, but most of the first printing was sold before the end of 1867. A second printing was made, but anyone who has read the first chapter of *The Origin of Species* may well feel that he need not plow through this expansion of the topic.

Although those two volumes as well as the first chapter of *The Origin of Species* were devoted more to animals than to plants, during that same period of the 1860s Darwin was also investigating and experimenting with some aspects of botany. Among the results of those activities are two relatively small books, one on the fertilization of orchids and one on climbing plants, the first published by Murray in 1862 and the second published first in 1865 as a long paper in the *Botanical Journal of the Linnean Society* and later with revision as a book published by Murray in 1875. Darwin also wrote numerous queries and accounts on botanical subjects published in various biological and horticultural journals and corresponded extensively on such subjects. The present brief chapter will reprint or excerpt some of these in illustration of the mature Darwin's development as a generalist in biological science and as a meticulous enquirer and experimenter in botany.

The following is a note by Darwin in the *Gardeners' Chronicle and Agricultural Gazette* of November 24, 1855—a journal in which he frequently published short notes.

As you have published notices by Mr. Berkeley and myself on the length of time seeds can withstand immersion in sea-water, you may perhaps like to hear, without minute details, the final results of my experiments. The seed of Capsicum, after 137 days' immersion, came up well, for 30 out of 56 planted germinated, and I think more would have grown with time. Of Celery only 6 out of some hundreds came up after the same period of immersion. One single Canary seed grew after 120 days, and some Oats half germinated after 120; both Oats and Canary seed came up pretty well after only 100 days. Spinach germinated well after 120 days. Seed of Onions, Vegetable Marrow, Beet, Orache and Potatoes, and one seed of Ageratum mexicanum grew after 100 days. A few, and but very few, seed of Lettuce, Carrot, Cress, and Radish came up after 85 days' immersion. It is remarkable how differently varieties of the same species have withstood the ill effects of the salt water; thus, seed of the "Mammoth White Broccoli" came up excellently after 11 days, but was killed by 22 days' immersion; "early Cauliflower" survived this period, but was killed by 36 days: "Cattell's Cabbage" survived the 36 days, but was killed by 50 days; and now I have seed of the wild Cabbage from Tenby growing so vigorously after 50 days, that I am sure that it will survive a considerably longer period. But the seed of the wild Cabbage was fresh, and some facts show me that quite fresh seed withstands the salt water better than old, though very good seed. With respect to an important point in my former communication of May 26th, permit me to cry *peccavi;* having often heard of plants and bushes having been seen floating some little distance from land, I assumed—and in doing this I committed a scientific sin—that plants with ripe seed or fruit would float at least for some weeks. I always meant to try this, and I have now done so with sorrowful result; for having put in salt-water between 30 and 40 herbaceous plants and branches with ripe seed of various orders, I have found that all (with the exception of the fruit of evergreens) sink within a month, and most of them within 14 days. So that, as far as I can see, my experiments are of little or no use (excepting perhaps as negative evidence) in regard to the distribution of plants by the drifting of their seeds across the sea. Can any of your readers explain the following sentence by Linnaeus, pointed out to me by Dr. Hooker, "Fundus maris semina non destruit"? Why does Linnaeus say that the bottom of the sea does not destroy seeds? The seeds which are often washed by the Gulf Stream to the shores of Norway, with which Linnaeus was well acquainted, float, as I have lately tried. Did he imagine that seeds were drifted along the bottom of the ocean? This does not seem probable, from the currents of the sea, at least many of them, being superficial. P.S. In my communication on Charlock seed lately printed by you, there is a misprint of "6 plants" for "6 plots of ground," which makes nonsense of the sentence.

Darwin was intensely interested in the survival and germination of seeds under various conditions and frequently discussed this subject. His interest was related to the biogeography of plants and their dispersal on land or over water. Most of the plants mentioned are generally known but I note that: "Orache" includes the many species of the genus *Atriplex,* which includes the greasewood and saltbush of our west; *Ageratum mexicanum* is a tropical American aster; "evergreens" here was later corrected as a peculiar misprint for *Euonymus,* a large group of plants with medicinal bark many of which are literally evergreens but not conifers. The reference in the last sentence is to a previous note in the same journal the point of which was that seeds of charlock had germinated after long burial in damp soil. Charlock is an old name for wild mustard. In a later, more technical paper read to (in 1856) and published by (in 1857) the Linnean Society, Darwin reported extensive experiments, jointly with the Reverend M. J. Berkeley, in which seeds of some of the many species tested germinated after more than a hundred days in sea water.

Here is a note published in the *Gardeners' Chronicle and Agricultural Gazette* of June 9, 1860.

I should be extremely much obliged to any person living where the Bee or Fly Orchis is tolerably common, if he will have the kindness to make a few simple observations on their manner of fertilisation. To render the subject clear to those who know nothing of botany, I must briefly describe what takes place in our common British Orchids. The pollen-grains form two pear-shaped masses; each borne on a foot-stalk, with a sticky gland at the end. The pollen masses are hidden in little pouches open in front. When an insect visits a flower, it almost necessarily, owing to the position of the parts, uncovers and touches the sticky glands. These firmly adhere to the head or body of the insect, and thus the pollen-masses are drawn out of their pouches, are dragged over the humid stigmatic surface, and the plant is fertilised. So beautifully are the relative degrees of adhesiveness of the gland, and of the grains of pollen to each other and to the stigmatic surface mutually adapted, that an insect with an adherent pollen-mass will drag it over the stigmas of several flowers, and leave granules of pollen on each. The contrivance by which the sticky glands are prevented from drying, and so kept always viscid and ready for action, is even still more curious; they lie suspended (at least in the two species which I have examined) in a little hemispherical cup, full of liquid, and formed of such delicate membrance, that the side projecting over the gangway into the nectary is ruptured transversely and depressed by the slightest touch; and then the glands, sticky and fresh out of their bath, immediately and almost inevitably come into contact with and adhere to the body which has just ruptured the cup. It is certain that with most of our common Orchids insects are absolutely necessary for their fertilisation; for without their agency, the pollen-masses are never removed and wither within their pouches. I have proved this in the case of *Orchis morio* and *mascula* by covering up plants under a bell-glass, leaving other adjoining plants uncovered; in the latter I found every morning, as the flowers became fully expanded, some of the pollen masses removed, whereas in the plants under the glass all the pollen-masses remained enclosed in their pouches.

Robert Brown, however, has remarked that the fact of all the capsules in a dense spike of certain Orchids producing seed seems hardly reconcileable with their fertilisation having been accidentally effected by insects. But I could give many facts showing how effectually insects do their work; two cases will here suffice; in a plant of *Orchis maculata* with 44 flowers open, the 12 upper ones, which were not quite mature, had not one pollen-mass removed, whereas every one of the 32 lower flowers had one or both pollen-masses removed; in a plant of *Gymnadenia conopsea* with 54 open flowers, 52 had their pollen-masses removed. I have repeatedly observed in various Orchids grains of pollen, and in one case *three* whole pollen-masses on the stigmatic surface of a flower, which still retained its own two pollen-masses; and as often, or even oftener, I have found flowers with the pollen-masses removed, but with no pollen on their stigmas. These facts clearly show that each flower is often, or even generally, fertilised by the pollen brought by insects from another flower or plant. I may add that after observing our Orchids during many years, I have never seen a bee or any other diurnal insect (excepting once a butterfly) visit them; therefore I have no doubt that moths are the priests who perform the marriage ceremony. The structure, indeed, of some Orchids leads to this same conclusion; for no insect without a very long and extremely fine proboscis could possibly reach the nectar at the bottom of the extremely long and narrow nectary of the Butterfly-Orchis; and entomologists have occasionally captured moths with pollen-masses adhering to them. If any entomologist reads this, and can remember positively having caught a moth thus furnished, I hope he will give its name, and describe exactly to which part of the moth's body the sticky gland adhered.

We may now turn to the genus Ophrys; in the Fly Orchis *(Ophrys muscifera)*, the pollen-masses, furnished with sticky glands, do not naturally fall out of their pouches, nor can they be shaken out; so that insect-agency is necessary, as with the species of the other genera, for their fertilisation. But insects here do their work far less effectually than with common Orchids; during several years, previously to 1858, I kept a record of the state of the pollen-masses in well-opened flowers of those plants which I examined, and out of 102 flowers I found either one or both pollen-masses removed in only 13 flowers. But in 1858 I found 17 plants growing near each other and bearing 57 flowers and of these 30 flowers had one or both pollen-masses removed; and as all the remaining 27 flowers were the upper and younger flowers, they probably would subsequently have had most of their pollen-masses removed, and thus have been fertilised. I should much like to hear how the case stands with the Fly Orchis in other districts; for it seems a strange fact that a plant should grow pretty well, as it does in this part of Kent, and yet during several years seldom be fertilised.

We now come to the Bee Orchis *(Ophrys apifera)*, which presents a very different case; the pollen masses are furnished with sticky glands, but differently from in all the foregoing Orchids, they naturally fall out of their pouches; and from being of the proper length, though still retained at the gland-end, they fall on the stigmatic surface, and the plant is thus self-fertilised. During several years I have examined many flowers, and never in a single instance found even one of the pollen-masses carried away by insects, or ever saw the flower's own pollen-masses fail to fall on the stigma. Robert Brown consequently believed that the visits of insects would be injurious to the fertilisation of this Orchis; and rather fancifully imagined that the flower resembled a bee in order to deter their visits. We must admit that the natural falling out of the pollen-masses of this Orchis is a special contrivance for its self-fertilisation; and as far as my experience goes, a perfectly successful contrivance, for I have always found this plant self-fertilised; nevertheless a long course of observation has made me greatly doubt whether the flowers of any kind of plant are for a perpetuity of generations fertilised by their own pollen. And what are we to say with respect to the sticky glands of the Bee Orchis, the use and efficiency of which glands in all other British Orchids are so manifest? Are we to conclude that this one species is provided with these organs for no use? I cannot think so; but would rather infer that, during some years or in some other districts, insects do visit the Bee Orchis and occasionally transport pollen from one flower to another, and thus give it the advantage of an occasional cross. We have seen that the Fly Orchis is not in this part of the country by any means sufficiently often visited by insects, though the visits of insects are indispensable to its fertilisation. So with the Bee Orchis, though its self-fertilisation is specially provided for, it may not exist here under the most favourable conditions of life; and in other districts or during particular seasons it may be visited by insects, and in this case, as its pollen masses are furnished with sticky glands, it would almost certainly receive the benefit of an occasional cross impregnation. It is this curious apparent contradiction in the structure of the Bee Orchis—one part, namely the sticky glands, being adapted for fertilisation by insect agency—another part, namely the natural falling out of the pollen-masses, being adapted for self-fertilisation without insect agency—which makes me anxious to hear what happens to the pollen-masses of the Bee Orchis in other districts or parts of England. I should be extremely much obliged to any one who will take the trouble to observe this point and to communicate the result to the *Gardeners' Chronicle* or to me.

This note was written while Darwin was working on his book on the fertilization of orchids and on cross-fertilization. It exemplifies one way in which Darwin repeatedly sought all available information on subjects of his researches. It is also an example of his clear and simple exposition when writing for nonspecialized readers. The Robert Brown mentioned had published a paper on "fecundation in the Orchideae and Asclepiadae' (orchids and milkweeds) in the *Transactions of the Linnean Society*.

The following pages are excerpts from a paper, "On the Two Forms, or Dimorphic Condition, in the Species of *Primula,* and on Their Remarkable Sexual Relations," read to the Linnean Society in 1861 and published in its transactions in 1862.

If a large number of Primroses or Cowslips *(P. vulgaris* and *veris)* be gathered, they will be found to consist, in about equal numbers, of two forms, obviously differing in the length of their pistils and stamens. Florists who cultivate the Polyanthus and Auricula are well aware of this difference, and call those which display the globular stigma at the mouth of the corolla "pin-headed" or "pin-eyed," and those which display the stamens "thumb-eyed." I will designate the two forms as long-styled and short-styled. Those botanists with whom I have spoken on the subject have looked at the case as one of mere variability, which is far from the truth.

In the Cowslip, in the long-styled form, the stigma projects just above the tube of the corolla, and is externally visible; it stands high above the anthers, which are situated halfway down the tube, and cannot be easily seen. In the short-styled form the anthers are attached at the mouth of the tube, and therefore stand high above the stigma; for the pistil is short, not rising above halfway up the tubular corolla. The corolla itself is of a different shape in the two forms, the throat or expanded portion above the attachment of the anthers being much longer in the long-styled than in the short-styled form. Village children notice this difference, as they can best make necklaces by threading and slipping the corollas of the long-styled flowers into each other. But there are much more important differences. The stigma in the long-styled plants is globular, in the short-styled it is depressed on the summit, so that the longitudinal axis of the former is sometimes nearly double that of the latter. The shape, however, is in some degree variable; but one difference is persistent, namely, that the stigma of the long-styled is much rougher: in some specimens carefully compared, the papillae which render the stigmas rough were in the long-styled form from twice to thrice as long as in the short-styled. There is another and more remarkable difference, namely, in the size of the pollen-grains. I measured with the micrometer many specimens, dry and wet, taken from plants growing in different situations, and always found a palpable difference. The measurement is best made with grains distended with water, in which case, the usual size of the grains from short-styled flowers is seen to be 10–11/7000 of an inch in diameter, and those from the longstyled about 7/7000 of an inch, which is in the proportion of three to two; so that the pollen-grains from the short stamens are plainly smaller than those from the long stamens which accompany the short pistil. When examined dry, the smaller grains from the long-styled plants are seen under a low power to be more transparent than the larger grains, and apparently in a greater degree than can be accounted for by their less diameter. There is also a difference in shape, the grains from the short-styled plants being nearly spherical, those from the long-styled being oblong with the angles rounded; this difference in shape disappears when the grains are distended with water. Lastly, as we shall presently see, the short-styled plants produce more seed than the long-styled.

To sum up the differences:—The long-styled plants have a much longer pistil, with a globular and much rougher stigma, standing high above the anthers. The stamens are short; the grains of pollen smaller and oblong in shape. The upper half of the corolla is more expanded. The number of seeds produced is smaller.

The short-styled plants have a short pistil, half the length of the tube of the corolla, with a smooth depressed stigma standing beneath the anthers. The stamens are long; the grains of pollen are spherical and larger. The tube of the corolla is of the same diameter till close to its upper end. The number of seeds produced is larger.

I have examined a large number of flowers; and though the shape of the stigma and the length of the pistil vary, especially in the short-styled form, I have never seen any transitional grades between the two forms. There is never the slightest doubt under which form to class a plant. I have never seen the two forms on the same plant. I marked many

Cowslips and Primroses, and found, the following year, that all retained the same character, as did some in my garden which flowered out of their proper season in the autumn. Mr. W. Wooler, of Darlington, however, informs us that he has seen the early blossoms on Polyanthuses which were not long-styled, but which later in the season produced flowers of this form. Possibly the pistils may not in these cases have become fully developed during the early spring. An excellent proof of the permanence of the two forms is seen in nursery gardens, where choice varieties of the Polyanthus are propagated by division; and I found whole beds of several varieties, each consisting exclusively of the one or the other form. The two forms exist in the wild state in about equal numbers; I collected from several different stations, taking every plant which grew on each spot, 522 umbels; 241 were long-styled, and 281 short-styled. No difference in tint or size could be perceived in the two great masses of flowers.

I examined many cultivated Cowslips (*P. veris*) or Polyanthuses, and Oxlips; and the two forms always presented the same differences, including the same relative difference in the size of the pollen-grains.

Primula Auricula presents the two forms; but amongst the improved fancy kinds the long-styled are rare, as these are less valued by florists, and seldomer distributed. There is a much greater relative inequality in the length of the pistils and stamens than in the Cowslip, the pistil in the long-styled form being nearly four times as long as in the short-styled, in which it is barely longer than the ovarium; the stigma is nearly of the same shape in both forms, but it is rougher in the long-styled, though the difference is not so great as in the two forms of the Cowslip. In the long-styled plants the stamens are very short, rising but little above the ovarium. The pollen-grains of these short stamens from the long-styled plants, when distended with water, were barely 5/6000 of an inch in diameter, whereas those from the long stamens of the short-styled plants were barely 7/6000, showing a relative difference of five to seven. The smaller grains of the long-styled plants were much more transparent, and before distention with water more triangular in outline than those of the other form. In one anomalous specimen with a long pistil, the stamens almost surrounded the stigma, so that they occupied the position proper to the stamens of the short-styled form; but the small size of the pollen-grains showed that these stamens had been abnormally developed in length, and that the anthers ought to have stood at the base of the corolla.

In the two forms of *Primula Sinensis*, the pistil is about twice as long in the one as in the other. The stigma of the long-styled varies much in shape, but is considerably more elongated and rougher than that of the short-styled, the latter being nearly smooth and spherical, but depressed on the summit. The shape of the throat of the corolla in the two forms differs as in the Cowslip, as does the length of the stamens. But it is remarkable that the pollen-grains of both forms, wet and dry, presented no difference in diameter; they vary somewhat in size, as do the pollen-grains of all the species, but in both forms the average diameter was rather above 10/6000 of an inch. There is one remarkable difference in the two forms of this species, namely (as we shall presently more fully see), that the short-styled plants, if insects be excluded and there be no artificial fertilization, are quite sterile, whereas the long-styled produce a moderate quantity of seed. But when both forms are properly fertilized, the short-styled flowers (as with Cowslips) yield more seed than the long-styled. In a lot of seedlings which I raised, there were thirteen long-styled and seven short-styled plants.

Of *Primula ciliata* a long-styled specimen, and of *P. ciliata,* var. *purpurpata,* a short-styled specimen, were sent me from Kew by Prof. Oliver. This case, however, is hardly worth giving, as the variety *purpurata* is said to be a hybrid between this species and *P. auricula;* and the height of the stamens in the one form does not correspond with the height of the stigma in the other, as they would have done had they been the same species. There was, however, the usual difference in the roughness of the stigmas in the two forms, and the pollen-grains, distended in water, measured 6/6000 and 4–5/6000 of an inch in diameter. Single trusses were sent me of *P. denticulata* and *P. Piedmontana* which were long-styled, and of *P. marginata* and *nivalis* which were short-styled; and the general character of the organs leaves hardly any doubt on my mind that these species are dimorphic. In a single flower of *P. Sibirica,* however, which was sent me from Kew, the stigma reached up to the base of the anthers; so that this species is not dimorphic, or not dimorphic as far as the length of the pistil and stamens are concerned, unless indeed this single specimen was anomalous, like that mentioned of *P. Auricula.*

We thus see that the existence of two forms is very general, if not universal, in the genus *Primula.* The simple fact of the pollen-grains differing in size and outline, and the stigma, in shape and roughness, in two sets of individuals of the same species, is curious. But what, it may be asked, is the meaning of these several differences? The question seems worthy of careful investigation, for, as far as I know, the use or meaning of dimorphism in plants has never been explained; hence, I will give my observations in detail, though I am far from supposing that all cases of dimorphism are alike. The first idea which naturally occurred was, that the species were tending towards a dioicous condition; that the long-styled plants, with their rougher stigmas, were more feminine in nature, and would produce more seed; that the short-styled plants, with their long stamens and larger pollen-grains, were more masculine in nature. . . .

We here have a case new, as far as I know, in the animal and vegetable kingdoms. We see the species of *Primula* divided into two sets or bodies, which cannot be called distinct sexes, for both are hermaphrodites; yet they are to a certain extent sexually distinct, for they require for perfect fertility reciprocal union. They might perhaps be called sub-dioicous hermaphrodites. As quadrupeds are divided into two nearly equal bodies

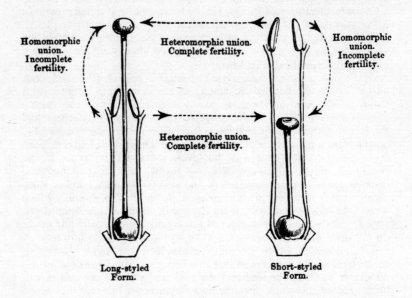

This woodcut was Figure 2 in a paper by Darwin on the dimorphic condition of the species of *Primula* (a genus of primroses) published by the Linnean Society in 1861. The legend was simply "heteromorphic and homomorphic unions." The point, as discussed in the accompanying text, is that in a single species of these plants the flowers are of two kinds (dimorphic). All the flowers are bisexual, that is, each produces both pollen (male) and ovules (female) in a single flower. In one of the morphs, at left in this figure, the style terminating in the stigma with ovules is long, but the stamens, which carry the anthers and produce pollen (male) are short. In the other, right in this figure, the style is short and the anthers are long. In both, self-fertilization or fertilization between flowers of the same morph (homomorphic) is possible but fertility is incomplete. However, fertilization between a long-styled and a short-styled flower, heteromorphic, is usual and is highly fertile. Darwin makes the point that in spite of the fact that these flowers are bisexual they are functionally almost dioecious ("dioicous" in the text, perhaps a misprint) or unisexual (each flower on each plant producing either ovules or pollen and not both).

of different sexes, so here we have two bodies, approximately equal in number, differing in their sexual powers and related to each other like males and females. There are many hermaphrodite animals which cannot fertilize themselves, but must unite with another hermaphrodite: so it is with numerous plants; for the pollen is often mature and shed, or is mechanically protruded, before the flower's own stigma is ready; so that these hermaphrodite flowers absolutely require for their sexual union the presence of another hermaphrodite. But in *Primula* there is this wide difference, that one individual Cowslip, for instance, though it can with mechanical aid imperfectly fertilize itself, for full fertility must unite with another individual; but it cannot unite with any individual in the same manner as an hermaphrodite Snail or Earth-worm can unite with any other one Snail or Earth-worm; but one form of the Cowslip, to be perfectly fertile, must unite with one of the other form, just as a male quadruped must and can unite only with a female.

I have spoken of the heteromorphic union in *Primula* as resulting in full fertility; and I am fully justified, for the Cowslips thus fertilized actually gave rather more seed than the truly wild plants—a result which may be attributed to their good treatment and having grown separately. With respect to the lessened fertility of the homomorphic unions, we shall appreciate its degree best by the following facts. Gärtner has estimated the degree of sterility of the union of several distinct species, in a manner which allows of the strictest comparison with the result of the heteromorphic and homomorphic unions of *Primula*. With *P. veris,* for every hundred seeds yielded by the heteromorphic unions, only sixty-four seeds were yielded by an equal number of good capsules from the homomorphic unions. With *P. Sinensis* the proportion was nearly the same—namely, as 100 to 62. Now Gärtner has shown that, on the calculation of *Verbascum lychnitis* yielding with its own pollen 100 seeds, it yields when fertilized by the pollen of *V. Phoeniceum* ninety seeds; by the pollen of *V. nigrum,* sixty-three seeds; by that of *V. blattaria,* sixty-two seeds. So again, *Dianthus barbatus* fertilized by the pollen of *D. superbus* yielded eighty-one seeds, and by the pollen of *D. Japonicus* sixty-six seeds, relatively to the 100 seeds reproduced by its own pollen. Thus we see—and the fact is highly remarkable—that the homomorphic unions relatively to the heteromorphic unions in *Primula* are more sterile than the crosses between several distinct species relatively to the pure union of those species.

The meaning or use of the existence in *Primula* in the two forms in about equal numbers, with their pollen adapted for reciprocal union, is tolerably plain; namely, to favour the intercrossing of distinct individuals. With plants there are innumerable contrivances for this end; and no one will understand the final cause of the structure of many flowers without attending to this point. I have already shown that the relative heights of the anthers and stigmas in the two forms lead to insects leaving the pollen of the one form on the stigma of the other; but, at the same time, there will be a strong probability of the flower's own pollen being likewise placed on the stigma. It is perfectly well known that if the pollen of several closely allied species be placed on the stigma of a distinct species, and at the same time, or even subsequently, its own pollen be placed on the stigma, this will entirely destroy the simultaneous or previous action of the foreign pollen. So again if the pollen of several varieties, including the plant's own pollen, be placed on the stigma, one or more of the varieties will take the lead and obliterate the effect of the others: but I have not space here to give the facts on which this conclusion is grounded. Hence we may infer as highly probable that, in *Primula,* the heteromorphic pollen which we know to be so much the most effective would obliterate the action of the homomorphic pollen when left on the flower's own stigma by insects; and thus we see how potent the dimorphic condition of the pollen in *Primula* will be in favouring the intercrossing of distinct individuals. The two forms, though both sexes are present in each, are in fact dioicous or unisexual. Whatever advantage there may be in the separation of the sexes, towards which we see so frequent a tendency throughout nature, this advantage has been here so far gained, that the one form is fertilized by the other, and conversely; and this is effected by the pollen of each form having less potency than that of the other on its own stigma.

Bearing on this view of the final cause of the dimorphism of the *Primulas,* there is another curious point. If we look at the right-hand figures of the four first lines in the previous tables of *P. Sinensis* and *veris* [omitted here], we shall see that one of the homomorphic unions, namely, the short-styled by its own-form pollen, is considerably more sterile than the other; and in *P. auricula,* though here there is no other homomorphic union as a standard of comparison, this union is likewise excessively sterile. That the fertility of this union is really less in a marked degree than in the other three unions, we have an independent proof in the seeds germinating less perfectly and much more slowly than those from the other unions. This fact is the more remarkable, because we have clearly seen that the short-styled form in the Cowslip in a state of nature is the most productive of seed. This form bears its anthers close together at the mouth of the corolla, and I observed long before I had ascertained the relative fertility of the four unions, in passing the proboscis of a dead Humble-bee or bristle down the corolla, that in this form the flower's own pollen was almost certain to be left on its own stigma; and, as I wrote down at the time, the chance of self-fertilization is much stronger in this than in the other form. On this view we can at once understand the good of the pollen of the short-styled form, relatively to its own stigma, being the most sterile; for this sterility would be the most requisite to check self-fertilization, or to favour intercrossing. Hence, also, it would appear that there are four grades of fertility from the four possible unions in *Primula;* of the two homomorphic unions, as we have just seen, one is considerably more sterile than the other. In the wild state we know that the short-styled plants are more fertile than the long-styled; and we may infer as almost certain, that in the wild state, when the flowers are visited by insects, as is absolutely necessary for the production of seed, and when pollen is freely carried from one form to the other, that the unions are heteromorphic; if so, there are two degrees of fertility in the heteromorphic unions, making altogether four grades of fertility.

Two or three other points deserve a passing notice. The question whether the Primrose and Cowslip (*P. vulgaris* and *veris*) are distinct species or varieties has been more disputed and experimented on than in any other plant. But as we now know that the visits of insects are indispensable to the fertilization of these plants, and that in all probability the heteromorphic pollen of a Primrose would be prepotent on the stigma of a Cowslip over the homomorphic pollen of a Cowslip, the numerous experiments which have been made, showing that Oxlips appear amongst the seedlings of Cowslips, cannot be trusted, as the parent plants do not appear to have been carefully protected from insects. I am far from wishing to affirm that pure Cowslips will not produce Oxlips, but further experiments are absolutely necessary. We may also suspect that the fact noticed by florists, that the varieties of the Polyanthus never come true from seed, may be *in part* due to their habitually crossing with other varieties of the Polyanthus.

The simple fact of two individuals of the same undoubted species, when homomorphically united, being as sterile as are many distinct species when crossed, will surprise those who look at sterility as a special endowment to keep created species distinct. Hybridizers have shown that individual plants of the same species vary in their sexual powers, so far that one individual will unite more readily than another individual of the same species with a distinct species. Seeing that we thus have a groundwork of variability in sexual power, and seeing that sterility of a peculiar kind has been acquired by the species of *Primula* to favour intercrossing, those who believe in the slow modification of specific forms will naturally ask themselves whether sterility may not have been slowly acquired for a distinct object, namely, to prevent two forms, whilst being fitted for distinct lines of life, becoming blended by marriage, and thus less well adapted for their new habits of life. But many great difficulties would remain, even if this view could be maintained.

Whether or not the dimorphic condition of the *Primulae* has any bearing on other points in natural history, it is valuable as showing how nature strives, if I may so express myself, to favour the sexual union of distinct individuals of the same species. The resources of nature are illimitable; and we know not why the species of *Primula* should have acquired this novel and curious aid for checking continued self-fertilization through the division of the individuals into two bodies of hermaphrodites with different sexual powers, instead of by the more common method of the separation of the sexes, or by the maturity of the male and female elements at different periods, or by other such contrivances. Nor do we know why nature should thus strive after the intercrossing of distinct individuals. We do not even in the least know the final cause of sexuality; why new beings should be produced by the union of the two sexual elements, instead of by a process of parthenogenesis. When we look to the state in which young mammals and birds are born, we can at least see that the object gained is not, as has sometimes been maintained, mere dissemination. The whole subject is as yet hidden in darkness.

In these excerpts one figure and eleven tables with statistical data on fertilization and seed production along with lengthy descriptions of procedures and results have been omitted here. The conclusions and interpretations are soundly based on those data and are clearly and interestingly covered by the excerpts here republished. The example shows Darwin as meticulous in observation and experimentation and as both logical and cautious in drawing conclusions. He states what he knows and can scientifically interpret, and he also states what he cannot, in this stage of knowledge, reasonably interpret. The points that still baffled him, notably regarding the origin and significance of sex, have been largely explained by genetical studies since his death.

Polyanthus and auricula are plants closely related or belonging to the primrose genus *Primula*. The common British primrose is *Primula veris,* there called a cowslip. The name oxlip was given to a different species of *Primula* or to some florists' hybrid primroses.

While Darwin was working intensely on fertilization and reproduction in plants, especially orchids and primroses but also a number of other groups, a young man named John Scott (1838–80) wrote him about those subjects in 1862. This initiated an exchange of correspondence that went on into the 1870s. Apart from technical points that they discussed, Darwin's letters to Scott reveal another side of his character: as a Nestor to a neophyte. This is illustrated by the following two extracts from Darwin's letters:

Down, Dec. 11th [1862].
I have read your paper with much interest. You ask for remarks on the matter, which is alone really important. Shall you think me impertinent (I am sure I do not mean to be so) if I hazard a remark on the style, which is of more importance than some think? In my opinion (whether or no worth much) your paper would have been much better if written more simply and less elaborated—more like your letters. It is a golden rule always to use, if possible, a short old Saxon word. Such a sentence as "so purely dependent is the incipient plant on the specific morphological tendency" does not sound to my ears like good mother-English—it

wants translating. Here and there you might, I think, have condensed some sentences. I go on the plan of thinking every single word which can be omitted without actual loss of sense as a decided gain. Now perhaps you will think me a meddling intruder: anyhow, it is the advice of an old hackneyed writer who sincerely wishes you well. Your remark on the two sexes counteracting variability in product of the one is new to me. But I cannot avoid thinking that there is something unknown and deeper in seminal generation. Reflect on the long succession of embryological changes in every animal. Does a bud ever produce cotyledons or embryonic leaves? I have been much interested by your remark on inheritance at corresponding ages; I hope you will, as you say, continue to attend to this. Is it true that female *Primula* plants always produce females by parthenogenesis? If you can answer this I should be glad; it bears on my *Primula* work. I thought on the subject, but gave up investigating what had been observed, because the female bee by parthenogenesis produces males alone. Your paper has told me much that in my ignorance was quite new to me. Thanks about *P. scotica*. If any important criticisms are made on the *Primula* to the Botanical Society, I should be glad to hear them. If you think fit, you may state that I repeated the crossing experiments on *P. sinensis* and cowslip with the same result this spring as last year—indeed, with rather more marked difference in fertility of the two crosses. In fact, had I then proved the *Linum* case, I would not have wasted time in repetition. I am determined I will at once publish on *Linum* . . .[1]

John Scott, a self-educated son of a farmer, early orphaned, was born in 1838, and was thus Darwin's junior by twenty-nine years. He was twenty-four years old and Darwin fifty-three when their correspondence started. Scott died in 1880, two years before Darwin. In 1862 Scott was working as a gardener in the botanical gardens at Edinburgh.

P. sinensis is another primrose, a Chinese species of *Primula*. *Linum* here mentioned as having been studied by Darwin and adding to his results with *Primula,* is a genus of flax and Darwin did soon publish on it.

Down, June 6th, 1863.
I fear that you think that I have done more than I have with respect to Dr. Hooker. I did not feel that I had any right to ask him to remember you for a colonial appointment: all that I have done is to speak most highly of your scientific merits. Of course this may hereafter fructify. I really think you cannot go on better, for educational purposes, than you are now doing,—observing, thinking, and some reading beat, in my opinion, all systematic education. Do not despair about your style; your letters are excellently written, your scientific style is a little too ambitious. I never study style; all that I do is to try to get the subject as clear

as I can in my own head, and express it in the commonest language which occurs to me. But I generally have to think a good deal before the simplest arrangement and words occur to me. Even with most of our best English writers, writing is slow work; it is a great evil, but there is no help for it. I am sure you have no cause to despair. I hope and suppose your sending a paper to the Linnean Society will not offend your Edinburgh friends; you might truly say that you sent the paper to me, and that (if it turns out so) I thought it worth communicating to the Linnean Society. I shall feel great interest in studying all your facts on *Primula,* when they are worked out and the seed counted. Size of capsules is often very deceptive. I am astonished how you can find time to make so many experiments. If you like to send me your paper tolerably well written, I would look it over and suggest any criticisms; but then this would cause you extra copying. Remember, however, that Lord Brougham habitually wrote everything important three times over. The cases of the *Primulæ* which lose by variation their dimorphic characters seem to me very interesting. I find that the mid-styled (by variation) *P. sinensis* is more fertile with own pollen, even, than a heteromorphic union! If you have time it will be very good to experiment on *Linum Lewisii.* I wrote formerly to Asa Gray begging for seed. If you have time, I think experiments on any peloric flowers would be useful. I shall be sorry (and I am certain it is a mistake on the part of the Society) if your orchid paper is not printed *in extenso.* I am now at work compiling all such cases, and shall give a very full abstract of all your observations. I hope to add in autumn some from you on *Passiflora.* I would suggest to you the advantage, at present, of being very sparing in introducing theory in your papers (I formerly erred much in Geology in that way): *let theory guide your observations,* but till your reputation is well established be sparing in publishing theory. It makes persons doubt your observations. How rarely R. Brown ever indulged in theory: too seldom perhaps! Do not work too hard, and do not be discouraged because your work is not appreciated by the majority.[2]

The opening three sentences refer to Scott's hope of getting away from a menial job in Scotland and perhaps to a more scientific position in the colonies of the then British Empire. In fact Darwin had written to Hooker, who had become a famous and influential botanist, strongly recommending Scott. Among things Darwin had written to Hooker about Scott were the statements that, "If he had leisure he would make a wonderful observer; to my judgment I have come across no one like him," and again, "I know nothing of him except from his letters; these show remarkable talent, astonishing perseverance, much modesty, and what I admire, determined difference from me on many points." Darwin's respect for Scott was instrumental in Hooker's obtaining for him an appointment in the Calcutta Botanic Garden in 1864. Darwin paid for Scott's voyage to India, and he refused to accept repayment later offered by Scott.

This letter of advice to a man younger than Darwin's first son is incidentally enlightening about Darwin's own attitude toward writing and theorizing. It is also still good advice for aspiring young scientists beginning their careers. In his next letter to Scott Darwin added the following good advice to a young scientist from an eminent one:

> By no means modify even in the slightest degree any [experimental or observational] result. Accuracy is the soul of Natural History. It is hard to become accurate; he who modifies a hair's breadth will never be accurate. It is a golden rule, which I try to follow, to put every fact which is opposed to one's preconceived opinion in the strongest light. Absolute accuracy is the hardest merit to attain, and the highest merit. Any deviation is ruin.

(Antievolutionists and among evolutionists those to some degree anti-Darwinian should take these admonitions to heart!)

References to *Primula* and *Linum* were sufficiently annotated in previous comments. *Passiflora* is a group of tropical, mainly American plants which include the passionflower. "Peloric" means appearance of regularity or symmetry in flowers usually irregular or asymmetrical. In this context *Primula,* which with respect to most flowers is abnormal (unusual) in respect to cross- or self-fertilization, is peloric in the relatively rare cases where it has the more usual arrangement.

Asa Gray was the most eminent American botanist of his century and a strong supporter of Darwin and Darwinism.

The Lord Brougham mentioned in this letter is Baron Brougham and Vaux (1778–1868), a famous jurist and politician. Although referred to in the past tense, he was still living when Darwin wrote this letter. In spite of his writing things "three times over" his style was considered "slovenly" by critics. The vehicle brougham was named for him. "R. Brown," also mentioned here on a previous page, is Robert Brown (1773–1858), librarian and later president of the Linnean Society. He was a botanist but he is remembered also as the discoverer and eponym of the Brownian movement of microscopic particles in a liquid.

Darwin's remark about having "formerly erred much in Geology" by youthfully introducing a theory that later was falsified certainly refers to his long paper on the "parallel roads" of Glen Roy in Scotland, published in the *Philosophical Transactions of the Royal Society* in 1839. These "roads" are wave-cut terraces which Darwin argued were indications that the sea was at these levels when they were formed. It was later found beyond doubt that they were beaches of a lake dammed by a high continental glacier. This was the most serious error Darwin ever made. He was so appalled by it that ever after he sought to obtain every possible observation, *both pro and con,* pertinent to a hypothesis or theory before publication. That was one of the factors in his long delay in publishing on evolution and natural selection until the amassed evidence was overwhelming, and none was contrary to his major conclusions.

In addition to the studies of plants that have been briefly exemplified in this chapter it should be noted that Darwin later followed these with studies on related or similar characteristics and activities of plants, all published by Murray: two books in 1875, and one each in 1876, 1877 and 1880. These are listed in the appendix. In the 1860s he was also gathering materials for *The Descent of Man,* to be considered in the next chapter, and for *The Expression of the Emotions in Man and Animals.*

The following excerpts from Darwin's autobiography sum up his work on plants in the period just reviewed here and later in the last years of his life.

On May 15th, 1862, my little book on the 'Fertilisation of Orchids,' which cost me ten months' work, was published: most of the facts had been slowly accumulated during several previous years. During the summer of 1839, and, I believe, during the previous summer, I was led to attend to the cross-fertilisation of flowers by the aid of insects, from having come to the conclusion in my speculations on the origin of species, that crossing played an important part in keeping specific forms constant. I attended to the subject more or less during every subsequent summer; and my interest in it was greatly enhanced by having procured and read in November 1841, through the advice of Robert Brown, a copy of C. K. Sprengel's wonderful book, 'Das entdeckte Geheimniss der Natur.' For some years before 1862 I had specially attended to the fertilisation of our British orchids; and it seemed to me the best plan to prepare as complete a treatise on this group of plants as well as I could, rather than to utilise the great mass of matter which I had slowly collected with respect to other plants.

My resolve proved a wise one; for since the appearance of my book, a surprising number of papers and separate works on the fertilisation of all kinds of flowers have appeared: and these are far better done than I could possibly have effected. The merits of poor old Sprengel, so long overlooked, are now fully recognised many years after his death.

During the same year I published in the 'Journal of the Linnean Society' a paper "On the Two Forms, or Dimorphic Condition of Primula," and during the next five years, five other papers on dimorphic and trimorphic plants. I do not think anything in my scientific life has given me so much satisfaction as making out the meaning of the structure of these plants. I had noticed in 1838 or 1839 the dimorphism of *Linum flavum,* and had at first thought that it was merely a case of unmeaning variability. But on examining the common species of Primula I found that the two forms were much too regular and constant to be thus viewed. I therefore became almost convinced that the common cowslip and primrose were on the high road to become diœcious;—that the short pistil in the one form, and the short stamens in the other form were tending towards abortion. The plants were therefore subjected under this point of view to trial; but as soon as the flowers with short pistils fertilised with pollen from the short stamens, were found to yield more seeds than any other of the four possible unions, the abortion-theory was knocked on the head. After some additional experiment, it became evident that the two forms, though both were perfect hermaphrodites, bore almost the same relation to one another as do the two sexes of an ordinary animal. With Lythrum we have the still more wonderful case of three forms standing in a similar relation to one another. I afterwards found that the offspring from the union of two plants belonging to the same forms presented a close and curious analogy with hybrids from the union of two distinct species.

In the autumn of 1864 I finished a long paper on 'Climbing Plants,' and sent it to the Linnean Society. The writing of this paper cost me four months; but I was so unwell when I received the proof-sheets that I was forced to leave them very badly and often obscurely expressed. The paper was little noticed, but when in 1875 it was corrected and published as a separate book it sold well. I was led to take up this subject by reading a short paper by Asa Gray, published in 1858. He sent me seeds, and on raising some plants I was so much fascinated and perplexed by the revolving movements of the tendrils and stems, which movements are really very simple, though appearing at first sight very complex, that I procured various other kinds of climbing plants, and studied the whole subject. I was all the more attracted to it, from not being at all satisfied with the explanations which Henslow gave us in his lectures, about twining plants, namely, that they had a natural tendency to grow up in a spire. This explanation proved quite erroneous. Some of the adaptations displayed by Climbing Plants are as beautiful as those of Orchids for ensuring cross-fertilisation. . . .

In the summer of 1860 I was idling and resting near Hartfield, where two species of Drosera abound; and I noticed that numerous insects had been entrapped by the leaves. I carried home some plants, and on giving them insects saw the movements of the tentacles, and this made me think it probable that the insects were caught for some special purpose. Fortunately a crucial test occurred to me, that of placing a large number of leaves in various nitrogenous and non-nitrogenous fluids of equal density; and as soon as I found that the former alone excited energetic movements, it was obvious that here was a fine new field for investigation.

During subsequent years, whenever I had leisure, I pursued my experiments, and my book on 'Insectivorous Plants' was published in July 1875—that is, sixteen years after my first observations. The delay in this case, as with all my other books, has been a great advantage to me; for a man after a long interval can criticise his own work, almost as well as if it were that of another person. The fact that a plant should secrete, when properly excited, a fluid containing an acid and ferment, closely analogous to the digestive fluid of an animal, was certainly a remarkable discovery.

During this autumn of 1876 I shall publish on the 'Effects of Cross and Self-Fertilisation in the Vegetable Kingdom.' This book will form a complement to that on the 'Fertilisation of Orchids,' in which I showed how perfect were the means for cross-fertilisation, and here I shall show how important are the results. I was led to make, during eleven years, the numerous experiments recorded in this volume, by a mere accidental observation; and indeed it required the accident to be repeated before my attention was thoroughly aroused to the remarkable fact that seedlings of self-fertilised parentage are inferior, even in the first generation, in height and vigour to seedlings of cross-fertilised parentage. I hope also to republish a revised edition of my book on Orchids, and hereafter my papers on dimorphic and trimorphic plants, together with some additional observations on allied points which I never have had time to arrange. My strength will then probably be exhausted, and I shall be ready to exclaim "Nunc dimittis."

Written May 1st, 1881.—'The Effects of Cross and Self-Fertilisation' was published in the autumn of 1876; and the results there arrived at explain, as I believe, the endless and wonderful contrivances for the transportal of pollen from one plant to another of the same species. I now believe, however, chiefly from the observations of Hermann Müller, that I ought to have insisted more strongly than I did on the many adaptations for self-fertilisation; though I was well aware of many such adaptations. A much enlarged edition of my 'Fertilisation of Orchids' was published in 1877.

In this same year 'The Different Forms of Flowers, &c.,' appeared, and in 1880 a second edition. This book consists chiefly of the several papers on Heterostyled flowers originally published by the Linnean Society, corrected, with much new matter added, together with observations on some other cases in which the same plant bears two kinds of flowers. As before remarked, no little discovery of mine ever gave me so much pleasure as the making out the meaning of heterostyled flowers.

The results of crossing such flowers in an illegitimate manner, I believe to be very important, as bearing on the sterility of hybrids; although these results have been noticed by only a few persons. . . .

In 1880 I published, with [my son] Frank's assistance, our 'Power of Movement in Plants.' This was a tough piece of work. The book bears somewhat the same relation to my little book on 'Climbing Plants,' which 'Cross-Fertilisation' did to the 'Fertilisation of Orchids;' for in accordance with the principle of evolution it was impossible to account for climbing plants having been developed in so many widely different groups unless all kinds of plants possess some slight power of movement of an analogous kind. This I proved to be the case; and I was further led to a rather wide generalisation, viz. that the great and important classes of movements, excited by light, the attraction of gravity, &c., are all modified forms of the fundamental movement of circumnutation. It has always pleased me to exalt plants in the scale of organised beings; and I therefore felt an especial pleasure in showing how many and what admirably well adapted movements the tip of a root possesses.[3]

Robert Brown has previously been identified here. C. K. Sprengel is Christian Konrad Sprengel (1750–1816) and the "discovered secret of nature," so named in the German title of a book published before Darwin was born, was that insects often pollinate flowers. The study of *Primula* has been sufficiently noticed previously in this chapter and that on *Linum* mentioned. *Lythrum* is a genus of plants commonly called loosestrife. *Drosera* is the genus of sundews, fascinating plants which, like Venus' flytrap, catch and digest insects.

Just one more point may be made here about Darwin's many and prolonged studies of plants. In studying the movements of plants he found that their response to gravity depended only on the tip of a rootlet, although the effect was somehow transmitted to other parts. He wrote that "the tip of the radicle [being] thus endowed . . . acts like the brain of one of the lower animals." This excited disbelief and even scorn in some botanists but some thirty years later the essentials of Darwin's hypothesis were confirmed. However his simile still need not be taken quite literally.

9

The Descent of Man

Except for footnotes, which have been omitted, the following is the complete text of Darwin's Introduction to *The Descent of Man, and Selection in Relation to Sex,* published in 1871.

The nature of the following work will be best understood by a brief account of how it came to be written. During many years I collected notes on the origin or descent of man, without any intention of publishing on the subject, but rather with the determination not to publish, as I thought that I should thus only add to the prejudices against my views. It seemed to me sufficient to indicate, in the first edition of my 'Origin of Species,' that by this work "light would be thrown on the origin of man and his history;" and this implies that man must be included with other organic beings in any general conclusion respecting his manner of appearance on this earth. Now the case wears a wholly different aspect. When a naturalist like Carl Vogt ventures to say in his address as President of the National Institution of Geneva (1869), "personne, en Europe au moins, n'ose plus soutenir la création indépendante et de toutes pièces, des espèces," it is manifest that at least a large number of naturalists must admit that species are the modified descendants of other species; and this especially holds good with the younger and rising naturalists. The greater number accept the agency of natural selection; though some urge, whether with justice the future must decide, that I have greatly overrated its importance. Of the older and honoured chiefs in natural science, many unfortunately are still opposed to evolution in every form.

In consequence of the views now adopted by most naturalists, and which will ultimately, as in every other case, be followed by others who are not scientific, I have been led to put together my notes, so as to see how far the general conclusions arrived at in my former works were applicable to man. This seemed all the more desirable, as I had never deliberately applied these views to a species taken singly. When we confine our attention to any one form, we are deprived of the weighty arguments derived from the nature of the affinities which connect together whole groups of organisms—their geographical distribution in past and present times, and their geological succession. The homological structure, embryological development, and rudimentary organs of a species remain to be considered, whether it be man or any other animal, to which our attention may be directed; but these great classes of facts afford, as it appears to me, ample and conclusive evidence in favour of the principle of gradual evolution. The strong support derived from the other arguments should, however, always be kept before the mind.

The sole object of this work is to consider, firstly, whether man, like every other species, is descended from some pre-existing form; secondly, the manner of his development; and thirdly, the value of the differences between the so-called races of man. As I shall confine myself to these points, it will not be necessary to describe in detail the differences between the several races—an enormous subject which has been fully discussed in many valuable works. The high antiquity of man has recently been demonstrated by the labours of a host of eminent men, beginning with M. Boucher de Perthes; and this is the indispensable basis for understanding his origin. I shall, therefore, take this conclusion for granted, and may refer my readers to the admirable treatises of Sir Charles Lyell, Sir John Lubbock, and others. Nor shall I have occasion to do more than to allude to the amount of difference between man and the anthropomorphous apes; for Prof. Huxley, in the opinion of most competent judges, has conclusively shewn that in every visible character man differs less from the higher apes, than these do from the lower members of the same order of Primates.

This work contains hardly any original facts in regard to man; but as the conclusions at which I arrived, after drawing up a rough draft, appeared to me interesting, I thought that they might interest others. It has often and confidently been asserted, that man's origin can never be known: but ignorance more frequently begets confidence than does knowledge: it is those who know little, and not those who know much, who so positively assert that this or that problem will never be solved by science. The conclusion that man is the co-descendant with other species of some ancient, lower, and extinct form, is not in any degree new. Lamarck long ago came to this conclusion, which has lately been maintained by several eminent naturalists and philosophers; for instance, by Wallace, Huxley, Lyell, Vogt, Lubbock, Büchner, Rolle, &c., and especially by Häckel. This last naturalist, besides his great work, 'Generelle Morphologie' (1866), has recently (1868, with a second edit. in 1870), published his 'Natürliche Schöpfungsgeschichte,' in which he fully discusses the genealogy of man. If this work had appeared before my essay had been written, I should probably never have completed it. Almost all the conclusions at which I have arrived I find confirmed by this naturalist, whose knowledge on many points is much fuller than mine. Wherever I have added any fact or view from Prof. Häckel's writings, I give his authority in the text; other statements I leave as they originally stood in my manuscript, occasionally giving in the foot-notes references to his works, as a confirmation of the more doubtful or interesting points.

During many years it has seemed to me highly probable that sexual selection has played an important part in differentiating the races of man; but in my 'Origin of Species' I contented myself by merely alluding to this belief. When I came to apply this view to man, I found it indispensable to treat the whole subject in full detail. Consequently the second part of the present work, treating of sexual selection, has extended to an inordinate length, compared with the first part; but this could not be avoided.

I had intended adding to the present volumes an essay on the expression of the various emotions by man and the lower animals. My attention was called to this subject many years ago by Sir Charles Bell's admirable work. This illustrious anatomist maintains that man is endowed with certain muscles solely for the sake of expressing his emotions. As this view is obviously opposed to the belief that man is descended from some other and lower form, it was necessary for me to consider it. I likewise wished to ascertain how far the emotions are expressed in the same manner by the different races of man. But owing to the length of the present work, I have thought it better to reserve my essay for separate publication.

"Carl" (usually written Karl) Vogt (1817–95) was a German zoologist who had worked on fossil fishes with Louis Agassiz. The quotation from his 1869 address in Geneva can be translated from French as "No one, in Europe at least, any longer dares to support the creation of species just so." It is interesting that his former associate, the elder Agassiz, continued all his life to be a firm antievolutionist. Jacques Boucher de Crèvecoeur de Perthes (1788–1868), to give him his full, resounding name, is generally credited with the discovery of artifacts indicating that man already existed in the Pleistocene, but that in itself had no bearing on having evolved from still earlier primates. Charles Lyell and T. H. Huxley have been noticed previously, Sir John Lubbock (1834–1913), who became the first Baron Avebury, was primarily a politician but he wrote popular books on natural history, including one in 1870, *The Origin of Civilization and the Primitive*

Condition of Man. Friedrich Karl Christian Ludwig Büchner (1824–99) was a physician and philosopher. I have not been able to place Rolle more precisely than Darwin does in a footnote styling him as Dr. F. Rolle and author of an 1869 book in German on mankind in the light of Darwinian doctrine.

Ernst Henrich Häckel, commonly spelled Haeckel, (1834–1919) was the most effusive and positive of all followers of Darwin. It now seems odd to find Darwin here taking him as superior in knowledge on some "doubtful or interesting points." In the present longer retrospect it seems that Haeckel tended to carry Darwinism to a fault, concocting evolutionary genealogies on inadequate or even incorrect evidence, which Darwin himself made every effort, usually successfully, to avoid. The title of Haeckel's major work can be literally translated as "Natural History of Creation," but it is a vehemently anticreationist work.

It should be noted that all the authorities here cited by Darwin as accepting the origin of man by evolution did so *after* the publication of *The Origin of Species* although the origin of man was not actually discussed in that book.

The reference to Sir Charles Bell in the last paragraph is to the Scottish anatomist who lived from 1774 to 1842 and thus died some years before Darwin published anything about evolution. He was, for his time and possibly for all time, the greatest neuroanatomist. He wrote the 1833 *Bridgewater Treatise* on *The Hand: its Mechanism and Vital Endowments as evincing Design,* but in 1806 he had published his *Anatomy and Philosophy of Expression.* It was to that work that Darwin was referring. Bell maintained that man has certain muscles solely for the expression of emotions and not present in any nonhuman species. That was for him an argument for special creation. Darwin long investigated the muscles involved in *"The Expression of the Emotions in Man and* [other] *Animals."* This grew into a long book published in 1872. Darwin concluded "that the study of the theory of expression confirms to a certain limited extent the conclusion that man is derived from some lower animal form." In reference to this work pioneer ethologist and Nobel Prize winner Konrad Lorenz (b. 1903) wrote in 1965 that, "I believe that even today we do not quite realize how much Charles Darwin knew."

In *The Descent of Man* Darwin started his discussion with the resemblances between man (that is, mankind) and what he tended to call "lower animals." Some of the main points made appear in the following excerpts:

The Bodily Structure of Man.—It is notorious that man is constructed on the same general type or model as other mammals. All the bones in his skeleton can be compared with corresponding bones in a monkey, bat, or seal. So it is with his muscles, nerves, blood-vessels and internal viscera. The brain, the most important of all the organs, follows the same law, as shewn by Huxley and other anatomists. Bischoff, who is a hostile witness, admits that every chief fissure and fold in the brain of man has its analogy in that of the orang; but he adds that at no period of development do their brains perfectly agree; nor could perfect agreement be expected, for otherwise their mental powers would have been the same. Vulpian remarks: "Les différences réelles qui existent entre l'encéphale de l'homme et celui des singes supérieurs, sont bien minimes. Il ne faut pas se faire d'illusions à cet égard. L'homme est bien plus près des singes anthropomorphes par les caractères anatomiques de son cerveau que ceux-ci ne le sont non seulement des autres mammifères, mais même de certains quadrumanes, des guenons et des macaques."[1]

Theodor Ludwig Wilhelm Bischoff (1807–82) was a German anatomist who studied and overemphasized the differences between man and apes. The extended quotation in French is from the work of Edme-Félix-Alfred Vulpian (1826–87), a Parisian physiologist and anatomist. This quotation may be translated into English as follows:

"The real differences that exist between the brain of man and that of the higher primates are quite small. One should not illude oneself in this respect. Man is much closer to the apes by the anatomical characters of his brain than these are not only to those of other mammals but even of some monkeys, of the guenons and of the macaques." ("Guenon" is a little-known English word, borrowed from French, used in this quotation to include about twelve species of African monkeys. "Macaque" is a general term for about thirteen species of somewhat similar monkeys in southern Asia, the East Indies, and some adjacent areas.) After this quotation, Darwin closed the discussion of anatomy of brains as follows: "But it would be superfluous here to give further details on the correspondence between man and the higher mammals in the structure of the brain and all other parts of the body." After brief comparisons of human and (other) animal diseases and reproduction, Darwin goes on, still briefly and still in Chapter I, to embryonic development.

Embryonic Development.—Man is developed from an ovule, about the 125th of an inch in diameter, which differs in no respect from the ovules of other animals. The embryo itself at a very early period can hardly be distinguished from that of other members of the vertebrate kingdom. At this period the arteries run in arch-like branches, as if to carry the blood to branchiæ which are not present in the higher vertebrata, though the slits on the sides of the neck still remain marking their former position. At a somewhat later period, when the extremities are developed, "the feet of lizards and mammals," as the illustrious Von Baer remarks, "the wings and feet of birds, no less than the hands and feet of man, all arise from the same fundamental form." It is, says Prof. Huxley, "quite in the later stages of development that the young human being presents marked differences from the young age, while the latter departs as much from the dog in its developments, as the man does. Startling as this last assertion may appear to be, it is demonstrably true."

After the foregoing statements made by such high authorities, it would be superfluous on my part to give a number of borrowed details, shewing that the embryo of man closely resembles that of other mammals. It may, however, be added, that the human embryo likewise resembles certain low forms when adult in various points of structure. For instance, the heart at first exists as a simple pulsating vessel; the excreta are voided through a cloacal passage; and the os coccyx projects like a true tail, "extending considerably beyond the rudimentary legs." In the embryos of all air-breathing vertebrates, certain glands, called the corpora Wolffiana, correspond with, and act like the kidneys of mature fishes. Even at a later embryonic period, some striking resemblances between man and the lower animals may be observed. Bischoff says "that the convolutions of the brain in a human fœtus at the end of the seventh month reach about the same stage of development as in a baboon when adult." The great toe, as Professor Owen remarks, "which forms the fulcrum when standing or walking, is perhaps the most characteristic peculiarity in the human structure;" but in an embryo, about an inch in length, Prof. Wyman found "that the great toe was shorter than the others; and, instead of being parallel to them, projected at an angle from the side of the foot, thus corresponding with the permanent condition of this part in the quadrumana." I will conclude with a quotation from Huxley, who after asking, does man originate in a different way from a dog, bird, frog or fish? says, "the reply is not doubtful for a moment; without question, the mode or origin, and the early stages of the development of man, are identical with those of the animals immediately below him in the scale: without a doubt in these respects, he is far nearer to apes than the apes are to the dog."

Rudiments.—This subject, though not intrinsically more important than the two last, will for several reasons be treated here more fully. Not one of the higher animals can be named which does not bear some part in a rudimentary condition; and man forms no exception to the rule. Rudimentary organs must be distinguished from those that are nascent; though in some cases the distinction is not easy. The former are either absolutely useless, such as the mammæ of male quadrupeds, or the incisor teeth of ruminants which never cut through the gums; or they are of such slight service to their present possessors, that we can hardly suppose that they were developed under the conditions which now exist. Organs in this latter state are not strictly rudimentary, but they are tending in this direction. Nascent organs, on the other hand, though not fully developed, are of high service to their possessors, and are capable of further development. Rudimentary organs are eminently variable; and this is partly intelligible, as they are useless, or nearly useless, and consequently are no longer subjected to natural selection. They often become wholly suppressed. When this occurs, they are nevertheless liable to occasional reappearance through reversion—a circumstance well worthy of attention.

The statement that human "ovules" (small ova) do not at all differ from those of other animals is either meant to be strictly confined to superficial aspects of ova in primates closely related to man or is exceptionally inaccurate if "other animals" is to be taken in a broader sense. Human ova are quite unlike those of most animals even superficially. Nevertheless human ova are evidence of man's relationship to apes, first of all, and to primates in general. This is emphasized by the post-Darwinian investigation of the chromosomes and genes in human and ape ova.

The bearing of embryology on evolution and on the descent of any particular species, here definitely applied to *Homo sapiens,* has a history that long antedates the recognition of evolution in its present sense. It dates from the *scala naturae,* the "ladder of nature," that organic beings form a graded sequence from lowest to highest. It was mainly Lamarck who brought this into an evolutionary context. Embryological observations derived from the *scala* the idea that higher organisms went through the stages of the lower steps of the ladder in the course of their development into adults. That could be viewed in a transcendental sense, evading scientific formulation by taking it simply as a law of nature, presumably created divinely or in some other sense supernaturally. It could, however, be viewed as evolutionary, producing the catch phrase "ontogeny repeats phylogeny," meaning that in the course of embryology some, many, or all species go through stages similar to those in the succession of their adult ancestors.

Karl Ernst von Baer (1792–1876), justly called "illustrious" in the preceding excerpt from Darwin, was a pioneer embryologist. His most important work, *Über die Entwickelungsgeschichte der Thiere* ("On the history of development of animals") was published in two parts in 1828 and 1837, thus long before Darwin's

The Origin of Species. He advanced four embryological "laws," which can be briefly restated as being that in the embryology of a species the most generalized characters appear first and the most specialized last, that as different species develop embryologically they depart more and more from generalized characters first common to them, and that therefore the early embryo of a "higher" (more specialized) animal is never like the adult of any other species but only like its embryo. Von Baer reacted strongly against the older idea of a *scala naturae* and against Lamarckian interpretation of it, and this biased him against any evolutionary interpretation although he lived seventeen years after *The Origin of Species* was published.

Louis Agassiz rejected von Baer's laws and reverted to, or retained, the idea of recapitulation: that embryonic sequences follow the adult sequences of earlier or lower animals. In his *Essay on Classification* published in 1857 he brought the fossil record—very poorly known at that time—into the discussion. He then maintained that ancient (extinct) forms do (or should) resemble embryonic stages in living animals. He took this as evidence against, not for, evolution. To him, "It exhibits everywhere the working of the same creative Mind, through all times and upon the whole surface of the globe." Darwin in *The Origin of Species,* only two years later, wrote of the supposed resemblance of extinct forms to modern embryos that, "Agassiz believes this to be a law of nature; but I am bound to confess that I only hope to see the law hereafter proved true." To Darwin this might have been further evidence of evolution, but as Darwin suspected it was not true. The truth of evolution depends on other and sounder grounds.

In *The Origin of Species* Darwin was involved with species in general, with particular species only exemplifying and confirming the act of evolution. In *The Descent of Man* he was applying the earlier conclusions to a particular species: *Homo sapiens*. In the brief excerpt about embryology in this connection Darwin seems to be wavering somewhat between two views which had not previously been combined in an evolutionary context. On one hand he thinks of recapitulation as a possible result and record of phylogeny, in nonevolutionary terms an embryological *scala naturae*. Haeckel's more extreme adoption of this view far out-Darwined Darwin. On the other hand Darwin here and elsewhere followed more closely the pre-evolutionist von Baer's view that embryos of modern or "higher" animals resemble embryos, not adults, of earlier or "lower" animals, and that the characteristics of the compared species diverge as they become adult. To Darwin, as to all biologists now, that was and is evidence that the species being compared evolved divergently from a common ancestor.

It may here be noted that in one of his innumerable notes Darwin had cautioned himself not to use the terms *higher* and *lower* in referring to kinds of organisms. Nevertheless he did frequently use them in his publications, especially when making comparisons involving mankind as compared with any related groups. Then *higher* generally meant more like humans, or especially cultured humans like proper Englishmen. Elsewhere it is often difficult to be sure of the meanings of these terms. *Higher* often means more and *lower* less complex in anatomy or sometimes in intelligence or in behavior. Sometimes *higher* means later and *lower* earlier in the history of life. *Higher* also may imply "specialized" and *lower* "primitive." ("Specialized" and "primitive" are words also inadequately defined.) One could wish that Darwin had followed his own admonition, and also that present-day biologists would do so.

The remarks on embryology are followed in Chapter I of *The Descent of Man* by a long passage on what Darwin calls rudimentary and nascent organs, the former, more fully discussed and more significant for the points Darwin is making, are considered as the retention of traits useful in ancestral or "lower" animals but of little or no essential use in man and here reduced to a rudimentary condition. Below I have excerpted only discussion of two sorts of "rudiments."

In man, the os coccyx, together with certain other vertebræ hereafter to be described, though functionless as a tail, plainly represent this part in other vertebrate animals. At an early embryonic period it is free and projects beyond the lower extremities. Even after birth it has been known, in certain rare and anomalous cases, to form a small external rudiment of a tail. The os coccyx is short, usually including only four vertebræ, all anchylosed together: and these are in a rudimentary condition, for they consist, with the exception of the basal one, of the centrum alone. They are furnished with some small muscles; one of which, as I am informed by Prof. Turner, has been expressly described by Theile as a rudimentary repetition of the extensor of the tail, a muscle which is so largely developed in many mammals.

The spinal cord in man extends only as far downwards as the last dorsal or first lumbar vertebra; but a thread-like structure (the *filum terminale*) runs down the axis of the sacral part of the spinal canal, and even along the back of the coccygeal bones.

The reproductive system offers various rudimentary structures; but these differ in one important respect from the foregoing cases. Here we are not concerned with the vestige of a part which does not belong to the species in an efficient state, but with a part efficient in the one sex, and represented in the other by a mere rudiment. Nevertheless, the occurrence of such rudiments is as difficult to explain, on the belief of the separate creation of each species, as in the foregoing cases. Hereafter I shall have to recur to these rudiments, and shall shew that their presence generally depends merely on inheritance, that is, on parts acquired by one sex having been partially transmitted to the other. I will in this place only give some instances of such rudiments. It is well known that in the males of all mammals, including man, rudimentary mammæ exist. These in several instances have become well developed, and have yielded a copious supply of milk. Their essential identity in the two sexes is likewise shewn by their occasional sympathetic enlargement in both during an attack of the measles.[2]

The two sorts of "rudiments" here discussed are so different in kind and import that they bear on two separate aspects of Darwin's exposition. One would hesitate now to call both kinds *rudiments,* a term now usually confined in biology to the beginnings of structures in an embryo or to vestiges of structures ancestrally but now no longer functional—still an ambiguous term but somewhat different from Darwin's usages.

First the coccyx, which is the lower termination of the human backbone. It is beyond doubt the homologue of the tail of such mammals as have tails. It is present in nearly the same form in the apes, which also have no functional or external tails. This is another indication that men and apes had a common ancestor, and also that still farther back in their phylogeny there were more monkeylike ancestors that did have tails. (Some macaques lack external tails, but this is a separate evolutionary development, as related macaques do have tails.) The coccyx serves no known or surmised function, and indeed can be quite disadvantageous on the fortunately rare occasions when it is painfully broken. It is better considered a vestige than a rudiment, and it is definite evidence for evolution from a tailed to an untailed condition, possibly by random genetic change but more likely by negative selection when conditions or habits of life made tails disadvantageous. (Positive selection favors anatomical or other characters that are adaptive or advantageous; negative selection tends to eliminate those that are maladaptive or disadvantageous.)

Darwin's second point here depends on the differences in forms and functions of surely or possibly homologous parts of males and females among humans. The physiological and embry-ological systems are closely similar in the two sexes of a single species except as regards their separate sexual roles and func-tions. Thus some aspect of the differentiation may well be accom-panied by partial retention of a characteristic essential in one sex, such as breasts and nipples in females, but neither necessary nor harmful in the other. This is not so much obvious evidence of evolution as it is clear evidence against special creation. There is here some parallel with the ridiculous but lengthy scholastic argument about whether Adam (or Eve, for that matter), never having been in a womb, had an umbilicus.

To this may be added the final paragraphs of Chapter I of *The Descent of Man:*

The bearing of the three great classes of facts now given is unmistak-able. But it would be superfluous fully to recapitulate the line of argument given in detail in my 'Origin of Species.' The homological construction of the whole frame in the members of the same class is intelligible, if we admit their descent from a common progenitor, to-gether with their subsequent adaptation to diversified conditions. On any other view, the similarity of pattern between the hand of a man or monkey, the foot of a horse, the flipper of a seal, the wing of a bat, &c., is utterly inexplicable. It is no scientific explanation to assert that they have all been formed on the same ideal plan. With respect to develop-ment, we can clearly understand, on the principle of variation superven-ing at a rather late embryonic period, and being inherited at a corre-sponding period, how it is that the embryos of wonderfully different forms should still retain, more or less perfectly, the structure of their common progenitor. No other explanation has ever been given of the marvellous fact that the embryos of a man, dog, seal, bat, reptile, &c., can at first hardly be distinguished from each other. In order to under-stand the existence of rudimentary organs, we have only to suppose that a former progenitor possessed the parts in question in a perfect state, and that under changed habits of life they became greatly reduced, either from simple disuse, or through the natural selection of those individuals which were least encumbered with a superfluous part, aided by the other means previously indicated.

Thus we can understand how it has come to pass that man and all other vertebrate animals have been constructed on the same general model, why they pass through the same early stages of development, and why they retain certain rudiments in common. Consequently we ought frankly to admit their community of descent; to take any other view, is to admit that our own structure, and that of all the animals around us, is a mere snare laid to entrap our judgment. This conclusion is greatly strengthened, if we look to the members of the whole animal series, and consider the evidence derived from their affinities or classification, their geographical distribution and geological succession. It is only our natural prejudice, and that arrogance which made our forefathers declare that they were descended from demi-gods, which leads us to demur to this conclusion. But the time will before long come, when it will be thought wonderful that naturalists, who were well acquainted with the comparative structure and development of man, and other mammals, should have believed that each was the work of a separate act of creation.

From that point Darwin progressed through a chapter "On the Manner of Development of Man from Some Lower Form," two chapters on "Comparison of the Mental Powers of Man and the Lower Animals," and one "On the Development of the Intellectual and Moral Faculties during Primeval and Civilised Times" and then to what for many will seem the real crux of the matter: "On the Affinities and Genealogy of Man." This contains the most positive statement that Darwin ever made on the more or less immediate ancestors of man:

And as man from a genealogical point of view belongs to the Catarhine or Old World stock [the Eurasian and African monkeys], we must conclude, however much the conclusion may revolt our pride, that our early progenitors would have been properly thus designated. But we must not fall into the error of supposing that the early progenitors of the whole Simian stock, including man, were identical with, or even closely resembled, any existing ape or monkey.

In conclusion to that chapter Darwin sketched more of the whole genealogy of man among the vertebrate animals.

Conclusion.—Von Baer has defined advancement or progress in the organic scale better than any one else, as resting on the amount of differentiation and specialisation of the several parts of a being,—when arrived at maturity, as I should be inclined to add. Now as organisms have become slowly adapted to diversified lines of life by means of natural selection, their parts will have become more and more differentiated and specialised for various functions from the advantage gained by the division of physiological labour. The same part appears often to have been modified first for one purpose, and then long afterwards for some other and quite distinct purpose; and thus all the parts are rendered more and more complex. But each organism still retains the general type of structure of the progenitor from which it was aboriginally derived. In accordance with this view it seems, if we turn to geological evidence, that organisation on the whole has advanced throughout the world by slow and interrupted steps. In the great kingdom of the Vertebrata it has culminated in man. It must not, however, be supposed that groups of organic beings are always supplanted, and disappear as soon as they have given birth to other and more perfect groups. The latter, though victorious over their predecessors, may not have become better adapted for all places in the economy of nature. Some old forms appear to have survived from inhabiting protected sites, where they have not been exposed to very severe competition; and these often aid us in constructing our genealogies, by giving us a fair idea of former and lost populations. But we must not fall into the error of looking at the existing members of any lowly-organised group as perfect representatives of their ancient predecessors.

The most ancient progenitors in the kingdom of the Vertebrata, at which we are able to obtain an obscure glance, apparently consisted of a group of marine animals, resembling the larvae of existing Ascidians. These animals probably gave rise to a group of fishes, as lowly organised as the lancelet; and from these the Ganoids, and other fishes like the Lepidosiren, must have been developed. From such fish a very small advance would carry us on to the Amphibians. We have seen that birds and reptiles were once intimately connected together; and the Monotremata now connect mammals with reptiles in a slight degree. But no one can at present say by what line of descent the three higher and related classes, namely, mammals, birds, and reptiles, were derived from the two lower vertebrate classes, namely, amphibians and fishes. In the class of mammals the steps are not difficult to conceive which led from the ancient Monotremata to the ancient Marsupials; and from these to the early progenitors of the placental mammals. We may thus ascend to the Lemuridae; and the interval is not very wide from these to the Simiadae. The Simiadae then branched off into two great stems, the New World and Old World monkeys; and from the latter, at a remote period, Man, the wonder and glory of the Universe, proceeded.

Thus we have given to man a pedigree of prodigious length, but not, it may be said, of noble quality. The world, it has often been remarked, appears as if it had long been preparing for the advent of man: and this, in one sense is strictly true, for he owes his birth to a long line of progenitors. If any single link in this chain had never existed, man would not have been exactly what he now is. Unless we wilfully close our eyes, we may, with our present knowledge, approximately recognise our parentage; nor need we feel ashamed of it. The most humble organism is something much higher than the inorganic dust under our feet; and no one with an unbiased mind can study any living creature, however humble, without being struck with enthusiasm at its marvellous structure and properties.[3]

A present-day anthropologist has called nineteenth-century ideas of the ancestry of man "fossil-free," but that is not wholly correct. Many fossils had been collected, described and named when Darwin wrote *The Descent of Man* but the fossil record was

still inadequate, as Darwin well knew and repeatedly emphasized. He knew and stated that a present living species, here
explicitly *Homo sapiens,* cannot be the literal descendant of any
other present species. Yet in the absence of a more extensive
fossil record he had to piece together the broad outlines of our
phylogeny largely in terms of surviving members of major
groups. The derivations one from another all occurred "at a
remote period" and from ancestral species that could turn out to
have been quite unlike living members of the classes, orders and
other broader groupings of related organisms. The fossil record
available in Darwin's day and well known to him did show the
sequence in time of the main classes of vertebrates: first fishes,
then amphibians, then reptiles and then mammals and birds at
about the same time geologically speaking. Middle Jurassic mammals had earlier been found and were recognized as such in
publication in 1824. The nearly complete skeleton of a likewise
middle Jurassic bird was found in 1861 and the find was adequately published in 1863, too late for the first edition of *The
Origin of Species,* but mentioned by name *(Archaeopteryx)* in the
fourth (1866) and subsequent editions. In its broader features
Darwin's sketch of human ancestry agreed with and was supported by the fossil record as it was known at that time.

Knowledge of the whole evolutionary sequence of organisms
never will be complete, for reasons already given by Darwin in
The Origin of Species. That knowledge has nevertheless become
enormously more extensive and more detailed since Darwin. We
now know from the fossil record not merely that fishes were
ancestral to amphibians but which fishes were ancestral to which
amphibians. We also know that "fishes" as known to Darwin
included an early group of jawless (agnathan) "fishes" ancestral
to the true or jawed fishes. We know closely, even though not in
the most specific detail, by what lines of descent mammals and
birds were derived from reptiles. It turns out that mammals arose
significantly earlier than birds, in the Triassic rather than the
Jurassic, but as the two origins were from decidedly different
reptiles and since birds, as such, obviously have no direct connection with human ancestry that sequence does not really matter
for Darwin's judgment of the descent of man.

For the line of descent within the order Primates, the fossil
record as known in Darwin's lifetime was so scant as to be almost
meaningless in this connection. That the sequence went through
the Prosimii, essentially what Darwin called "Lemuridae" and
the Anthropoidea, which divided into New World and Old World

monkeys, and from the Old World monkeys (the Catarrhini) into apes and men was based by Darwin and his contemporaries almost entirely on the comparative anatomy of the living representatives of those groups. Now, however, there is extensive fossil evidence for that filiation.

A supposed discovery of fossil human, or humanoid, remains was made as far back as 1700, a skull fragment from near Stuttgart. For a long time such finds were not of well-established antiquity or were not clearly distinct from modern man, or both. Through the nineteenth century and well into the twentieth such questionable finds continued to be made in some numbers. The only surely early (Pleistocene) finds distinctly different from most if not all living humans made during Darwin's lifetime were those of the Neanderthals, so called because first found in 1856 in the Neander valley in Germany. (*Thal* is an obsolete spelling of the German word *Tal,* meaning "valley.") That is perforce the only fossil member of the human family ever referred to by Darwin. In *The Descent of Man* he first cites James Cowles Prichard (1786–1848) as being "persuaded that the present inhabitants of Britain have 'much more capacious braincases' than the ancient inhabitants"—a poorly supported opinion—and Darwin goes on to say that, "Nevertheless it must be admitted that some skulls of very high antiquity, such as the famous one of Neanderthal, are well developed and capacious." The Neanderthal populations, which were rather widespread in the Pleistocene of Eurasia, had somewhat flatter skulls and heavier brow ridges than are usual in living humans but had brains equally large or even slightly larger than in most present populations. Anthropologists used to give new specific, generic, or even family names to almost all their finds of fossil humanoids, but the present consensus is that the Neanderthals were only a subspecies, *Homo sapiens neanderthalensis,* which either became extinct or merged with other *Homo sapiens* by interbreeding.

This is not the place to extend discussion of the now innumerable discoveries of close relatives and ancestors of *Homo* as fossils in rocks of increasing remoteness in time. Everyone who reads newspapers or books now knows at least the names of *Pithecanthropus erectus* (now called *Homo erectus*) found in Java in 1894 and subsequently also in China and in Africa, and knows also of *Australopithecus africanus* found in South Africa in 1925. Both are near, if not precisely in, the main line of evolution leading to *Homo sapiens.* It seems lately that seldom a year and hardly a month passes without still older discoveries. The line has now been followed back some millions of years into the late Miocene, when our ancestors already walked erect but had brains the size of apes' brains. Recent finds of this sort are mostly in eastern Africa, and even older and more decidedly apelike probable ancestors also turn up there, but most of these have been found in southern Asia. It is highly unlikely that either area can be considered "the birthplace of man," as the various species surely ranged widely in the Old World but were more often entombed and more often became accessible as fossils in some areas than in others. There is some quibbling over nomenclature or other details, but there is no serious doubt that fossils now fully attest our community of origin with the apes.

Fully two-thirds of the work published with the dual name *The Descent of Man, and Selection in Relation to Sex* is devoted to the latter subject. The two parts are to some extent connected by a discussion of differences among human races, which Darwin considered inadequately explained by natural selection but probably better by sexual selection. On this distinction just two paragraphs from the general summary at the end of the whole work will be excerpted.

Sexual selection depends on the success of certain individuals over others of the same sex, in relation to the propagation of the species; whilst natural selection depends on the success of both sexes, at all ages in relation to the general conditions of life. The sexual struggle is of two kinds; in the one it is between individuals of the same sex, generally the males, in order to drive away or kill their rivals, the females remaining passive; whilst in the other, the struggle is likewise between the individuals of the same sex, in order to excite or charm those of the opposite sex, generally the females, which no longer remain passive, but select the more agreeable partners. This latter kind of selection is closely analogous to that which man unintentionally, yet effectually, brings to bear on his domesticated productions, when he preserves during a long period the most pleasing or useful individuals, without any wish to modify the breed.

The laws of inheritance determine whether characters gained through sexual selection by either sex shall be transmitted to the same sex, or to both; as well as the age at which they shall be developed. It appears that variations arising late in life are commonly transmitted to one and the same sex. Variability is the necessary basis for the action of selection, and is wholly independent of it. It follows from this, that variations of the same general nature have often been taken advantage of and accumulated through sexual selection in relation to the propagation of the species, as well as through natural selection in relation to the general purposes of life. Hence secondary sexual characters, when equally transmitted to both sexes can be distinguished from ordinary specific characters only by the light of analogy. The modifications acquired through sexual selection are often so strongly pronounced that the two sexes have frequently been ranked as distinct species, or even as distinct genera. Such strongly-marked differences must be in some manner highly important; and we know that they have been acquired in some instances at the cost not only of inconvenience, but of exposure to actual danger.[4]

While working on the subject of sexual selection Darwin wrote to one of his regular correspondents, J. Jenner Weir (1822–94; an amateur naturalist and a civil servant in the Custom House), "You will not be able to read all my book—too much detail." To that some later readers of it, or parts of it, have said "Amen!" Julian Huxley in 1938 wrote that, "None of Darwin's theories have been so heavily attacked as that of sexual selection." But Ernst Mayr (b. 1904) noted in 1972 in a symposial book largely devoted to sexual selection that, "The vitality of the principle is best documented by the large number of recent review papers or chapters in general books."

Darwin's original discussion of this subject is to some extent responsible for later disputes and complications. He found it improbable that natural selection, alone, accounts for the origins of *different* human races, but almost all of the rest of his "too much detail" has to do with differences between males and females of the *same* races or species in a great variety of animals. Some but probably not all of the differences among human races appear to have been adaptive when and where the races arose and thus may be considered at least in part as results of natural selection in Darwin's strict sense. It is, however, hard to see how differentiation between the sexes within a given population could itself have produced racial diversity. Nevertheless if sexual selection does occur in a genetically varied population, as Darwin's examples do indicate, then within that population some of the genetic variants, among both females and males, will tend to have more descendants than others. As we now see it, that is the same process as natural selection, and sexual selection, when significant in evolution, is simply another of the many factors involved in natural selection in general.

10

Darwin's Last Years and Place in History

It is impossible to include here more than summaries and excerpts from Darwin's many books, but all are listed in the appendix and most have been mentioned in the present text. Two others, perhaps the least important but both interesting for different reasons, may here be noted. One was a life of Charles Darwin's grandfather, *Erasmus Darwin,* originally written in German by Ernst Krause (1839–1903) who used the pseudonym Carus Sterne. Charles Darwin had Krause's text translated into English, and in 1879 he added to it a sketch of Erasmus' "character and habits." In translation from Krause this book contained the remark that, "Erasmus Darwin's system was in itself a most significant step in the path which his grandson [Charles] has opened up for us, but to wish to revive it at the present day as has actually been attempted, shows a weakness of thought and a mental anachronism which no one can envy." Samuel Butler (1835–1902), best known now as the author of *Erewhon* (1872) and *The Way of All Flesh* (published posthumously in 1903), also published in 1879 *Evolution Old and New* which supported the views of Erasmus Darwin on evolution and attacked those of Charles Darwin. Butler accused Krause and Darwin of a plot against him and, as Darwin wrote in his autobiography, he "abused me with almost insane virulence." Darwin was tempted to answer back, but Huxley calmed him down by quoting from Goethe "that every whale has its louse," obviously casting Darwin as the whale and Butler as the inevitable louse. The account of this was one of the passages expunged by the family from the first publication of Darwin's autobiography.

The second book to be noted here was the last that Darwin wrote. He mentioned this in his autobiography as follows:

"I have now (May 1, 1881) sent to the printers the MS. of a little book on 'The Formation of Vegetable Mould, through the Action of Worms.' This is a subject of but small importance; and I know not whether it will interest any readers, but it has interested me. It is the completion of a short paper read before the Geological Society more than forty years ago, and has revived old geological thoughts."[1]

The "little book" here mentioned was Darwin's last book. When he sent the manuscript to the printers he had less than a year to live. As first written the autobiography was dated "August 3rd, 1876," but this excerpt is from an addition written on the date given for delivery of the manuscript: May 1, 1881. The paper of "more than forty years ago" was "On the Formation of Mould" read to the Geological Society of London on November 1, 1837, and published in its *Transactions* in 1840. The point was that the origin of so-called vegetable mould was the probability "that every particle of earth forming the bed from which the turf in old pasture land springs, has passed through the intestines of worms; and hence the term 'animal mould' would in some respects be more appropriate than that of 'vegetable mould.' " The evidence suggested that stones resting on top of the soil had slowly been lowered into it by the activities of worms below the stones. To test this Darwin placed a "wormstone" on top of the lawn back of Down House, over soil in which worms were active, and in the course of years the stone was indeed lowered. (Visitors to Down House will find a "wormstone" on that ground, but the original stone disappeared during the later occupations of the house and the present stone was not placed there until 1929.) Despite Darwin's doubts the book did interest many readers. Francis Darwin noted that between November 1881 and February 1884 (the latter date almost two years after Darwin's death) 8,500 copies had been sold.

Although he was there referring especially to reviews of *The Origin of Species* the following sums up Darwin's reaction to reviews and to criticism in general:

Hardly any point gave me so much satisfaction when I was at work on the 'Origin,' as the explanation of the wide difference in many classes between the embryo and the adult animal, and of the close resemblance of the embryos within the same class. No notice of this point was taken, as far as I remember, in the early reviews of the 'Origin,' and I recollect expressing my surprise on this head in a letter to Asa Gray. . . . I had materials for a whole chapter on the subject, and I ought to have made the discussion longer; for it is clear that I failed to impress my readers; and he who succeeds in doing so deserves, in my opinion, all the credit.

This leads me to remark that I have almost always been treated honestly by my reviewers, passing over those without scientific knowledge as not worthy of notice. My views have often been grossly misrepresented, bitterly opposed and ridiculed, but this has been generally done, as I believe, in good faith. On the whole I do not doubt that my works have been over and over again greatly overpraised. I rejoice that I have avoided controversies, and this I owe to Lyell, who many years ago, in reference to my geological works, strongly advised me never to get entangled in a controversy, as it rarely did any good and caused a miserable loss of time and temper.

Whenever I have found out that I have blundered, or that my work has been imperfect, and when I have been contemptuously criticised, and even when I have been overpraised, so that I have felt mortified, it has been my greatest comfort to say hundreds of times to myself that "I have worked as hard and as well as I could, and no man can do more than this." I remember when in Good Success Bay, in Tierra del Fuego, thinking (and, I believe, that I wrote home to the effect) that I could not employ my life better than in adding a little to Natural Science. This I have done to the best of my abilities, and critics may say what they like, but they cannot destroy this conviction.[2]

Darwin did make one exception to his belief in the good faith of critics opposed to him, but this was expunged from Francis Darwin's publication of the autobiography. The exception was St. George Jackson Mivart (1829–1900). Mivart was a biologist who was converted to Roman Catholicism and tried to reconcile evolution and religion, but he was opposed to natural selection and was among the most bitter opponents of both Darwin and Huxley. Nevertheless he was excommunicated for liberalism and repudiation of the church's authority. Darwin did avoid public controversy, but privately he did not forget or forgive what he considered unjustified attacks by Mivart, Owen, Butler and a few others.

Darwin's self-analysis in his autobiography is of special interest. Much of it is included in the following excerpt:

I have now mentioned all the books which I have published, and these have been the milestones in my life, so that little remains to be said. I am not conscious of any change in my mind during the last thirty years, excepting in one point presently to be mentioned; nor, indeed, could any change have been expected unless one of general deterioration. But my father lived to his eighty-third year with his mind as lively as ever it was, and all his faculties undimmed; and I hope that I may die before my mind fails to a sensible extent. I think that I have become a little more skilful in guessing right explanations and in devising experimental tests; but this may probably be the result of mere practice, and of a larger store of knowledge. I have as much difficulty as ever in expressing myself clearly and concisely; and this difficulty has caused me a very great loss of time; but it has had the compensating advantage of forcing me to think long and intently about every sentence, and thus I have been led to see errors in reasoning and in my own observations or those of others.

There seems to be a sort of fatality in my mind leading me to put at first my statement or proposition in a wrong or awkward form. Formerly I used to think about my sentences before writing them down; but for several years I have found that it saves time to scribble in a vile hand whole pages as quickly as I possibly can, contracting half the words; and then correct deliberately. Sentences thus scribbled down are often better ones than I could have written deliberately.

Having said thus much about my manner of writing, I will add that with my large books I spend a good deal of time over the general arrangement of the matter. I first make the rudest outline in two or three pages, and then a larger one in several pages, a few words or one word standing for a whole discussion or series of facts. Each one of these headings is again enlarged and often transferred before I begin to write *in extenso*. As in several of my books facts observed by others have been very extensively used, and as I have always had several quite distinct subjects in hand at the same time, I may mention that I keep from thirty to forty large portfolios, in cabinets with labelled shelves, into which I can at once put a detached reference or memorandum. I have bought many books, and at their ends I make an index of all the facts that concern my work; or, if the book is not my own, write out a separate abstract, and of such abstracts I have a large drawer full. Before beginning on any subject I look to all the short indexes and make a general and classified index, and by taking the one or more proper portfolios I have all the information collected during my life ready for use.

I have said that in one respect my mind has changed during the last twenty or thirty years. Up to the age of thirty, or beyond it, poetry of many kinds, such as the works of Milton, Gray, Byron, Wordsworth, Coleridge, and Shelley, gave me great pleasure, and even as a schoolboy I took intense delight in Shakespeare, especially in the historical plays. I have also said that formerly pictures gave me considerable, and music very great delight. But now for many years I cannot endure to read a line of poetry: I have tried lately to read Shakespeare, and found it so intolerably dull that it nauseated me. I have also almost lost my taste for pictures or music. Music generally sets me thinking too energetically on what I have been at work on, instead of giving me pleasure. I retain some taste for fine scenery, but it does not cause me the exquisite delight which it formerly did. On the other hand, novels which are works of the imagination, though not of a very high order, have been for years a wonderful relief and pleasure to me, and I often bless all novelists. A surprising number have been read aloud to me, and I like all if moderately good, and if they do not end unhappily—against which a law ought to be passed. A novel, according to my taste, does not come into the first class unless it contains some person whom one can thoroughly love, and if a pretty woman all the better.

This curious and lamentable loss of the higher æsthetic tastes is all the odder, as books on history, biographies, and travels (independently of any scientific facts which they may contain), and essays on all sorts of subjects interest me as much as ever they did. My mind seems to have become a kind of machine for grinding general laws out of large collections of facts, but why this should have caused the atrophy of that part of the brain alone, on which the higher tastes depend, I cannot conceive. A man with a mind more highly organised or better constituted than mine, would not, I suppose, have thus suffered; and if I had to live my life again, I would have made a rule to read some poetry and listen to some music at least once every week; for perhaps the parts of my brain now atrophied would thus have been kept active through use. The loss of these tastes is a loss of happiness, and may possibly be injurious to the intellect, and more probably to the moral character, by enfeebling the emotional part of our nature.

My books have sold largely in England, have been translated into many languages, and passed through several editions in foreign countries. I have heard it said that the success of a work abroad is the best test of its enduring value. I doubt whether this is at all trustworthy; but judged by this standard my name ought to last for a few years. Therefore it may be worth while to try to analyse the mental qualities and the conditions on which my success has depended; though I am aware that no man can do this correctly.

I have no great quickness of apprehension or wit which is so remarkable in some clever men, for instance, Huxley. I am therefore a poor critic: a paper or a book, when first read, generally excites my admiration, and it is only after considerable reflection that I perceive the weak points. My power to follow a long and purely abstract train of thought is very limited; and therefore I could never have succeeded with metaphysics or mathematics. My memory is extensive, yet hazy: it suffices to make me cautious by vaguely telling me that I have observed or read something opposed to the conclusion which I am drawing, or on the other hand in favour of it; and after a time I can generally recollect where to search for my authority. So poor in one sense is my memory, that I

have never been able to remember for more than a few days a single date
or a line of poetry.

Some of my critics have said, "Oh, he is a good observer, but he has
no power of reasoning!" I do not think that this can be true, for the
'Origin of Species' is one long argument from the beginning to the end,
and it has convinced not a few able men. No one could have written it
without having some power of reasoning. I have a fair share of invention,
and of common sense or judgment, such as every fairly successful
lawyer or doctor must have, but not, I believe, in any higher degree.

On the favourable side of the balance, I think that I am superior to the
common run of men in noticing things which easily escape attention, and
in observing them carefully. My industry has been nearly as great as it
could have been in the observation and collection of facts. What is far
more important, my love of natural science has been steady and ardent.

This pure love has, however, been much aided by the ambition to be
esteemed by my fellow naturalists. From my early youth I have had the
strongest desire to understand or explain whatever I observed,—that is,
to group all facts under some general laws. These causes combined have
given me the patience to reflect or ponder for any number of years over
any unexplained problem. As far as I can judge, I am not apt to follow
blindly the lead of other men. I have steadily endeavoured to keep my
mind free so as to give up any hypothesis, however much beloved (and I
cannot resist forming one on every subject), as soon as facts are shown
to be opposed to it. Indeed, I have had no choice but to act in this
manner, for with the exception of the Coral Reefs, I cannot remember a
single first-formed hypothesis which had not after a time to be given up
or greatly modified. This has naturally led me to distrust greatly deduc-
tive reasoning in the mixed sciences. On the other hand, I am not very
sceptical,—a frame of mind which I believe to be injurious to the
progress of science. A good deal of scepticism in a scientific man is
advisable to avoid much loss of time, but I have met with not a few men,
who, I feel sure, have often thus been deterred from experiment or
observations, which would have proved directly or indirectly service-
able.[3]

Thus in expected privacy Darwin was capable of evaluating
what he considered his bad as well as his good points. The extent
of modesty in a man who knew that he was famous may seem
almost excessive or even feigned, but anyone truly without his
own axe to grind must find it a genuine part of Darwin's character.

The person who usually read aloud to Darwin "a surprising
number" of romantic novels was his wife, Emma. During much of
his life at Down House this became a regular routine during his
usual afternoon rest. It is said that he often fell asleep during the

reading but that Emma would continue lest her stopping might awaken him.

The autobiography ends with the following paragraph:

Therefore my success as a man of science, whatever this may have amounted to, has been determined, as far as I can judge, by complex and diversified mental qualities and conditions. Of these, the most important have been—the love of science—unbounded patience in long reflecting over any subject—industry in observing and collecting facts—and a fair share of invention as well as of common sense. With such moderate abilities as I possess, it is truly surprising that I should have influenced to a considerable extent the belief of scientific men on some important points.[4]

Early in 1882 Darwin's almost lifelong illness was exacerbated by symptoms of heart disease, but as late as March 27, 1882, he was able to write an almost cheery acknowledgment of a letter from his "dear old friend," Huxley. He died at about 4 P.M. on April 19, 1882. The family wanted him to be buried at Downe, but a group of members of parliament, led by Sir John Lubbock, successfully petitioned the Dean of Westminster that he be buried in Westminster Abbey.

In this connection Sir John wrote as follows to Darwin's son William:

House of Commons, April 25, 1882.
My Dear Darwin,—I quite sympathise with your feeling, and personally I should greatly have preferred that your father should have rested in Down amongst us all. It is, I am sure, quite understood that the initiative was not taken by you. Still, from a national point of view, it is clearly right that he should be buried in the Abbey. I esteem it a great privilege to be allowed to accompany my dear master to the grave.
Believe me, yours most sincerely,
John Lubbock.[5]
W. E. Darwin, Esq.

His grave is under the north aisle of the nave, near that of Sir Isaac Newton and others worthy of his company. During his lifetime Darwin received many academic honors, but it is extraordinary and in retrospect it is a disgrace to Great Britain that the only national honor he ever received was given to his dead body.

Darwin justly remarked in letters and in his autobiography that some of his critics misrepresented his views. They are still frequently misrepresented or at least misunderstood today, especially by those opposed to him on religious grounds but sometimes even by a few among the many who consider themselves his followers. To the first it will be news that Darwin was not an atheist, and also that he did not say that man descended from an ape. On the former point, in 1879, toward the end of his life, he wrote to J. Fordyce, who was preparing a book about skepticism, that:

> What my own views may be is a question of no consequence to anyone but myself. But, as you ask, I may state that my judgment often fluctuates . . . In my most extreme fluctuations I have never been an Atheist in the sense of denying the existence of a God.

On the latter point, as previously stated here, Darwin believed that the living apes are the closest relatives of man still extant and that on this evidence man and apes had an ancient ancestor in common. Whether that common ancestor might be called in the vernacular an ape or a monkey, or for that matter something else, Darwin did not state.

Another error is considering "Darwinism" as synonymous with "evolution." There were evolutionists before Darwin, including his own grandfather, as he well knew and clearly stated. There have also been evolutionists after Darwin who have not been Darwinians in any strict sense of that word.

In correction of some misconceptions of certain more recent evolutionists, even some who do consider themselves Darwinians or Neo-Darwinians, Darwin did not believe or say that:

All characteristics of organisms are adaptive.

All rates of evolution were slow in respect to geological time.

Species were never static for geologically long times.

All "variations" in species or other populations are slight.

Natural selection is the exclusive means of evolutionary change.

It is true that Darwin's most influential work was *The Origin of Species* and that the Darwinian revolution in human thought and knowledge arose from his insistence and evidential support that evolution is a fact of nature and has been throughout the history of life. Yet it has been one of the purposes of this book to show that Darwin was an able and important scientist in fields only indirectly or not at all connected with organic evolution. He would have been a great naturalist, although not a revolutionary one, if he had never studied evolution and written on it.

The establishment of organic evolution as a fact was the greatest achievement of Darwin and his most important legacy to later generations, even though some people have rejected this legacy. Knowledge of evolution has itself evolved and will continue to do so. Unless you have read everything that Darwin wrote—and few have done so even among Darwin's devoted followers—Darwin knew some things that you do not know. An occasional later reputation as a scientist or especially as an evolutionist has been based on the "discovery" of things that Darwin already knew. Among the examples supporting that statement are such "discoveries" as that when closely related populations come in contact with each other they tend either to merge or to diverge, that natural selection occurs both within and between species, or that there is an interplay between speciation and extinction.

It is also true that any student of the various branches of natural history knows a good many things that Darwin did not know. It is now a century since Darwin died. Studies in the diverse fields of all his works have not stood still, and any well-instructed schoolchild knows things that Darwin did not know. We know more now about both of the two most important things that Darwin *did* know: evolution occurred; natural selection was its most important guiding force. It has been said on occasion—including the occasion of the centenary of publication of *The Origin of Species*—both that neither of these is true and that one or both are true but were known before Darwin. As I have said elsewhere, "It is naive to proclaim as a 'discovery' that Darwin did not live in a vacuum and that he resembled everyone else who ever lived in that his ideas had origins"—I iterate now that Darwin, too, knew this and fully recognized it. To go on, I added, "In fact, despite Darwin's plain debt to others, his thought was unusually original. He would still be a great historical figure even if that were not true, because it is a historical fact that general acceptance of evolution by biologists stems from him, that it was he and no other who did open wide this door to a new world."

The only objective facts that really had previously had some weight against the accumulation of evidence for evolution were the myriads of adaptive relationships between living organisms and their environments in the broadest sense of the word *environments*. It really is evident that this connection requires either supernatural creation or natural evolution. With some, but few, hints from the past Darwin saw natural selection as essential for the connection. This view has been opposed in various ways, but without logically reasoned success. The operation of natural selection turns out to be far from simple, but the reasons for it are simple and indisputable. If populations of organisms vary, and they do. If much of their variation is clearly heritable, and it is. If populations often or usually can expand so rapidly that only a fraction of the offspring can live to adulthood and then themselves reproduce, and that is almost invariably true. And finally if the survivors generally have somewhat different heritable traits than those who do not survive, and that is clearly usual in natural populations, in animal and plant breeding, and in laboratory, and it is — then natural selection not only may but must occur.

The theories of evolution and of natural selection thus stood on grounds not scientifically assailable even as Darwin left them. However, as Darwin realized, fuller understanding of evolution must eventually depend on knowledge of just how heredity occurs and how it introduces and perpetuates the variation within and between populations on which natural selection acts. Darwin made an attempt in this direction in 1868 when in the second volume of *The Variation of Animals and Plants under Domestication* he advanced a hypothesis of "pangenesis." By this he meant the presence of hypothetical particles, which he called "gemmules," present in all parts of an organism and carried by the blood to the reproductive organs and hence transmitted to offspring. Thus not only the characters inherited by the parents but also those acquired by them could be passed on. In this connection Darwin quoted Whewell to the effect that "Hypotheses may often be of service to science, when they involve a certain incompleteness, and even of error." There is a modern view, not always rigidly acceptable, that formal hypotheses and theories should be falsifiable. Darwin advanced pangenesis explicitly as a falsifiable hypothesis, and in due course, long after his death, this one was definitely falsified. On the other hand both evolution and natural selection are falsifiable, and since none of the strenuous efforts made and thousands of relevant observable facts learned have failed to falsify them, they stand as facts in vernacular but also correctly scientific usage.

The full falsification of the existence of hypothetical, unobserved gemmules and of any other hypothesis involving the inheritance of acquired characters was rather slowly reached as increasing knowledge was gained about how in fact inheritance does occur and about the relationship of this to evolution. As here noted previously, Mendel's work could have opened a small door leading to that relationship, but neither Mendel nor for many years anyone else went through that door. Mendel himself was a strong antievolutionist and remained so not only in the short period of his experimentation but also for the rest of his life, which extended two years after Darwin's. The word *genetic* originally meant merely the origin (of anything) and was apparently first specifically applied in biology by Darwin, but the science of genetics in the present sense of the word and especially as a science connected to evolution properly dates from about 1900 when the German botanist Karl Correns (1864–1933), the Dutch botanist Hugo De Vries (1848–1935), and the Austrian botanist Erich Tschermak von Seysenegg (1871–1962) performed experiments similar to those of Mendel, a similarity that came as a surprise to them. The incidental rediscovery of "Mendel's laws" is not so pertinent here as the fact that now evolution was considered in connection with this approach to heredity.

It was unfortunate that De Vries chose for his experiments evening primroses of the genus *Oenothera*. (This is not closely related to the true primroses, notably the cowslip or genus *Primula* on which Darwin worked, as noted here in Chapter 8.) De Vries found that crossing plants of his evening primroses sometimes produced offspring so unlike the parental generation that he considered them different species arising by what he called "mutation," a word even then with a somewhat tangled history. De Vries and a number of other geneticists in the first twenty years or so of the twentieth century maintained that species normally arose by such abrupt mutations and hence that Darwinian natural selection postulated as working mainly on relatively small variations, could not determine the direction of evolution. Neo-Darwinians, however, maintained with Darwin that the abrupt changes found by De Vries and of the sort that Darwin called "sports" could rarely if ever give rise in one step to a specific population reproductively isolated from the parental generation. It was eventually found that *Oenothera* has a complex and rare mixture of different kinds of hereditary changes. It is also fairly obvious that the origins and changes of adaptation cannot have as a general or usual origin the adventitious appearance of large mutations not induced by and seldom if ever compatible with adaptation.

It was gradually learned, in what came to be called Mendelian genetics, that some processes of heredity are explicable only by the existence in reproductive cells, generally ova and sperm, of discrete units with effects on the development and offspring of the next generation. These units, for a time hypothetical, were called "genes." It was successively demonstrated that they are in the microscopic, often filamentlike bodies called chromosomes, present in most but not quite all living cells of organisms. Some genes, at first recognized by effects such as different eye colors, could be located in sequences in chromosomes. Further studies enabled experimenters to define them in chemical terms as segments in stringlike arrangements along chromosomes. The very long chemical formulas have now been determined in many instances. They have been found to be in what may be called a code, which by transference determines the chemistry of other reactive molecules, generally proteins, some of which are catalysts or enzymes. The genes are the principal, but not always the only, controls in heredity which determine structures and functions in organisms. There are various complications which need not be considered here, where we are concerned with the development of evolutionary theory and their relationship to Darwinian evolutionism.

The main point here is the origin of heritable variation in species as essential for the operation of natural selection. It has already been discussed that Darwin did not succeed in this, but that his failure in this one point does not contradict the fact of evolution or the theory of natural selection. From the present genetic point of view heritable variation must generally involve changes in the nature, arrangement, number or interaction of genes. In sexually reproducing organisms, in both plants and animals, offspring usually inherit one set of chromosomes, and hence one set of genes, from each sex in their parentage. (There are exceptions, but these are not relevant here.) Cells of sexually produced organisms thus generally have two sets of chromosomes which match on the whole but are extremely unlikely to be identical. This is in itself a source of variation that can be acted on by natural selection, a fact that goes part of the way toward explaining the evolutionary origin of sex.

In its narrowest sense mutation involves point changes within one segment of the part of a chromosome that is coded for a particular gene. For a time it was thought that each gene and each mutation had a single effect, an idea engendered by the fact that in strictly "Mendelian" procedures each gene was recognized by some one evident effect. It was found, however, that a gene usually has multiple effects and that any particular characteristic of an organism is usually affected by multiple genes. Thus even though genes are discrete, nonblending units, the whole genetic system in an organism is a single interacting complex. Morever some genes affect others, turning them on (active) or off (inactive) and timing them in the process of embryology and growth. There are also some chemically analyzable parts of chromosomes that have no known effect, that seem to be blanks in the code system, although of course this may mean only that their action or function has not been determined in the present state of knowledge. There are also genetic processes in which segments of one of a pair of chromosomes may be transferred to the other; the arrangement of genes in a chromosome may be changed; or the number of chromosomes may be changed. These effects also result in genetic variation among the members of a specific population. It has been experimentally demonstrated that these changes, too, may be subjected to natural selection.

Most of such changes in genes and in genetic systems as a whole have small individual effects. If the effects are large, on the scale of Darwin's "sports" or De Vries's "mutations," they are usually maladaptive or lethal. It is so improbable as to be virtually impossible that multiple gene mutations producing a new genetic system and thus a new species should all occur simultaneously. This problem for speciation in a single leap (saltation) led a brilliant early geneticist, Richard Goldschmidt (1878–1958), to formulate a hypothesis of saltation even more drastic than that of De Vries. His view was that while the gene or point mutations usually studied by "Mendelian" geneticists are involved in variation at and below the level of species, the more important changes, macroevolution as opposed to microevolution, occurred by single "systemic" mutations which remake the genetic system all at once. There has been some confusion of this view with the quite different single gene mutations that have strongly marked effects. The latter do occur, but as noted above they are not likely to have played a usual role in evolution. Goldschmidtian "systemic mutations" are not definitely known ever to have occurred, and they probably have not.

There was thus considerable confusion among geneticists and other biologists who were students of evolution about the relationship between their subjects. Genetics, as the term is now understood, did not really exist during Darwin's lifetime. In its early development its exponents also were not really clear and decidedly not in agreement about its application to evolutionary theory as such. Although there were some Neo-Lamarckians to the contrary, the one thing that geneticists early did agree on and which they definitely established was that acquired characters were not heritable. This was non-Darwinian to the extent that Darwin, like virtually all his predecessors and contemporaries, did give a place, even though a definitely minor one, to the inheritance of acquired characters. In other respects the geneticists could be rather clearly arrayed somewhat loosely in two schools. One was anti-Darwinian in their belief that gene mutation was the prime force in evolution and in their opposition to, or simply neglect of, natural selection. The other school was Neo-Darwinian in study of the possible or probable interaction of genetic variation and evolution. Out of this in the 1930s a synthesis began to emerge among geneticists about their experimental and statistical evidence. What they called Mendelism could be seen—contrary to Mendel himself—as a major part of the basis for evolution. Among those who took this stand one of the first was the Russian S. J. Chetverikov (1880–1959); soon followed by Theodosius Dobzhansky (1900–1975), also Russian by birth but American for most of his life; by the British R. A. Fisher (1890–1962), E. B. Ford (b. 1901), J. B. S. Haldane, (1892–1964), and Julian Huxley; and by the American Sewall Wright (b. 1889). In the 1940s systematics was brought into the growing synthesis by the (German-born) American Ernst Mayr, paleontology by the author of the present book, and botany by G. Ledyard Stebbins (b. 1906). Since then so many researchers in all those and other fields have enriched the synthesis and in some respects modified it that it would be impossible to list them here. All the syntheticists have taken evolution as a fact, proved such by Darwin, and have definitely but in somewhat varying ways and degrees taken Darwinian natural selection as a guiding force in evolution.

Twentieth-century developments in geology and paleontology have also had a decided bearing on the status of Darwin's views in these fields of evolutionary studies. During the nineteenth century much of the strongest opposition to Darwin was led by the British physicist Baron Kelvin, born William Thomson (1824–1907). His premise was that the earth began as a molten ball and had been cooling ever since its creation. From this Kelvin made successive, different calculations as to the number of years necessary for the earth to have cooled to its present temperature, which would for Kelvin also be the time elapsed since the Creation. In 1862 he held that the still rather uncertain data would allow no more than 400,000,000 years for this figure. In 1868 he asserted that the duration of life on the earth, if not that of the earth itself, could not be more than 100,000,000 years. In 1876 he put the upper limit at 50,000,000 years. In 1881 his variously calculated estimates put the age between 20 million and 50 million years, and his final figure in 1897 narrowed that to between 20 million and 40 million but in his opinion nearer 20 than 40. Some geologists, owerawed by Kelvin's mathematical virtuosity, felt constrained to accept his steadily lowered estimates. The prestigious American geologist Clarence King (1842–1901) by some modification of Kelvin's premises and calculations reached a figure between 22 million and 24 million years, which was happily approved by Kelvin. On the other hand what may be called Lyellian geologists, including of course Lyell himself and Charles Darwin as a geologist, were reluctant to accept such low estimates and viewed them with suspicion without being able to refute them conclusively. It is of some incidental interest that George Darwin (1845–1912), Charles Darwin's second son and a noted mathematician and astronomer, reinforced Kelvin from a different standpoint. Later, however, he did say that the earth might be as old as "1,000 million" years.

Not only as a geologist but especially as an evolutionary biologist, Charles Darwin stubbornly refused to accept such low figures as Kelvin's for the age of the earth and more particularly for the duration of life on it. Darwin believed that the evolution of such varied and extremely numerous species, both extant and extinct, would have required a longer time than even Kelvin's earliest and largest estimates. Darwin was right, and he even made some broad estimates of geological dates in years not extremely far off dates now known, but he died long before this was definitely established.

Radioactivity was discovered in 1903 by Pierre Curie (1859–1906). This completely invalidated Kelvin's premise of steady cooling of a once molten earth. In 1904 that was pointed out by Ernest Rutherford (1871–1937), the great British physicist born in New Zealand but having most of his professional career in England. Kelvin attended Rutherford's lecture in which he announced this conclusion, but Kelvin remained unconvinced, and he died three years later still of his old opinion. He also remained a staunch anti-Darwinian and a devotee of Paley's 1794 creationist book. (Even today there are some physicists, as ignorant of biology and geology as Kelvin was, who cling to Paley but who repudiate Kelvin by insisting on ages for the earth even smaller than Kelvin's by several degrees of magnitude.)

As early as 1905 Rutherford suggested that radioactivity in minerals might provide a way to determine the age of the earth. It was another British physicist, Robert John Strutt (1875–1947), later Baron Rayleigh, who in 1905 first applied this suggestion directly to the age of a mineral. His result was an astonishing 2 billion years. Later using other minerals he also obtained dates for several geological periods from the Paleozoic and later eras. Such results were embarrassing for contemporaneous geologists. On the whole they had found Kelvin's calculated ages far too short. Now they found Strutt's and his early followers' ages far too long. It is true that the results of the calculations by Strutt and his early followers were open to doubt on various counts and involved some errors, but on the whole they were at or near the now confirmed order of magnitude. Throughout the present century geological dating, involving an increasingly varied number of mostly radiometric methods, has become steadily more precise. The geological time scale, earlier indicating only the sequence of rocks and their contained fossils, has now been reasonably equated with their ages and lengths in years. Throughout this century the reliably known ages have increased rather steadily, and confirmed ages of rocks now at the surface of the earth are well over 3 billion years. There are known fossils somewhat over that date, so that life is known to have existed and evolution to have involved no less than about 3.2 billion years, and possibly somewhat more. The origin of the solar system and hence of the earth as a distant planet is less closely dated but evidence mainly from meteorites indicates it as approximately 4.5 billion years.

Darwin did not give any numerical values for rates of evolution. He did not have a reliable time scale for this purpose, and the fossil record although clearly indicative of broad features of evolutionary change was inadequate for detailed rates of evolution within lines of descent. Also, as Darwin himself noted, he was not mathematically learned or inclined. Knowledge of the fossil record will always perforce be incomplete in some respects, but it increased enormously in the century after Darwin's death in 1882. That and the development of a reasonably accurate time scale has made possible the calculation of rates of evolution at various levels and in lineages with increasingly good fossil sequences. This has confirmed and made more definite the fact stated by Darwin in less precise and nonmathematical terms that rates of evolution have varied greatly in different groups of organisms and at different times. Darwin often wrote of evolution as "gradual" and as occurring through long periods of time. *Gradual* means "step by step." It is not an expression of rate: slow or fast. Darwin did make it reasonably clear that gradual evolution was usually by small steps, which could be faster or slower, and indeed that evolutionary change can be nil for considerable periods of time. He adumbrated, at least, the present conception of evolution as involving an interaction of hereditary variation—genetics in modern times—and environment in its broadest sense. He saw evolution, as almost all biologists still do, as having a tempo largely affected by rates of environmental change, from nil if adaptation was effective and environment stable to rapid if environmental change was rapid, or to cessation (extinction) if environmental change was so rapid that genetic change under natural selection could not keep up with it. I do not find that Darwin clearly noted one aspect of natural selection now firmly established: that it can prevent instead of directing evolutionary changes. This, sometimes called stabilizing selection or centripetal selection, means that in a well-adapted species and a fairly stable environment it is the modal and not the more deviant variants that will usually have more offspring. Darwin was also aware that the steps in evolution could conceivably be large at times, but he thought, as have most later evolutionists, that this has not been the usual mode of evolution.

It is not entirely clear in Darwin's works but is not a contradiction of any of his expressed views that adaptation from one kind of environment or adaptive niche to another, while still gradual in the sense of proceeding in small steps from one generation to another, is commonly more rapid than the preceding and following phases. In the 1940s during the development of the synthetic theory this was discussed and called "quantum evolution," meaning a rapid shift from one adaptive zone to another. Lately the same process has been called "punctuated evolution" as distinct from "equilibrium," meaning the absence of much or of any change in the intervals between "punctuations." This has led to some apparent disagreement and unnecessary argument. "Punctuated equilibrium" has been advanced as a replacement of synthetic theory or Neo-Darwinism, these being tagged as "stabilist." The authors of this view have considered stabilism as constant, slow change of whole species through long spans of geological time. They thus created a dichotomy which, like most dichotomies, is merely the dialectic separation of the two extremes of a continuum. Slow evolutionary change or no change at all in a span of geological time has certainly occurred and so has exceptionally rapid change in a usually shorter span, but so have all the intermediates between those extremes and all the combinations of the two. This perception has a sound base in Darwinian evolutionism and in the synthetic theory that developed beyond that base.

Another objection brought first against Darwinian natural selection and later against the genetical basis of variation in populations also requires some brief notice here. The earlier objection was that variants selected for are not always clearly adaptive and the later form of essentially the same objection was that genetic mutations are random. That requires better understanding of what "random" means in this connection. It means that mutations are not necessarily, in fact are not usually, in a direction favorable for adaptation or the "survival of the fittest." Mutations may have environmental causes, for instance from radiation, but they are not adaptively either for or against those causes. Evolution is affected but is not directed by the environment. Natural selection prunes out mutations or variants definitely misadapted. This is not a negative process, as claimed by some of Darwin's critics, but a positive one as it promotes the formation and retention of harmonious genetic systems.

A point not quite clear in Darwin's work but, one might say, lurking in it is that natural selection is not the only restraint on the direction taken by evolution. Another strong restraint is the fairly obvious fact that evolutionary change can occur only on the basis of what is actually present in the evolving population. Thus the possible avenues of change depend quite largely on the whole *past* history of the group of organisms involved.

This account of Darwin's place in the history of science can well close with two quotations. The first is from Sir Gavin de Beer (1899–1972), who after a discussion of how new points of view emerge added the following:

This is what relativity did to Newton's physics and future research will do to Darwin's evolution. It is part of the achievement of both these men that they not only made fundamental discoveries but opened up whole new fields of research that had never been thought of before and in which further advances in knowledge can be made.

And a final thought, from Theodosius Dobzhansky:

The true greatness of a scientist may lie in the fact that his work carries the seeds of its own obsolescence.

APPENDIX A

The Works of Charles Darwin

A. BOOKS PUBLISHED DURING HIS LIFETIME

1839. *Narrative of the Surveying Voyages of His Majesty's Ships Adventurer and Beagle, between the Years 1826 and 1836, Describing their Examination of the Southern Shores of South America, and the Beagle's Circumnavigation of the Globe.* 3 volumes. London: Colburn. (Volume 3 is by Darwin and was reprinted in the following separate form.)

1839. *Journal of Researches into the Geology and Natural History of the Various Countries Visited by H.M.S. Beagle, under the command of Captain FitzRoy, R.N., from 1832–36.* London: Colburn. (This is Darwin's part of the *Narrative;* it has been referred to as *Journal of Researches.*)

1839, 1840, 1841, 1842, 1843. *The Zoology of the Voyage of H.M.S. Beagle, under the Command of Captain FitzRoy, R.N., during the Years 1832 to 1836.* Edited and Superintended by Charles Darwin. London: Smith, Elder. (Published in five parts, on the dates shown; the parts have seven other authors, but each part has notes and other contributions by Darwin.)

1842. *The Structure and Distribution of Coral Reefs. Being the First Part of the Geology of the Voyage of the Beagle.* London: Smith, Elder.

1844. *Geological Observations on the Volcanic Islands, Visited during the Voyage of H.M.S. Beagle, Being the Second Part of the Geology of the Beagle.* London: Smith, Elder.

1845. *The Voyage of the Beagle.* London: Murray. (A revised edition of the 1839 *Journal of Researches;* it has frequently been reprinted, usually with this shortened title.)

1846. *Geological Observations on South America. Being the Third Part of the Geology of the Voyage of the Beagle.* London: Smith, Elder.

1851. *A Monograph of the Fossil Lepadidae; or Pedunculated Cirripedes of Great Britain.* London: Palaeontographical Society.

1851. *A Monograph of the Sub-Class Cirripedia, with Figures of All the Species. The Lepadidae: or Pedunculated Cirripedes.* London: Ray Society.

1854. *A Monograph of the Fossil Balanidae and Verrucidae of Great Britain.* London: Palaeontographical Society.

1854. *A Monograph of the Sub-Class Cirripedia, with Figures of All the Species. The Balanidae (or Sessile Cirripedes): the Verrucidae, etc.* London: Ray Society.

1859. *On the Origin of Species by Means of Natural Selection, or the Preservation of Favoured Races in the Struggle for Life.* London: Murray. (Revisions by Darwin have been specified in the preceding text; this is the work generally reprinted simply as *The Origin of Species*.)

1862. *On the Various Contrivances by which British and Foreign Orchids are Fertilized by Insects, and on the Good Effects of Intercrossing.* London: Murray.

1865. *The Movements and Habits of Climbing Plants.* London: Linnean Society.

1868. *The Variation of Animals and Plants under Domestication.* 2 volumes. London: Murray.

1871. *The Descent of Man, and Selection in Relation to Sex.* 2 volumes. London: Murray. (Later usually in a single volume.)

1872. *The Expression of the Emotions in Man and Animals.* London: Murray.

1875. *Insectivorous Plants.* London: Murray.

1875. *The Movements and Habits of Climbing Plants.* London: Murray. (A revised version of the long Linnean Society paper of 1865.)

1876. *The Effects of Cross and Self Fertilization in the Vegetable Kingdom.* London: Murray.

1877. *The Different Forms of Flowers on Plants of the Same Species.* London: Murray.

1879. *Erasmus Darwin. Preliminary Notice.* London: Murray. (On Charles's grandfather, written with Ernst Krause.)

1880. *The Power of Movement in Plants.* London: Murray. (With the assistance of Charles's son Francis.)

1881. *The Formation of Vegetable Mould through the Action of Worms, with Observations on their Habits.* London: Murray.

B. SHORTER PUBLICATIONS DURING DARWIN'S LIFE

These number over 150 and were published in many different journals from 1835, when Darwin was still on the *Beagle,* to 1882, the year of Darwin's death. They have been collected, annotated and reprinted in the following work:

1977. *The Collected Papers of Charles Darwin.* Edited by Paul H. Barrett; with a Foreword by Theodosius Dobzhansky. 2 volumes. Chicago: University of Chicago Press.

C. SOME OF THE IMPORTANT WRITINGS OF CHARLES DARWIN PUBLISHED SINCE HIS DEATH

1877. *The Life and Letters of Charles Darwin Including an Autobiographical Chapter.* Edited by his son Francis Darwin. 3 volumes. London: Murray. (There is also a later American edition in two volumes.)

1903. *More Letters of Charles Darwin. A Record of His Work in a Series of Hitherto Unpublished Letters.* Edited by Francis Darwin, Fellow of Christ's College, and A. C. Seward, Fellow of Emmanuel College, Cambridge. 2 volumes. London: Murray. (There is also an American edition of the same date.)

1909. *The Foundations of the Origin of Species by Charles Darwin.* Edited by Francis Darwin. Cambridge: Cambridge University Press. (This contains the full texts of Darwin's sketch of 1842 and extended essay of 1844.)

1958. *Evolution by Natural Selection.* Prefaced and edited by Gavin de Beer. Cambridge: Cambridge University Press. (This also includes the sketch of 1842 and essay of 1844 reedited from Francis Darwin, with some other matter.)

1958. *The Autobiography of Charles Darwin, 1809–1882, with the Original Omissions Restored.* Edited with Appendix and Notes by his granddaughter Norah Barlow. London: Collins. (There is also a 1959 American edition.)

1975. *Charles Darwin's Natural Selection, being the Second Part of His Big Species Book Written from 1856 to 1858.* Edited from manuscript by R. C. Stauffer. Cambridge: Cambridge University Press.

(Darwin also left many letters not included in the two collections cited above and masses of notes which have been published more or less piecemeal and not yet all collected and collated.)

D. SOME BOOKS ON DARWIN'S LIFE

There are almost innumerable books on Darwin's life as a whole, on aspects of it and on its outcome. I have here selected just a few that I can especially recommend. Here authors are in alphabetical order.

Appleman, Philip, ed. 1979. *Darwin.* 2nd ed. New York: W. W. Norton & Co. (Selections from Darwin, but mostly contemporaneous and later discussions.)

de Beer, Gavin. 1963. *Charles Darwin. Evolution by Natural Selection.* Garden City: Doubleday & Co. (Biography.)

Hull, David. 1974. *Philosophy of Biological Science.* Englewood Cliffs: Prentice-Hall. (General, but Darwin as a central figure.)

Huxley, Julian and Kettlewell, H. B. D. 1965. *Charles Darwin and His World.* London: Thames and Hudson. (Biography, richly illustrated.)

Keynes, R. D., ed. 1979. *The Beagle Record. Selections from the Original Pictorial Records and Written Accounts of the Voyage of H.M.S. Beagle.* Cambridge: Cambridge University Press.

Manier, Edward. 1978. *The Young Darwin and His Cultural Circle.* Dordrecht and Boston: D. Reidel.

Moore, Ruth. 1955. *Charles Darwin. A Great Life in Brief.* New York: Alfred A. Knopf.

Ruse, Michael. 1979. *The Darwinian Revolution. Science Red in Tooth and Claw.* Chicago: University of Chicago Press. (Good historical-philosophical discussion with a misleading subtitle.)

Vorzimmer, Peter J. 1970. *Charles Darwin: The Years of Controversy. The Origin of Species and its Critics 1859–1882.* Philadelphia: Temple University Press.

E. A FEW SELECTED RECENT BOOKS ON EVOLUTION IN GENERAL.

Dobzhansky, T., Ayala, F. J., Stebbins, G. L. and Valentine, J. W. 1977. *Evolution.* San Francisco: W. H. Freeman and Company.

Futuyama, D. J. 1979. *Evolutionary Biology.* Sunderland: Sinauer Associates.

Simpson, G. G. 1967. *The Meaning of Evolution.* Revised edition. New Haven and London: Yale University Press.

APPENDIX B

A Note on Species, Nomenclature, and Classification

Darwin's most influential book is called *The Origin of Species,* and the term "species" is used by all biologists and by everyone interested in nature. Its definition and application are nevertheless complicated and often debatable.

A colloquial definition of the word "species," which, by the way, is the same in singular and plural, is given in a recent dictionary (Random House) as, "a class of individuals having some common characteristics or qualities; distinct sort or kind." For systematists, the scientists whose business is to distinguish, name, and classify species, that definition is not usable. The problems involved are so complex and so variable in different cases that much has been written and there are many differences of usage and opinion in this respect. The most recent (1982) definition of a species by a competent systematist of living animals (Mayr) is: "A species is a reproductive community of populations (reproductively isolated from others) that occupies a specific niche in nature." For a majority of species these characteristics cannot be observed. They can only be inferred from a variety of observations. An evolutionary definition (by me) is: "An evolutionary species is a lineage (an ancestral descendant sequence of populations) evolving separately from others and with its own unitary evolutionary role and tendencies." This, too, cannot be directly observed in usual instances but must be inferred. In fact, although there are other approaches, the recognition of a population as a species almost always depends on observation of its characteristics, mostly anatomical in fossils,

213

within a sample of a population. If, then, another population, which may or may not be different in space or, for fossils, in time, is clearly distinct in some of those characteristics, it will usually be considered a different species. The ability to make such a distinction in a convincing and workable way is a matter of insight and experience, hence the not entirely facetious remark that "A species is a species if a competent specialist says it is." To become a "competent specialist" takes intelligence, discipline, and time. Hence the value to Darwin and to *The Origin of Species* that Darwin spent much of his time for eight years studying barnacles. (See Chapter 6 of this book.)

To be discussed, or even thought about, species must have names. From ancient times and well into the eighteenth century the relatively few species discussed were simply described. For purposes of scholarly communication among Renaissance and later savants with different languages, such descriptions were written in Latin. As the number of known species multiplied, eventually into millions, it became necessary to have some more abbreviated way of designating them. This was standardized by a Swedish botanist who wrote under the Latinized name of Carolus Linnaeus (1707–1778). His solution to the problem, which we still use, was to give each species a double or binomial name. The first is the name of a genus (plural genera) and is to be treated or considered as a Latin noun. It is always capitalized and usually italicized. The second or specific name is also considered as Latin and is also in italics if the generic name is, but is not now capitalized. It is usually an adjective but may also be a noun or adjective in the genitive (or possessive) case or occasionally another noun in what, if you are a grammarian, you will call apposition with the generic name. Our own specific name, dating from Linnaeus, 1758, is *Homo sapiens,* from Latin *homo,* "human being" (including women; in Latin the word for "man" excluding "woman" is *vir*), and *sapiens,* also Latin and meaning "wise." (Well, even jokesters must admit that "homo" is wiser than most other animals.) Names of genera are often of Greek origin, Latinized. In this book *Macrauchenia,* found by Darwin and named by Owen, is an example.

If, as has happened rather often through the years, different genera or species are given the same name, the first one published is retained and the other or others have to be changed. If, as has occurred even more often, the same genus or species has been given more than one name, again the first one published is retained and the others just become invalid synonyms of it.

With so many genera and species to name, possibilities became limited, and current rules permit using derivatives from any language and even meaningless combinations of any two or more letters provided that we pretend that they are Latin. It is recommended, but not required, that names should not suggest "a bizarre, comical, or otherwise objectionable meaning." For example, I once found a very ancient, big fossil snake in a locality in Patagonia known in local Spanish as Cañadón Vaca, "cow canyon," and I named it *Madtsoia bai* from the Patagonian Tehuelche Indian words *mad,* "valley," *tsoi,* "cow," and *bai,* "grandfather," because it was so old. (I was not then a grandfather myself, as I am now multiply.) Or for another example, which should perhaps be condemned as "objectionable" but hasn't been, the great American paleontologist E. D. Cope (1840–1897) named a species of fossil mammals from New Mexico *Anisonchus cophater. Anisonchus* is perfectly good Latinized Greek referring to the uneven size of cusps on the teeth, but for Cope *cophater* was pronounced "Cope-hater" in honor of his unfriendly rival Othniel Charles Marsh (1831–1899). Then, too, there is a whole group of rodents named Franimorpha by the expert on fossil rodents Albert Elmer Wood (born 1910) and meaning literally "Fran-shaped." "Fran" is the nickname of Albert's wife Frances, but she is not in the least rodent-shaped.

In addition to genera and species systematists use a hierarchic arrangement of increasingly higher or more comprehensive groups, also adopted and complicated from Linnaeus. In such an arrangement each rank or level of the hierarchy includes all those below it. From the top down the simplest form of the Linnaean hierarchy now in general use is kingdom-class-order-family-genus-species. It is usual now to insert various other steps between these and thus make the sequence more detailed. Without such complications our position in the hierarchy is kingdom Animalia, class Mammalia, order Primates, family Hominidae, genus *Homo,* species *Homo sapiens.* In such an arrangement all the names above genus must be considered Latin plurals.

Notes

CHAPTER 2

1. Darwin's text as published in the *Journal of the Proceedings of the Linnean Society (Zoology),* Vol. 3 (1859), pp. 259–67.
2. *The Life and Letters of Charles Darwin Including an Autobiographical Chapter,* ed. Francis Darwin, 3 vols. (London: Murray, 1893), 1:442.
3. Ibid., pp. 467–68.

CHAPTER 3

1. *Life and Letters,* 1:23–49.

CHAPTER 4

1. *Life and Letters,* 1:49–53. Slightly excised account from "Autobiography."
2. *Journal of Researches,* 1st ed. (London: Colburn, 1839), pp. 11–12.
3. Ibid., pp. 589–91.
4. Ibid., pp. 95–99.
5. Ibid., pp. 180–81.
6. Ibid., pp. 208–11.
7. Ibid., pp. 249–50.
8. Ibid., pp. 389–91.
9. Ibid., pp. 403–4.
10. Ibid., pp. 454–55.
11. Ibid., pp. 460–62.
12. Ibid., pp. 474–75.
13. *The Zoology of the Voyage of H.M.S. Beagle,* 5 vols. (London: Smith, Elder, 1840), 2:99–100.

CHAPTER 5

1. *The Structure and Distribution of Coral Reefs,* 2nd ed. rev. (London: Smith, Elder, 1842), pp. 98–103.
2. *More Letters of Charles Darwin,* ed. Francis Darwin and A. C. Seward, 2 vols. (London: Murray, 1903), 1:30.

CHAPTER 6

1. *Life and Letters,* 1:66–67.
2. Ibid., pp. 314–17.
3. Ibid., pp. 67–69.

CHAPTER 7

1. *The Origin of Species,* 6th ed. rev. (London: Murray, 1872), pp. 2–5. This edition differs little from the first.
2. Ibid., pp. 18–20.
3. Ibid., pp. 55–56.
4. Ibid., pp. 57–60.
5. Ibid., pp. 73–75.
6. Ibid., pp. 94–100.
7. Ibid., 1st ed. (1859), pp. 116–25.
8. Ibid., 6th ed., pp. 495–505.

CHAPTER 8

1. *More Letters of Charles Darwin,* 1:219–21. First paragraph of a letter from Darwin to Scott written on December 11, 1862.
2. *More Letters of Charles Darwin,* 2:322–23. Letter from Darwin to Scott dated June 6, 1863.
3. *Life and Letters,* 1:73–75, 77–79.

CHAPTER 9

1. *The Descent of Man,* 2 vols. (London: Murray, 1871).
2. Ibid., pp. 409–10.
3. Ibid., pp. 527–28.
4. Ibid., p. 916.

CHAPTER 10

1. *Life and Letters*, 1:79.
2. Ibid., pp. 72–73.
3. Ibid., pp. 79–83.
4. Ibid., pp. 85–86.
5. Ibid., 2:532.

GEORGE GAYLORD SIMPSON, doyen of American paleontologists, has served during his distinguished career at the American Museum of Natural History as well as Columbia and Harvard universities. His many books include *The Meaning of Evolution*, *Concession to the Improbable,* and *Splendid Isolation*. Recently retired from the faculty of the University of Arizona, Dr. Simpson lives in Tucson with his wife, Dr. Anne Roe.

HEALTHY IS BEAUTIFUL

Shape Up Within & Without

Whatever your interests, whatever your needs,
Pocket Books has the best books to help you look good
and feel good.

____45363	**BACKACHE: STRESS & TENSION** H. Kraus, M.D.	$2.50
____47199	**BODYBUILDING FOR EVERYONE** Lou Ravelle	$2.95
____46941	**CARLTON FREDERICK'S CALORIE &** **CARBOHYDRATE GUIDE** Carlton Fredericks	$2.95
____44787	**COMPLETE ILLUSTRATED BOOK OF YOGA** Swami Vishnudevananda	$3.50
____49702	**CONSUMER GUIDE TO A FLATTER STOMACH**	$2.95
____49407	**DICTIONARY OF NUTRITION** Richard Ashley & Heidi Duggal	$3.50
____47794	**FAMILY MEDICAL ENCYCLOPEDIA** J. Schifferes, Ph.D.	$4.95
____47433	**HEALTH & LIGHT** John Ott	$2.95
____44049	**HOW TO STOP SMOKING** Herbert Brean	$2.50
____47210	**JOY OF RUNNING** Thaddeus Kostrubala	$2.95
____47222	**TOTAL FITNESS IN 30 MINUTES A WEEK** Laurence E. Morehouse, Ph.D.	$3.50

778